1st International Workshop on Nakba Narratives as Language Resources (Nakba-NLP 2025)

Abu Dhabi, United Arab Emirates
20 January 2025

ISBN: 979-8-3313-1372-2

Printed from e-media with permission by:

Curran Associates, Inc.
57 Morehouse Lane
Red Hook, NY 12571

CURRAN ASSOCIATES INC. proceedings.com

Some format issues inherent in the e-media version may also appear in this print version.

Printed with permission by Curran Associates, Inc. (2026)

For permission requests, please contact the Association for Computational Linguistics at the address below.

Association for Computational Linguistics
209 N. Eighth Street
Stroudsburg, Pennsylvania 18360

Phone: 1-570-476-8006
Fax: 1-570-476-0860

acl@aclweb.org

Additional copies of this publication are available from:

Curran Associates, Inc.
57 Morehouse Lane
Red Hook, NY 12571 USA
Phone: 845-758-0400
Fax: 845-758-2633
Email: curran@proceedings.com
Web: www.proceedings.com

The 31st International Conference on Computational Linguistics

1st International Workshop on Nakba Narratives as Language Resources (Nakba-NLP 2025)

Proceedings of the workshop

Edited by:

Mustafa Jarrar, Nizar Habash, Mo El-Haj, Amal Haddad Haddad, Zeina Jallad, Camille Mansour, Diana Allan, Paul Rayson, Tymaa Hammouda, Sanad Malaysha

January 20, 2025
https://sina.birzeit.edu/nakba-nlp/

Order copies of this and other ACL proceedings from:

Association for Computational Linguistics (ACL)
209 N. Eighth Street
Stroudsburg, PA 18360
USA
Tel: +1-570-476-8006
Fax: +1-570-476-0860
acl@aclweb.org

Preface

Welcome to the 1st International Workshop on Nakba Narratives as Language Resources (Nakba-NLP 2025), co-located with the 31st International Conference on Computational Linguistics (COLING 2025). Nakba-NLP 2025 was held virtually on January 20, 2025.

The narratives of the (ongoing) Palestinian Nakba hold immense historical, cultural, literary, and academic value. Preserving this content and empowering it with AI tools is vital to ensure its accessibility and usability for present and future generations. Nakba narratives and testimonies exist in diverse formats such as manuscripts, books, audio recordings, novels, and films, making their conversion into machine-understandable formats a significant challenge. Establishing accessible archives and well-annotated collections is crucial for researchers and historians to validate and share meaningful information.

This workshop aims to explore how artificial intelligence, natural language processing, and corpus linguistics can assist in understanding, disseminating, and preserving Nakba narratives and testimonies. The goal is to create accessible, comprehensive, and well-annotated collections that empower researchers and historians to validate and share critical insights derived from these data. The workshop targets datasets and narratives in Arabic, English, and other languages.

This year's workshop featured a total of 18 submissions, 14 submissions were accepted. The accepted papers are authored by 43 scholars representing diverse perspectives from 11 different countries, including the Egypt, France, Germany, Lebanon, Malta, Netherlands, Palestine, Spain, Turkey, USA, and UK. This highlights the international reach and collaborative spirit of the workshop. Each submission to the workshop was evaluated by at least two reviewers who were members of the Program Committee.

The Nakba-NLP 2025 workshop featured a keynote address and a panel discussion. Ilan Pappé, a renowned historian and political scientist from the University of Exeter, specializing in the Nakba, delivered the keynote address titled "*The Words Laundrette: Unmasking Bias and Propaganda in the Discourses on the Ongoing Nakba*". In his address, Pappé delved into how language is used, shaped, and contested within political and cultural narratives surrounding the Nakba—providing critical insights directly applicable to the role of NLP in analyzing such complex discourses.

The panel discussion, "*Digital Archives and Cultural Heritage in the LLM Era*," brought together leading experts, including Dawn Knight, Antonio Moreno Sandoval, Muhammad Abdul-Mageed, and Mustafa Jarrar. Their thought-provoking dialogue explored the rapidly evolving interplay between digital archives, cultural heritage, Large Language Models and Multimodal Large Models, highlighting the field's pressing challenges and transformative opportunities.

We would like to thank everyone who submitted a paper to the workshop and to all the members of the Program Committee.

Workshop organizers

Workshop Page: `https://sina.birzeit.edu/nakba-nlp`

Organizing Committee

Nakba-NLP 2025:

Organising Committee & Workshop Chairs:

Mustafa Jarrar (Birzeit University, Palestine)
Nizar Habash (New York University Abu Dhabi, UAE)
Mo El-Haj (Lancaster University, UK)
Amal Haddad Haddad (Universidad de Granada, Spain)
Zeina Jallad (Harvard Law School, USA)
Camille Mansour (Institute for Palestine Studies, Lebanon)
Diana Allan (McGill University, Canada)
Paul Rayson (Lancaster University, UK)
Tymaa Hammouda (Birzeit University, Palestine)
Sanad Malaysha (Birzeit University, Palestine)

Programme Committee:

Abdelkader El Mahdaouy (Mohamed VI polytechnic University)
Abdellah El Mekki (Mohammed VI Polytechnic University)
Abdelrahim Qaddoumi (NYU)
Abdulrahman Abdulsalam (University of Utah)
Abed Alhakim Freihat (University of Trento)
Adnan Yahya (Birzeit University)
Ala Alazzeh (Birzeit University)
Ali AlKhathlan, (King Abdulaziz University)
Almoataz B. Al-Said, (Cairo University)
Amr Keleg (The University of Edinburgh)
Areej Jaber (Technical University Khadouri)
Ashraf Elnagar (University of Sharjah)
Ayah Soufan (Strathclyde University)
Azzeddine Mazroui (University Mohammed First)
Badr AlKhamissi (EPFL)
Baker Abdalhaq (Annajah National University)
Basem Ezbidi (Birzeit university)
Bassam Haddad (University of Petra)
Bayan AbuShawar (Al Ain University)
Dana Abdulrahim (University of Bahrain)
Dima Taji (Charles University)
ElMoatez Billah Nagoudi (The University of British Columbia)
Eyad Elyan (Robert Gordon University)
Fadhl Eryani (University of Tübingen)
Fadi Zaraket (American University of Beirut)
Faisal Awartani (Insights for Research Polling and Training)
Fatemah Husain (Kuwait University)
Fatima Haouari (Qatar University)
Fethi Bougares (LIUM- Le Mans Université)
Fouzi Harrag (Ferhat Abbas University)
Ghassan Mourad (libanese university)
Go Inoue (Mohamed bin Zayed University of Artificial Intelligence)
Habiba Dahmani (Mohamed Boudiaf University)
Haithem Afli (ADAPT Centre, Munster Technological University)

Hamada Nayel (Benha University)
Ibrahim Abu Farha (University of Sheffield)
Imed Zitouni (Google)
Imene Bensalem (Constantine 2 University)
Injy Hamed (Institute for Natural Language Processing, University of Stuttgart)
Kamel Gaanoun (National Institute of Statistics and Applied Economics)
Kamel Smaili (LORIA)
Kaoukab Chebaro (Columbia University)
Karim Bouzoubaa (Mohammed V University in Rabat)
Khaled Shaalan (The British University in Dubai)
Khalid Choukri (ELRA/ELDA) Khalil Mrini (Bytedance)
Khloud Al Jallad (SySSR)
Labib Arafeh (AlQuds University)
Lama Nachman (Intel Labs)
Lamia Hadrich-Belguith (ANLP Research Group, MIRACL Lab, FSEGS, Sfax University)
Majdi Sawalha (The University of Jordan)
Manar Alkhatib (British University in Dubai)
Maram Hasanain (Qatar Computing Research Institute)
Mo El-Haj (Lancaster University)
Mohamed Lichouri (Centre de Recherche Scientifique et Technique pour le Développement de la Langue Arabe (CRSTDLA)
Mohamed Yahya, (NLP Researcher)
Mohammad Abuoudeh (Al Hussein Bin Talal University)
Mohammed Attia (Google Inc.)
Mohammed Khalilia (Birzeit University)
Mohammed Salah Al-Radhi (Budapest University of Technology and Economics)
Mona Baker (University of Oslo)
Moustafa Al-Hajj (Lebanese University)
Muhammad Abdul-Mageed (The University of British Columbia)
Munir Fakher Eldin (Birzeit University)
Munther Dahleh (MIT)
Nada Ghneim (Damascus University)
Omar Shehabi (Yale Law School)
Omar Tesdell (Birzeit University)
Omar Trigui (University of Sousse in Tunisia)
Owen Rambow (Stony Brook University)
Radi Jarrar (Birzeit University)
Radwan Tahboub (Palestine Polytechnic University)
Raia Abu Ahmad (DFKI)
Reem Suwaileh (Qatar University)
Saad Ezzini (Lancaster University)
Sabri Boughorbel (Qatar Computing Research Institute)
Sahar Ghannay (CNRS, LISN)
Salima Harrat (ENS Bouzaréah, Algiers)
salima mdhaffar (LIA - University of Avignon)
Samhaa R. El-Beltagy (Newgiza University/Optomatica)
Sari Hanafi (American University of Beirut)
Seif Mechti (ISSEPS)
Serin Atiani (Princess Sumaya University for Technology)
Shady Elbassuoni (American University of Beirut)
Sultan Alrowili (University of Delaware)

Susan Akram (Boston University)
Tamer Elsayed (Qatar University)
Thaher Gharabeh (University of Granada)
Violetta Cavalli-Sforza (Al Akhawayn University)
Wajdi Zaghouani (Northwestern University Qatar)
Walid Magdy (The University of Edinburgh)
Wassim El-Hajj (American University of Beirut)
Watheq Mansour (The University of Queensland)
Wissam Antoun (Inria)
Yahya Mohamed Elhadj (Arab Center for Research and Policy) Studies

Table of Contents

Time Activity & Authors

09:00 - 09:20 **Opening Session**: Welcome by Workshop Chairs Mustafa Jarrar and Camille Mansour

09:20 - 09:40 **Talk 1**: Integrating Argumentation Features for Enhanced Propaganda Detection in Arabic Narratives on the Israeli War on Gaza.
Authors: Sara Nabhani, Claudia Borg, Kurt Micallef, Khalid Al-Khatib.
Paper ID: 18

09:40 - 10:00 **Talk 2**: Multilingual Propaganda Detection: Exploring Transformer-Based Models mBERT, XLM-RoBERTa, and mT5.
Authors: Mohamed Ibrahim Ragab, Ensaf Hussein Mohamed and Walaa Medhat.
Paper ID: 12

10:00 - 10:20 **Talk 3:** Bias Detection in Media: Traditional Models vs. Transformers in Analyzing Social Media Coverage of the Israeli-Gaza Conflict.
Authors: Marryam Yahya Mohammed, Esraa Ismail Mohamed, Mariam Nabil Esmat, Yomna Ashraf Nagib, Nada Ahmed Radwan, Ziad Mohamed Elshaer and Ensaf Hussein Mohamed.
Paper ID: 16

10:20 - 10:40 **Talk 4**: The Missing Cause: An Analysis of Causal Attributions in Reporting on Palestine.
Authors: Paulina Garcia Corral, Hannah Bechara, Krishnamoorthy Manohara and Slava Jankin
Paper ID: 15

10:40 - 11:00 **Talk 5**: Deciphering Implicatures: On NLP and Oral Testimonies.
Authors: Zainab Sabra
Paper ID: 4

11:00 - 11:15 Coffee Break

11:15 - 12:30 **Panel Discussion**: Digital Archives and Cultural Heritage in the LLMs Era. **Panel Chair:** Mo El-Haj
Muhammad Abdul-Mageed, The University of British Columbia, Canada.
Antonio Moreno Sandoval, Autonomous University Madrid, Spain.
Dawn Knight, Cardiff University, UK.
Mustafa Jarrar, Birzeit University, Palestine.

12:30 - 13:00 Lunch Break

13:00 - 13:15 **Talk 6:** Sentiment Analysis of Nakba Oral Histories: A Critical Study of Large Language Models.
Authors: Huthaifa I. Ashqar
Paper ID: 7

13:15 - 13:30 **Talk 7:** Arabic Topic Classification Corpus of the Nakba Short Stories.
Authors: Osama Hamed and Nadeem Zaidkilani.
Paper ID: 9

13:30 - 13:45 **Talk 8**: Exploring Author Style in Nakba Short Stories: A Comparative Study of Transformer-Based Models.
Authors: Osama Hamed and Nadeem Zaidkilani.
Paper ID: 10

13:45 - 14:00 Coffee Break

14:00 - 14:20 **Talk 9:** NakbaTR: A Turkish NER Dataset for Nakba Narratives.
Authors: Esma Fatıma Bilgin Tasdemir and Şaziye Betül Özateş.
Paper ID: 17

14:20 - 14:40 **Talk 10:** The Nakba Lexicon: Building a Comprehensive Dataset from Palestinian Literature.
Authors: Izza AbuHaija, Salim Al Mandhari, Mo El-Haj, Jonas Sibony and Paul Rayson.
Paper ID: 8

14:40 - 15:00 **Talk 11:** Cognitive Geographies of Catastrophe Narratives: Georeferenced Interview Transcriptions as Language Resource for Models of Forced Displacement.
Authors: Annie K. Lamar, Rick Castle, Carissa Chappell, Emmanouela Schoinoplokaki, Allene M. Seet, Amit Shilo and Chloe Nahas.
Paper ID: 6

15:00 - 15:20 **Talk 12:** Collective Memory and Narrative Cohesion: A Computational Study of Palestinian Refugee Oral Histories in Lebanon.
Authors: Ghadir A. Awad, Tamara N. Rayan, Lavinia Dunagan and David Gamba.
Paper ID: 13

15:20 - 15:40 **Talk 13:** A cultural shift in Western perceptions of Palestine.
Authors: Terry Regier and Muhammad Ali Khalidi.
Paper ID: 5

15:40 - 16:00 **Talk 14:** Detecting Inconsistencies in Narrative Elements of Cross Lingual Nakba Texts.
Authors: Nada Hamarsheh, Zahia Elabour, Aya Murra and Adnan Yahya.
Paper ID: 11

16:00 - 17:00 **Keynote**: The Words Laundrette: Unmasking Bias and Propaganda in the Discourses on the Ongoing Nakba By Ilan Pappe.

17:00 - 17:15 Closing Remarks and Wrap-Up

Deciphering Implicatures: On NLP and Oral Testimonies

Zainab Sabra
Department of Philosophy, Erasmus University of Rotterdam/ Rotterdam, Netherlands
Department of Philosophy, American University of Beirut / Beirut, Lebanon
sabra@esphil.eur.nl

Abstract

The utterance of a word does not intrinsically convey its intended force. The semantic of utterances is not shaped by the precise references of the words used. Asserting that "it is shameful to abandon our country" does not merely convey information; rather, it asserts an act of resilience. In most of our exchanges, we rarely utilize sentences to describe reality or the world around us. More frequently, our statements aim to express opinions, to influence, or be influenced by others. Words carry more than just their syntax and semantics; they also embody a pragmatic normative force. This divergence between literal and conveyed meaning was depicted in the literature of philosophy of language as the difference between sentence meaning and speaker meaning. Where the former is the literal understanding of the words combined in a sentence, the latter is what the speaker is trying to convey through her expression. In order to derive the speaker meaning from the sentence meaning, J.L. Austin relied on conventions, whereas H.P. Grice relied on conventional and nonconventional implicatures. This paper aims to decipher how we can infer speaker's meaning from sentence meaning and thereby capture the force of what has been articulated, focusing specifically on oral testimonies. I argue that oral testimonies are forms of speech acts that aim to produce normative changes. Following this discussion, I will examine various natural language processing (NLP) models that make explicit what is implicit in oral testimonies with its benefits and limitations. Lastly, I will address two challenges, the former is related to implicatures that are not governed by conventions and the latter is concerned with the biases inherent in hermeneutical approaches.

1 Introduction

'You do not suppose that you can learn, or I explain, any subject of importance all in a moment; at any rate, not such a subject as language, which is, perhaps, the very greatest of all'-Socrates.

The utterance of a word does not intrinsically convey its intended force. For instance, when Nayfah Abd al Tayih[1], one of the testimony givers in the Al Jana collection found in Palestinian Oral history Archives, expresses, "عار علينا نترك بلدنا" ("Shame on us if we leave our homeland"), or when Fatime Abd al Samad[2], another testimony giver in the same archive, states,"هذا واجبي لازم أقوم في" ("This is my duty, and I must fulfill it"), what is produced is not merely sound waves traveling through the air. The meaning of these utterances is not shaped by the precise references of the words used. For example, asserting that "it is shameful to abandon our country" does not merely convey information; rather, it asserts an act of resilience. In most of our exchanges, we rarely utilize sentences to describe reality or the world around us. More frequently, our statements aim to express opinions, to influence, or be influenced by others. Words carry more than just their syntax and semantics; they also embody a pragmatic normative force. This paper aims to decipher how we can infer speaker meaning from sentence meaning and thereby capture the force of what has been articulated, focusing specifically on oral testimonies. The first section will establish the semantic theory that characterizes linguistic practices as normative, drawing upon existing literature in speech act theory. I will argue that oral testimonies should be considered as forms of speech acts. The second section will address the indeterminacy of the implications of what is said, providing tools to clarify such indeterminacies, specifically through the examination of conventional and conversational implicatures. Follow-

[1]Palestinian Oral History Archives, American University of Beirut, Al Jana, Nakba Collection, recorded 06/1997

[2]Palestinian Oral History Archives, American University of Beirut, Al Jana, Nakba Collection, recorded 07/1997

Proceedings of the Proceedings of the 1st International Workshop on Nakba Narratives as Language Resources, pages 1–8
January 20, 2025.

ing this discussion, I will examine various natural language processing (NLP) models that that facilitate the work of researchers in the field of oral history. Lastly, I will address two challenges, the former is related to implicatures that are not governed by conventions and the latter is concerning the biases inherent in hermeneutical approaches.

2 Saying is Doing: On the normative aspect of language

In the literature of the philosophy of language, the force of a word, known as illocutionary force, is central to speech act theories. J. L. Austin, in *How to Do Things with Words*, defines this force as follow:

> The utterance of the sentence is part of, the doing of an action, which again would not normally be described as... merely saying something. The action which is performed when we say something is an illocutionary act; for example, informing, ordering, warning, undertaking (Austin, 1965).

Speech can be viewed as a normative vehicle aimed at transitioning from a set of entitlements that enable the speaker to articulate a sentence toward instituting normative changes in the status quo. The former will be referred to as the input of speech, while the latter will be regarded as the output of speech. The input is the set of entitlements, conditions and circumstances that gives credibility to the speaker as a proper speaker i.e. one can only pronounce a couple husband and wife if he is a registered priest. The output is the normative changes the utterance institutes i.e. once the priest utters the expression then the couple are socially and legally referred to as a married couple. Since the input of the expression is governed by a set of norms that enable the utterance in question, and the output of the expression is the normative changes it invokes in the status quo then linguistic practices can only be understood within a normative social structure. Language is used as a tool to mitigate normative societal practices by inducing normative changes such as asserting a commitment is taken as a justification for your future behavior, making a promise is taken as producing expectations for the hearer, issuing an order is taken as inducing a feeling of obligation in the hearer etc. Linguistic activities are interwoven with nonlinguistic activities.

Applying the dichotomy between input and output, we can analyze the relevant testimonies in the following manner. Fatime is a testimony giver in a collection of archive that aim to provide the oral history of Palestinians since pre 1948. Fatime's set of input is successfully met, as she is a Palestinian, she was living in A'akka in 1948 and she was chosen by the interviewer to be a testimony giver. In addition, the fact that she was resisting leaving her house behind, ensuring that she gets all her family members from under the rubble, insures that Fatime is a legitimate candidate to deliver a testimony about her perspective on what her duty is. The output of the testimony in question does not only serve to mirror a reality about the facts that unfolded back then but rather it is an authoritative claim that assert her commitment towards her family members and her household. In this specific explication we can depict the interaction between the linguistic and nonlinguistic aspects of oral testimonies. In order for us to be able to recognize the output of the speech and give its proper normative aspect -as a prescription rather than a description- it is essential to be familiar with the context in question.

2.1 The illocutionary Force and the Indeterminacy of Hermeneutics

> The illocutionary force of an utterance determines the type of illocutionary act being performed. A single sentence can be used with varying illocutionary forces; for instance, the phrase 'It is raining' may function as an assertion, a conjecture, or a question (Searle, 1969).

If you are asking someone about the weather and they answer 'It is raining', you take their assertion as reporting a fact about the weather. If a child asks her father whether she can play outdoors and he answers that 'It is raining', then his answer is a rejection to the proposal. For the hearer to accurately derive what is implied from what is said, immersion in the context surrounding the conversation is essential. This context can be analogous to a stage in a theater, where each prop, costume, and bodily gesture contributes to the audience's understanding of the actor. The more the scene unfolds and the mise en scène is revealed, the clearer the meaning behind the actor's expressions becomes and the better the audience can pick from the different possibilities of illocutionary outcome. To fully comprehend the speaker's utterance, one must be familiar with her identity (Who is making the utterance?), her personality (Is she typically sarcastic, serious, or witty?), and the situational and historical background. This list of contextual elements is not fixed; it is adaptable based on the aims of the analysis. On another note, the context encompasses not only the speaker but also the audience, whose state of mind can influence interpretation—what one listener finds offensive, another might find humorous. Thus, the aforementioned list which would help in deriving what was meant from what was said should include information about the speaker, the hearer, and the dynamics of their interaction.

Given the peculiarity of oral testimonies the characteristics of the context are adapted to answer the following questions:: a) the identity of the researcher which answers to the question: Who is she affiliated with? What is the aim of her study?, b) the identity of the testimony giver (the narrator): Based on what was she chosen to give a testimony? What were her relevant social and historical condition?, c)the audience the listeners of the audio or readers of the transcript: To whom is this narrative directed? What is their background information? The contextual elements presented contributes the semantic dimension of the testimony given. The plasticity of its semantic value is but an indication of the coupling between words and society.

Given the indeterminacy of the hermeneutical scheme in question one needs to have some basic assumption to avoid a case of 'Téléphone cassé' where the more the expression is repeated the farther we dive away from the initial speaker meaning. H. P. Grice in Logic and conversation distinguishes between sentence meaning and speaker meaning. The former pertains to the literal meaning of the utterance, while the latter refers to the intended meaning conveyed by the speaker. A proper understanding of the speaker meaning requires an understanding of the implications of what was said. For the hearer to be able to derive the implications implicit in the discourse some basic assumptions need to relied on.

2.2 Deriving what is not said but rather implied

Grice introduces the cooperative principle as a guiding tenet for effective communication:

> Make your conversational contribution such as is required, at the stage at which it occurs, by the accepted purpose or direction of the talk exchange in which you are engaged(Grice, 1991) .

The primary assumption necessary for grasping the implications of an utterance is that the speaker is cooperating with the listener. When Nayfah claimed "عار علينا نترك بلدنا" after she was asked about the imbalance of power between the colonizer and the colonized, if the assumption is solely descriptive we will not be able to derive the true meaning of what was said. Nayfah's speech act is an assertion which serves as a commitment that justifies her action. The connection between saying and doing is revealed through the lens of the cooperative principle. It is only by taking into consideration the context in question that we can recognize the implication of Nayfah's utterance.

2.3 On Conventional and Conversational Implicature

Some of the implications between what is said and what is implied are conventional i.e. the relation between what is said and what is implied can be easily grasped for anyone familiar with the conventions in question. Other implications are non-conventional, Grice refers to these as conversational implicature. He describes them as a

> certain subclass of non-conventional implicature which I shall call conversational implicatures, as being essentially connected with certain general features of discourse (Grice, 1991).

The common norm underlying both conventional and nonconventional implicature is that the speaker is being cooperative with the direction of the talk exchange. Since the former is conventional then it should follow some explicit norms and rituals. Grice identifies four maxims that underpin cooperative principle: 1)Quantity: make your contribution as informative as required, 2)Quality: do not say that which you believe is false,3)Relation: your utterance should be relevant to the stage of the talk exchange you've reached and 4)Manner: avoid any obscurity or ambiguity in your speech exchange(Grice, 1991) . These maxims are not found apriori, they are routed in societal practices and constitute the precondition of making a meaningful talk. Since they are derived from empirical observations that make a talk exchange efficient, then there is the possibility that a speaker can violate, exploit or dismiss at least one of the maxims.

Other types of implications are conversational. Whenever at least one of these maxims is violated, the resulting instance can be identified as a conversational implicature. Unlike conventional implicatures, the conversational implicature is not a direct inference from conventions in question but rather it presupposes the exploitation of the conventions making it more difficult for the hearer to naturally derive the speaker meaning from the sentence literal meaning. This requires additional interpretative effort to understand what is being conveyed. In deciphering such meanings, Searle and Austin emphasize the importance of factual background information, the principle of cooperation, and the conditions outlined in the theory of speech acts. Grice, however, highlights the role of intuition

> The presence of conversational implicature must be capable of being worked out; for even if it can in fact be intuitively grasped, unless the intuition is replaceable by an argument, the implicature will not count as a conversational implicature: it will be a conventional implicature (Grice, 1991).

3 Digitalized Oral testimonies

Whether it is the power of conventions or that of intuition, what was mentioned above is but a proof of the complexities reigning the realm of semantics. William Schneier in *Oral History in the Age of Digital Possibilities* highlights the complexity in the epistemic approach towards the narrative. The oral historian must not only comprehend the voice of the narrator but also ensure that the force behind this voice is preserved in the written narrative.. He claims 'I have gained a strong appreciation for the value of hearing accounts many times over, and in different contexts, in order to understand the meaning and to recognize multiple meanings, depending on context and audience' (Nyhan and Flinn, 2016). One has to be aware how easily one can make assumption about meaning. It should be as well clear that the variety of ways in which people use and understand oral narrative give birth to different accounts of the same discourse said or written. In order to make sure that the narrative is authentic to what was narrated, what needs to be preserved is the interchange between the researcher and the researched, the historical background in question, the nuances of oral narratives, the conventional meaning of the words used and the context at hand, while ensuring that the Gricean principle and maxims are being observed.

3.1 Oral History: Written or Heard?

> The human voice consist of carefully crafted and culturally shaped pressure waves traveling through the air in the form of words, woven together in the form of a story (Boyd, 2014).

The story, shaped through the act of narrating, must be preserved in the written narrative while considering the factors discussed earlier. To fully capture the force of spoken language, it is often more effective to listen to the recording—especially if it is in the listener's native language—than to rely solely on the written account. Spoken words tend to be clearer and convey more nuances and sentiments than written ones. The innovation and advancement of technology have introduced new methods for preserving oral testimonies. From microphones and recording machines to wax cylinders, algorithms, software, digital archives, and technological progress has made it increasingly practical to preserve and disseminate these narratives. The internet, in particular, has become an invaluable tool for making recordings accessible to the public. Palestinian Oral History Archive (POHA) is an example of a solid database that preserves more than 1000 hours of testimonies narrated by first generation Palestinians and other Palestinian communities displaced in Lebanon. The digital platform created for this archive allows users easy access to numerous recordings 'the eyewitness narratives of first generation refugees have been instrumental to the survival of the cultural geography of spaces, traditions and histories from pre-1948 Palestine'(mentioned in the collection). This digitization of the material is an invaluable innovation that ensured the flourishing of oral history in the digital world. Instead of merely reading narrative, audiences now have the opportunity to engage directly with the actual recordings. It is not only the recording that was preserved but also the life story of the participants as they were narrated. Their memory, their past and their life story were protected and made available to the public, only a click away from immersing themselves in the compelling stories.

> Oral history... is the verdict of those who weren't there on those who were (Nyhan and Flinn, 2016).

Systems such as Oral History Metadata Synchronizer (OHMS) provide a new opportunities that makes the access to oral testimonies even more user friendly. Navigating these recordings reveals textual titles and sets of keywords that correspond to specific segments within the audio. This feature is beneficial for researchers, enhancing the efficiency of their research work. Instead of spending countless hours listening to entire testimonies to extract relevant information for their study, researchers can now browse through keywords, listen to the corresponding segment and build their analyses more effectively. The advantages of a metadata synchronizer are evident in the Palestinian Oral History Archive (POHA). Each interview in this extensive database is accompanied by a time-coded transcript, enabling researchers to click on specific keywords corresponding to particular time segments in the recording. The primary benefit of metadata synchronizers lies in their ability to allow researchers proficient in the narrator's language to directly listen to the recording. This user-friendly, firsthand access is the most effective way for researchers familiar with the language of the discourse to fully grasp the implications of the uttered sentences. After providing the researcher an easy access to the recorded testimonies, it is her role to capture conversational implicatures or address potential biases.

While the advantages of OHMS are clear, they primarily function as a search engine for those who are familiar with and immersed in the language of the speaker. As a Lebanese researcher, I was impressed by the ease of accessing various recordings. The indexing system allowed me to focus on specific segments relevant to my studies. I encountered no difficulty in understanding the content, being a native Arabic speaker and familiar with the sociopolitical context of the interviews. There are two significant challenges: listening to the testimonies requires more time than reading the narrative, and, more importantly, not all scholars are familiar with or immersed in the narrator's language. This raises an important concern: how can one achieve a comprehensive understanding of what is narrated from looking at the narrative (whether translated to one's native language or not)? Additionally, how can a transcript fully capture the hermeneutics of spoken language?

4 On Natural Language Processing: What is natural about natural language?

What distinguishes language processing applications from other data processing systems is their use of knowledge of natural language (Keselj, 2009). This approach does not focus solely on the formal understanding of language as developed by philosophers like Gottlob Frege and Bertrand Russell, but rather emphasizes the informalist aspect of language. Grice presents two accounts that are relevant to our subject of study. On one hand in the literature of philosophy of language, the formalists employ formal devices such as $\wedge, \vee, \exists, \forall$ to represent their counterparts in natural language such as 'and, or, there exists, for all'. Words that do not conform to this formal structure are often viewed as exceptions to be minimized or disregarded. However, following our initial examination, which centers on language as a speech act and grounds semantics in the illocutionary force attached to an utterance, we depart from a strictly formalist view. As Grice notes,

> language serves many important purposes besides those of scientific inquiry. There are very many inferences and arguments expressed in natural language and not in terms of these devices, that are nevertheless recognizably valid (Grice, 1991).

If we adopt a formalist approach to natural language, it would seem plausible that any algorithm could accurately depict the semantics of our speech. However, given that we do not take this approach, the task of preserving the natural language of oral testimonies becomes significantly more complex. As previously noted, context plays an indispensable role in determining the semantic value of an utterance. Therefore, any model employed for this purpose must be enhanced with deep learning capabilities, particularly those equipped with word sense disambiguation (WSD) tasks—i.e. the task of selecting the correct sense of a word within a given context.

Before detailing the specific tasks that an NLP model should encompass, it is important to reiterate the context we are addressing: individuals who prefer reading the transcript or those unfamiliar with the original language and thus rely on a translated transcript. For this to be feasible, the initial model must be capable of converting speech into text. Automatic Speech Recognition (ASR), a subset of natural language processing, performs this function by transcribing spoken words into text, thereby facilitating analysis, search, and archiving. The technologies under ASR uses machine learning algorithms to convert spoken language into text. It recognizes audio input, identifies the phonetic components of the segments, and transcribes them into written words (Keselj, 2009).

For the native speaker, incorporating the audio with the text presents the ideal scenario which will provide a rigorous framework in truly capturing the illocutionary force of oral testimonies. However, it is the case that most researchers are not familiar with the native language of the narrator. To preserve the hermeneutics of narrated content, particularly in terms of conventional and conversational implicatures for a foreign language, a speech-to-text model alone is insufficient. In most cases, the challenge extends beyond phonetics, morphology, and syntax to encompass semantics and pragmatics.

To adequately capture these multilayers of meaning, an NLP model incorporating deep learning architectures and techniques is necessary. Deep learning in natural language processing features a multidimensional approach that assists the reader in interpreting the speaker's intended meaning. Phonetics, which studies linguistic sounds and their relationship to written words, is a foundational component in any NLP system. Morphology, the study of the internal structure of words, is also crucial, as it helps link words to sounds and understand their composition—an essential step for interpreting word meanings and grammatical structures. Lastly, syntax is vital for discerning the structural relationships among words in a sentence, laying the groundwork for an accurate representation of both meaning and context.

4.1 On the pragmatics of the expression

If we stop at this point, we achieve only a formal understanding of natural language. However, as previously mentioned, natural language—especially in the context of oral history— cannot be fully understood through formal language alone. To capture the nuances necessary for comprehending conventional and conversational implicatures, an NLP model must incorporate characteristics that allow readers of transcripts to grasp these deeper meanings. This is achievable through the following two essential components: semantics and pragmatics. The study of semantics, grounded in Frege's compositionality thesis from *Begriffsschrift* (1879), posits that the sense of a compound expression is determined by the senses of its constituents. In the context of deep learning, semantics involves the analysis of word meanings and how they combine to convey the meaning of a sentence. However, even at this level, the generated output primarily captures the sentence meaning. To move beyond this and capture the normative aspects of discourse, deep learning models integrate pragmatics. Pragmatics situates the use of language within a broader context, allowing the analysis of linguistic discourse to extend beyond isolated sentences and incorporate the standards and conventions that shape communication (Goyal et al., 2018).

Deep learning models encompass the five characteristics outlined above, enabling them to capture nuanced meanings and their relationships to text, as well as perform sentiment analysis that makes explicit the emotions implicit within an utterance. BERT (Bidirectional Encoder Representations from Transformers) is an example of a model that can support the analysis of text generated by ASR. BERT's bidirectional understanding of sentences—analyzing both preceding and following text—allows it to contextualize meaning within a broader discursive framework. The capacity for sentiment analysis is particularly vital in testimonies that shape the life story of the narrator. BERT-based models provide summaries of lengthy testimonies while emphasizing key events and themes. By fine-tuning BERT for sentiment analysis, it becomes possible to identify emotional tones within testimonies, such as anger, fear, and more. The dual capacity for generating concise summaries and conducting sentiment analysis equips researchers with tools that not only enhance efficiency but also offer insights into the semantic nuances of discourse, which can shift depending on emotional variations. Recognizing sentiments is particularly important, as it aids researchers in understanding the implications of the narrator's speech. For example, the statement, "Shame on us to leave our country" when expressed in a tone of sadness and helplessness, may suggest that the narrator feels forcibly displaced and powerless. Conversely, if the same statement is delivered with anger, it could reflect the narrator's stance on resistance and resilience. By using ASR to transcribe spoken words into written text and employing BERT to interpret both the explicit content and the implicit meanings within the text, a comprehensive approach can be achieved. This method is especially beneficial for non- native speakers, enabling them to engage more effectively with the narratives conveyed.

NLP offers a powerful tool that has made the history of oral testimonies more accessible to the public. For listeners immersed in the language being narrated, systems like OHMS provide the advantage of a user-friendly archive, complete with keywords and titles that correlate with their exact timing in testimony segments. For those unfamiliar with the language, combining ASR with BERT can facilitate a deeper hermeneutical understanding, helping to interpret what is implied but not explicitly stated. However, whether the listener is an AI model or a human, deriving the meaning of what is said (illocutionary force) comes with its own set of obstacles. In the final section of my paper, I discuss two challenges: one specific to AI and non-native readers, and another that considers the possibility of a bias-free epistemic approach to the utterances of the narrator.

5 Challenges to be resolved

5.1 On the unpredictability of conversational implicatures

As previously discussed, some implicatures are conventional while others are conversational. Referring to conventions means referring to a set of rules and rituals that, through repeated use over time, form a pattern known as 'conventions.' It is relatively straightforward for an NLP model to identify such patterns and infer the conventions. Similarly, for a foreign listener, an immersion in the native speaker's community over time can facilitate the recognition of these patterns and the abstraction of conventions. Therefore, grasping conventional implicature requires a degree of immersion in the other's community to predict the meaning behind spoken language, a possible task that both NLP models and human effort can achieve.

Conversational implicatures on the other hand are intrinsically non-conventional and do not adhere to predictable patterns. An AI trained to make connections based on pattern recognition would struggle to capture the essence of conversational implicature. By definition, Grice introduces conversational implicature as a move that exploits established norms. When narrating one's story, it is inevitable that both conventional and conversational implicatures will occur. While capturing the former allows for the preservation of the illocutionary force governed by patterns, failing to mirror the latter results in an incomplete representation of the illocutionary force generated by conversational implicatures. As a result, the hermeneutical account derived from conversational implicatures is often less precise and clear.

5.2 On biases inherent in the discursive practices

The second challenge pertain to the presence of bias on a human and AI level. Miranda Fricker a feminist philosopher introduced in her book *Epistemic Injustice, Power and the Ethics of Knowing*, the concept of epistemic injustice. Her focus is on the concept of injustice in the epistemic activity that harms the individual in her capacity as a knower. For the purposes of this paper, which centers on oral testimonies, the focus will be on testimonial injustice, one of the key forms of epistemic injustice.

Epistemic and linguistic conduct are immersed in the context of social power i.e. the ability to exert force and constraint on the other. The ability to assert authority is essential to discursive practices as some are distinguished as authoritative discourse whereas others as marginalized discourse. Fricker defines identity power as

> a form of social power which is directly dependent upon shared social-imaginative conceptions of social identities of those implicated in the particular operation of power... That governs for example what it means to be a woman or a man, or what it is or means to be gay or straight, young or old, and so on (Fricker, 2007).

Constructed social identities, such as being labeled a 'refugee' or an 'Arab,' create prejudices that impact how individuals are perceived. When these prejudices lead the hearer to assign less credibility to the speaker than warranted, it constitutes testimonial injustice. Such biases are not exclusive to human interactions but also extend to AI. The NLP models under consideration build implicatures based on social patterns, which are often laden with identity power and prejudices. If the database includes inherent prejudices, the AI model will inevitably replicate these biases.

A notable example outside the realm of oral testimonies occurred in 2015 when Google's algorithm mistakenly labeled images of Black individuals as gorillas. This error was rooted in the lack of diversity within the training datasets. A similar issue arises in the context of oral testimonies, where AI tools risk misrepresenting narratives by perpetuating gender biases embedded in stereotypical language patterns within the data. For instance, even when a male nurse and a female doctor were intentionally identified as such, the AI system continued to associate the roles with traditional stereotypes, labeling the nurse as female and the doctor as male. Consequently, AI models reflect and perpetuate the social biases inherent in the conventional patterns they are trained on.

6 Conclusion

In navigating the interplay between oral testimonies, natural language processing, and hermeneutics, we are reminded that language is not merely a vehicle for information but a dynamic, context-dependent tool shaped by the voices that tailor it. This paper has explored how NLP models, when combined with deep learning, can serve as powerful resources for capturing both the explicit and implicit content of spoken narratives. However, the complexities in deriving conversational implicatures and the biases that underpin both human and AI hermeneutical scheme present significant challenges. To engage meaningfully with oral testimonies, particularly in diverse linguistic and cultural landscapes, we must be vigilant of the limitations and assumptions embedded in our approaches. Only through recognizing these complexities that we can strive for an epistemic practice that respects the speaker's voice and preserves the force of their words. Addressing these challenges demands a commitment to refining NLP models, not only to replicate patterns but to approach the nuanced approach of understanding—where words, identity, and meaning converge in testimonies.

Acknowledgments

I would like to acknowledge the directors of Palestine Oral History Archive at the American University of Beirut without which the work on Palestinian oral testimonies wouldn't have been possible. Their wide collection offered me a substantial platform in developing my ideas. I would also like to extend my heartfelt gratitude to Mousa Mohammadian, Lena Dadourian and Dala Fakhredine for the stimulating conversations that significantly contributed to the refinement of my ideas. I am grateful to Mohamad Sabra for his support in allowing me the time and space necessary to complete this work.

References

John Langshaw Austin. 1965. How to do things with words. the william james lectures delivered at harvard university in 1955.

Douglas A Boyd. 2014. *Oral history and digital humanities: voice, access, and engagement*. Springer.

Miranda Fricker. 2007. *Epistemic injustice: Power and the ethics of knowing*. Oxford University Press.

Palash Goyal, Sumit Pandey, and Karan Jain. 2018. Deep learning for natural language processing. *New York: Apress*.

Paul Grice. 1991. *Studies in the Way of Words*. Harvard University Press.

Vlado Keselj. 2009. Book review: Speech and language processing by daniel jurafsky and james h. martin. *Computational Linguistics*, 35(3).

Julianne Nyhan and Andrew Flinn. 2016. *Computation and the humanities: towards an oral history of digital humanities*. Springer Nature.

John R Searle. 1969. Speech acts: An essay in the philosophy of language. *Cambridge University*.

A cultural shift in Western perceptions of Palestine

Terry Regier
Department of Linguistics
UC Berkeley
terry.regier@berkeley.edu

Muhammad Ali Khalidi
Department of Philosophy
CUNY Graduate Center
makhalidi@gc.cuny.edu

Abstract

We argue that a cultural shift in Western perceptions of Palestine began in the late 1990s to 2000s, leading to increased openness to Palestinian perspectives, including awareness of the Nakba. We present 3 computational analyses designed to test this idea against data from the 2020 Google Books English dataset. The results support the claim of a cultural shift, and help to characterize that shift.

Introduction

In the West today, there is some awareness of the Nakba — the displacement and dispossession through violence of Palestinian Arab society in 1948 (Zureiq, 1948). This awareness is evident from references to the Nakba in discussion of the current war in Gaza, and from the fact that a major computational linguistics conference is hosting a workshop on Nakba narratives. But not long ago, things were different. In her book *Perceptions of Palestine*, written from a U.S. perspective, Christison (1999, p. 2) remarked:

> The dispossession and dispersal of the Palestinians in 1948 has always been and to a great extent remains "an unrecognizable episode," as [Malcolm] Kerr put it, even for most informed Americans . . . — unrecognizable in the sense not only that the dispossession has been forgotten but also that it is seldom recognized to be the ultimate cause of the conflict.

From today's perspective, these remarks seem dated, and it is striking that the author does not use the word *Nakba* in a direct reference to that historical event. In contrast, several books published in English since then have the word *Nakba* (Arabic for *catastrophe*) in their title (e.g. Sa'di and Abu-Lughod, 2007; Masalha, 2012; Abdo and Masalha, 2018; Allan, 2021). Thus it appears that the Nakba has become more prominent in the West, both as a recognized historical event and as a word, than it was not too long ago. Why is this?

We pursue the hypothesis that a cultural shift occurred in the late 1990s to 2000s, resulting in greater Western openness to Palestinian perspectives — including but not limited to awareness of the Nakba. On this hypothesis, the shift emerged in opposition to a dominant view that is indifferent or hostile to Palestinian perspectives, and that views Palestine and Palestinians from the outside, as a problem, and in terms of the so-called "conflict". The collision of these two views can be seen in current tensions in the West surrounding the Palestine question; our hypothesis concerns the origins of the more Palestine-sympathetic view.

Our study connects to prior computational work that has explored linguistic reflections of dehumanization (Mendelsohn et al., 2020; Caporusso et al., 2024). We emphasize in particular the feature of negative evaluation, which has been engaged in this prior work, and also the notions of psychological distancing and denial of subjectivity that have been identified as features of dehumanization (Opotow, 1990; Haslam, 2006) but have received less attention in computational work. A related body of work explores bias and propaganda in news media (e.g. Hamborg et al., 2019), and a line of this work has specifically addressed representations of the Palestine question in the news, in the context of the current war on Gaza (e.g. Zaghouani et al., 2024) and the 2014 Gaza war (Al-Sarraj and Lubbad, 2018). With respect to a cultural shift in Western perceptions of Palestine, Telhami (2018, 2020) and Serhan (2023) argued for a recent shift in the U.S., based on polling data, and Regier (2016) presented evidence that the term *the Nakba* entered the English language around 1998, and proposed that this might have signalled the beginning of a general shift. Regier and Khalidi (2024) provided an initial test of that proposal, based on historical

Proceedings of the Proceedings of the 1st International Workshop on Nakba Narratives as Language Resources, pages 9–17
January 20, 2025.

patterns of language use, suggesting support for it. However they did so briefly, in a few paragraphs in a non-peer-reviewed publication, with technical detail limited to 2 footnotes. Our study tests the same hypothesis in detail; the specific analyses we report here are novel.

In what follows, we first describe the data on which we rely, and then test the hypothesis of a general cultural shift in a series of 3 studies of increasingly fine temporal grain, asking: (**Study 1**) Was there a general shift?; (**Study 2**) If so, was the shift historically unusual?; (**Study 3**) Is such a shift supported by the first appearance of specific English words in a Palestinian context? We then conclude, and consider limitations of this work.

Data

We drew on data from the 2-gram subset of the Google Books English corpus (Michel et al., 2011), Version 20200217,[1] which we took to be reasonably representative of elite Western language use. We are aware of concerns surrounding this dataset, in particular relating to its change in composition over time, for example due to changes in the degree of representation of scientific work and fiction (e.g. Pechenick et al., 2015; Schmidt et al., 2021). In an attempt to address these concerns, we restricted attention to a subset of the overall 2-gram dataset: those bigrams in which the first term is a national adjective (explicitly marked as an adjective with the suffix *_ADJ*), and the second term is any noun (marked with the suffix *_NOUN*) composed of lower-case characters, which excludes proper names.[2] This yielded a dataset of bigrams such as *Korean students*, *Nigerian government*, *Israeli delegation*, *Palestinian territories*, etc., holding frequency counts for each bigram for each year. We also restricted the years under consideration to 1948 (the year of the Nakba) through 2019 (the last year covered by the dataset). We refer to this restricted subset as the *bigram dataset*. The restriction to (national adjective, noun) pairs is intended to reduce any influence of a change in composition of the larger dataset over time: while an influx of scientific publications or fiction could skew the overall Google Books dataset by increasing the frequency of certain terms, it seems less likely that it would substantially skew a subset of that dataset that is composed only of bigrams of this character. When we calculate the relative frequency of a target bigram, we normalize using only the frequencies of bigrams in this bigram dataset. Figure 1 shows such relative frequency traces over time for the term *Palestinian* (i.e. *Palestinian* * where * is any noun), and for *Palestinian nakba*. The time period highlighted in pink (1998-2012) shows an increase in usage for *Palestinian*, and a sharp increase from near zero for *Palestinian nakba*. On this basis, we take 1998-2012 to be a target period of apparently greater attention to Palestinians, and we test the hypothesis of a cultural change during that period.

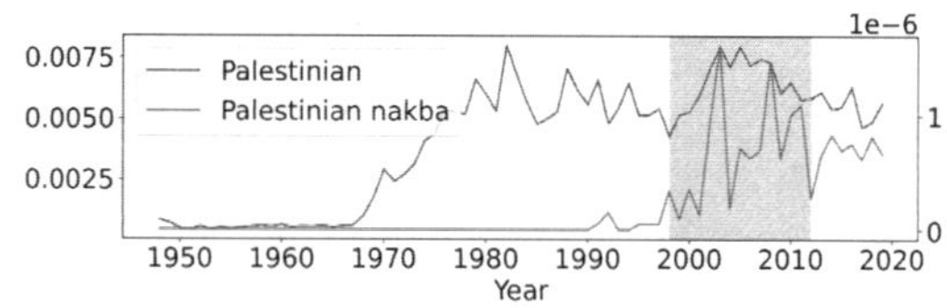

Figure 1: Relative frequency over time for *Palestinian* (left y-axis) and *Palestinian nakba* (right y-axis), in the subset of the Google Ngram dataset that we use: the "bigram dataset". The time period in pink is 1998-2012.

Study 1: A general cultural shift?

If there was a general cultural shift, then there should be expressions other than *the Nakba* or *Palestinian nakba* that: (1) increased in frequency during the target period, (2) are still in use, and (3) convey openness to Palestinian perspectives. To identify those words that increased in frequency in a Palestinian context during the target period, and that remained high-frequency afterwards, we extracted from the bigram dataset those nouns n that appeared in the bigram "Palestinian n" disproportionately more often after the target period than before it. The target period is 1998-2012, so we defined two periods on either side of it: the distant past, which we call "then", defined as 1948-1997, and the recent past, which we call "now", defined as 2013-2019. We calculated, for each noun n that appears in a bigram of the form "Palestinian n", the log of the likelihood ratio:

$$G(n, \text{now}) = \log_2 \frac{p(\text{Palestinian } n|\text{now})}{p(\text{Palestinian } n|\text{then})} \quad (1)$$

where the two conditional probabilities are estimated as relative frequencies based on corpus counts in the bigram dataset, and with normalization also based on counts in the bigram dataset,

[1] http://storage.googleapis.com/books/ngrams/books/20200217/eng/eng-2-ngrams_exports.html.

[2] When listing words here, we omit the *_ADJ* and *_NOUN* suffixes for readability.

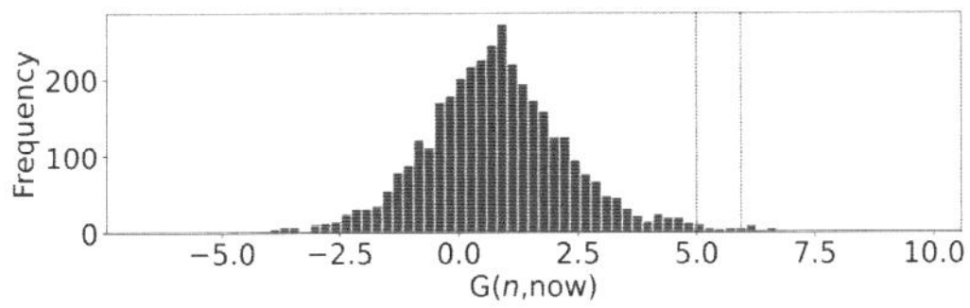

Figure 2: The histogram shows $G(n, \text{now})$ for all nouns n that are modified by the national adjective *Palestinian* in the bigram dataset. The red line marks this quantity for the noun *nakba*, and the green line marks $G(n, \text{now}) = 5$, which means that the bigram probability for "Palestinian n" is $2^5 = 32$ times greater in the recent than in the distant past. Of the full set of 3698 nouns, 64, or 1.7%, are at or above this value.

with add-one smoothing applied to all corpus counts. $G(n, \text{now})$ measures the extent to which a given noun n was more frequent in a Palestinian context in the recent than in the distant past, and Tenenbaum and Griffiths (2001) argue that this quantity, the log of the likelihood ratio, captures the cognitive notion of being a good example of a category — in this case, the category of the recent rather than the distant past. Thus, nouns with high values for $G(n, \text{now})$ should be good examples (hence the letter G), or prototypical, of text from the recent rather than the distant past.[3]

The results of this analysis are shown in Figure 2. It can be seen that *nakba* (red line) is an extreme example of a word that showed increased relative frequency in a Palestinian context during the recent past compared with the distant past; thus, the bigram *Palestinian nakba* is identified as prototypical of the recent past, among bigrams starting with *Palestinian*. At the same time, *nakba* is not the only such extreme example. The green line in the figure marks a value that is lower than that for *nakba*, but high enough that only a small fraction of all nouns is at or above this value (see caption). The 64 words in this upper tail are listed in the top panel of Table 1, in order of decreasing $G(n, \text{now})$, i.e. decreasing prototypicality with respect to the recent past. A number of these newly prominent words capture a view of Palestinians from "up close," without much psychological distancing. This can be seen in words (other than *nakba*) that explicitly adopt Palestinian perspectives, as one would expect if there had been a general cultural shift, e.g. *sumud* (Arabic for steadfastness), *keffiyeh, intifadas*, words that highlight Palestinian subjectivity, e.g. *subjectivity, testimonies, narratives*, and words that capture ordinary human interests e.g. *football, restaurants, filmmakers*. Another theme represented here is that of the internet, e.g. *internet, website, hackers*; this is significant because it has been suggested (Regier, 2016; Regier and Khalidi, 2024) that the advent of the internet may have facilitated a cultural shift in Western perceptions of Palestine, by opening up access to information from a wide range of sources that previously would have been difficult to find. Overall, there seems to be a tendency for the newly prominent words to capture Palestinian perspectives from "up close", i.e. with minimal psychological distance, and thus in a way that emphasizes Palestinian humanity, i.e. the opposite of dehumanization.[4]

The bottom panel of the same table shows the 64 nouns n that appear in the highest frequency bigrams of the form "Palestinian n" for the same period, i.e. 2013-2019, listed in order of descending frequency. This is conceptually distinct from the words with greatest prototypicality for that period just seen in the top panel, and the contents of the high-frequency list contrast with the prototypical words. The high-frequency list contains many words that capture the dominant view of Palestinians "from the outside", i.e. with greater psychological distance – and in fact as a *problem*, which word is included in the list, along with words that, while not necessarily expressing psychological distance, do not express closeness, e.g. *state, people, conflict, issue, refugees*. There is no overlap between the two lists, although *intifadas* (note the plural, only applicable since 2000) appears in the first list, and *intifada* appears in the second. This lack of overlap indicates that the newly prominent words are not extremely prominent in absolute terms. There are some apparent exceptions to the general tendencies noted above — e.g. *intifada* among the high-frequency words, and *corruption* among the newly prominent words — but the general tendencies themselves seem at least qualitatively apparent.

We take these findings to support the view that there was a recent general cultural shift in Western

[3]We used this method rather than that of Monroe et al. (2008) because this method is simpler and has an independent connection to the cognitive notion of being a good example.

[4]As a control, we re-ran the same analysis but on nouns following the national adjective *American* (cf. Mendelsohn et al., 2020). The American list of the top 64 nouns contained many not found on the Palestinian list, e.g. *millennials, subprime, cybersecurity, cisgender, megachurches*. The lists for the two national adjectives contained the following nouns in common: *jihadist, jihadists, jihadi, website, websites, internet, indigeneity*; thus, these words highlight shared themes.

Newly prominent: hip queers intifadas hackers indigeneity gays masculinity jihadist internet rappers bid victimhood modernity spaces stakeholders accession cartoon rapper commemoration corruption jihadists website space rap patriation cleric football telecommunications custodianship filmmaking reform mobility testimonies restaurants shahid sumud nakba polling subjectivity textbook cinemas spouses practitioners coordinator websites keffiyeh imam presidency facilitators classrooms airspace narratives livelihoods campaigners filmmakers jihadi print standoff textbooks imams colonial cinema reforms statebuilding
High frequency: state people conflict refugees territories cause population women refugee society citizens issue resistance leadership territory land question nationalism children problem identity side groups rights leaders community struggle terrorists peace villages leader civilians economy suicide self statehood prisoners uprising communities factions politics residents organizations security history village movement youth woman delegation students areas case government workers militants terrorism lands minority intifada police cities context families

Table 1: **Top**: Nouns that were newly prominent in a Palestinian context as of 2013-19, and thus prototypical of that period rather than the distant past, listed by decreasing prototypicality. **Bottom**: Nouns that were high-frequency in a Palestinian context during the same period, 2013-19.

(specifically Anglophone) perceptions of Palestine, exemplified by newly prominent words that often convey openness to Palestinian perspectives, and psychological closeness to Palestinian experience, in contrast with high-frequency words from the same period, which do not show these features as clearly. This pattern suggests that the cultural shift was real but not especially high-profile at the time. Instead, it can be characterized as a quiet precursor to today's prominence for some of the same ideas, in the context of a continuing dominant view that is not particularly receptive to Palestinian perspectives.

Study 2: Was the shift historically unusual?

For a cultural shift to be noteworthy, it should be unusual — specifically it should be the case that the kinds of changes observed during that period are not observed regularly during earlier historical periods. To test whether this is the case, we ran variants of the analysis from Study 1 above, which picked out words that were newly prominent in a period of interest, but now for systematically varying target periods. Specifically, we conducted such analyses for several target decades: the 1960s, 1970s, 1980s, 1990s, 2000s, and 2010s. For each decade, the past or "then" period lasted from 1948 up until the last year before the target decade, and the "now" period covered the years of that decade.[5] A difference from the analysis in Study 1 is that here we compare an earlier time period with the decade immediately following it — whereas in the original analysis we compared time periods on either side of a specified target period. We adopt the form of analysis we do here because the original analysis spanned a large time range, and we wished to move to a temporally finer grain, to pinpoint more specifically when changes happened.

For each target decade, and for each *Palestinian*-modified noun n in that decade, we obtained the quantity $G(n, \text{now})$ as defined above, with the "now" period being the target decade and the "then" period being the period leading up to it, as just described. This is a measure of the extent to which the bigram "Palestinian *n*" is more frequent in the target decade, relative to the preceding period. Table 2 shows, for each decade, the top 50 nouns that were found to be newly prominent in a Palestinian context for that decade, in order of decreasing $G(n, \text{now})$.[6] Especially in earlier decades, there are several words relating to Judaism, e.g. *talmud, yeshiva, targum, gemara*. Many of the other words align with what one might expect given the historical record of the Palestinian national movement: *revolution, liberation, commando, guerillas, resistance* in the 1960s, when the PLO was first formed and began to assume prominence; *hijackings, hijackers, skyjackers* in the 1970s; *intifada, uprising, protestors* in the 1980s, at the time of the First Intifada; *spokeswoman, tracks, ministries, governance* in the 1990s, at the time the Madrid and Oslo processes. The 2000s are of particular interest because our target period (1998-2012) falls mostly within this decade. Here, the newly-prominent Palestinian words show a conflicting mix of perspectives, perhaps reflecting change in progress. On the one hand, we see the unfortunately familiar theme of violence, presumably because of

[5]For example, for the 1960s, "then" = 1948-1959 and "now" = 1960-1969; for the 1970s, "then" = 1948-1969 and "now" = 1970-1979, etc.

[6]All words listed in this table had $G(n, \text{now})$ values well above zero, i.e. all showed a substantial increase in frequency during the target decade, relative to the preceding period. These words include a few misspellings and partial words, presumably reflecting OCR errors: *lssue* (with a lower-case L, rather than issue), *confl* (presumably part of conflict).

1960-1969: revolution liberation commando guerillas resistance guerilla organisations laissez action freedom exodus fighter fedayin entity intellectuals guerrilla partisans commandos kerygma consciousness level schoolgirls commandoes guerrillas sign diaspora ampulla bourgeoisie patriots congress oak talmud yeshiva activist personality struggle organizations individual identity demands graduates targum saboteurs concept revolutionaries potential brigades fragment males grievances
1970-1979: objectives news camps splinter attempt mini targets bases rejectionists voice diplomacy dimension demonstrations acts hijackers component approach attempts Issue statelet desire quarter reconciliation autonomy selfrule coexistence militiamen leaderships recognition operation dialogue presence resolutions hijackings perceptions role peoplehood dissidents involvement bomb gemara summit participation reporter clashes concentration murder skyjackers spokesmen distinctiveness
1980-1989: dies cartoonist protester intifadah uprising businesses constants taxi folktale fida'iyyin boycott neighborhoods Issues communication reunification scarves anthem marketing collaborator rioting separatists infighting departure unionists intifada evacuation shells infrastructure passenger analyst intifadeh decisionmaking mujahidin rioters protesters nonviolence entrepreneur missile decisionmakers interdependence savings genocide boyfriend agenda assaults cars childhood step sample fringe
1990-1999: tourism track spokeswoman tracks subcontractors debts preventive adm ministries residency donor governance knife television islands bantustans selfgovernance hanging empowerment groundwater police grassroots jails websites management voter trucks worshipers businesspeople polls patriarchy capacities mufti nakba histories Intifada engagement paramilitaries pork airport negotiator demilitarization publics investment custody lesbians plates democratization stateless expenditure
2000-2009: hackers intifadas jihadists mortar moms reform rappers jihadist imams gays patriation modernity corruption reforms shahid queers hip website landholder masculinity airspace internet sniper textbook firebrand suicide textbooks cartoon spouses cinemas custodianship homicide schoolbooks victimhood pollster presidency apologists facilitators contiguity cleric coordinator bombers classrooms medics schoolboys nakba rapper reformers premier descendants
2010-2019: indigeneity accession bid hip internet kitchen queers presidents dessert football rap push application hagiography plaintiffs conict rapper websites rabbinic keffiyeh subjectivity campuses museum operative stakeholders spaces masculinity space collective victimhood schism commemoration restaurants food claimants mobility practitioners filmmaking st confl meals web cartoon campaigners telecommunications cuisine interviewees applications foods rappers

Table 2: Nouns that were newly prominent in a Palestinian context in several target decades, and thus prototypical of that decade rather than the preceding past, listed by decreasing prototypicality for each decade.

the events of the Second Intifada (*sniper, suicide, bombers*). On the other hand, there are a number of words that suggest an awareness of Palestinian perspectives and concerns; these include *nakba*, and also *contiguity*, and arguably *moms, medics, cinemas*. Also of note are e.g. *website, internet, hackers*, which, as noted above, likely reflect the advent of the internet, a possible mechanism for the proposed cultural shift. In contrast, the 2010s appear to be a period in which newly prominent words more consistently reflect Palestinian perspectives and experiences. Of note, 7 of the top 50 newly prominent words in this decade, or 14%, concern food: *kitchen, dessert, restaurants, food, meals, cuisine, foods*. There are very few food-related words in other decades (but see *pork* in the 1990s) — this development, along with other words from this decade, suggests a move away from viewing Palestinians as a political problem, and toward viewing them "up close" as normal human beings with normal interests such as food, and suggests more generally a new openness to and interest in Palestinian culture.

We supplemented this qualitative analysis with a quantitative one. Specifically, we assessed the valence, positive or negative, of each noun (without the adjective *Palestinian*) via sentiment analysis.[7] We used this to classify each of the words in Table 2 above, and noted what proportion of the top 50 words per decade had positive sentiment. The results are shown in Figure 3; Fisher's exact test conducted on the counts underlying those proportions indicated a significant association ($p < 0.025$, 2-tailed) between positive sentiment and the 2010s, compared with the 1960s-2000s pooled together.

[7]We considered several sentiment analysis methods and eventually settled on DistilBERT base uncased finetuned SST-2, based on DistilBERT (Sanh et al., 2019) and made available by HuggingFace. The model accepts text as input (in our case a single noun) and returns a sentiment classification (positive or negative) together with a score showing the probability of the positive or negative classification. We found that all nouns in our data were classified as either very strongly positive or very strongly negative, such that the score added negligible information, and so we retained only the positive/negative classification and not the score. We compared the coverage and classifications of this model with those of two crowd-sourced sentiment lexicons, the NRC Word-Emotion Association Lexicon, or EmoLex (Mohammad and Turney, 2013), and the NRC VAD Lexicon (Mohammad, 2018), and found that: (1) DistilBERT covered approximately twice as many of the nouns in our data as did the crowd-sourced lexicons; (2) DistilBERT and EmoLex agreed in their negative/non-negative classifications for 86% of the nouns they both covered; and (3) the results we report here are qualitatively unchanged if EmoLex or VAD are used instead of DistilBERT, with attention restricted to the words covered by those lexicons.

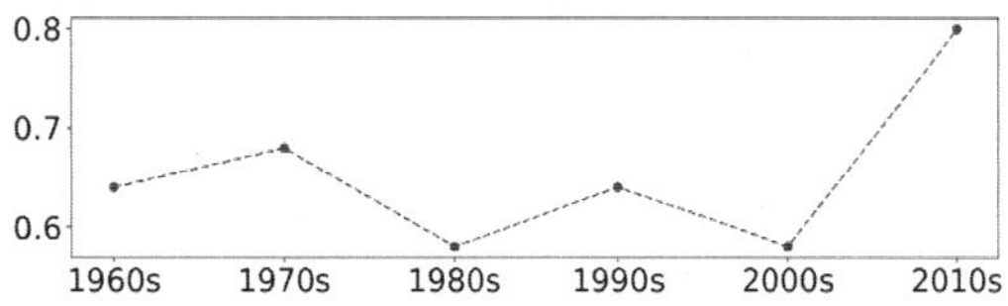

Figure 3: Proportion of the top 50 nouns that are newly prominent in a Palestinian context that have positive valence, per decade. The words analyzed here are those shown in Table 2.

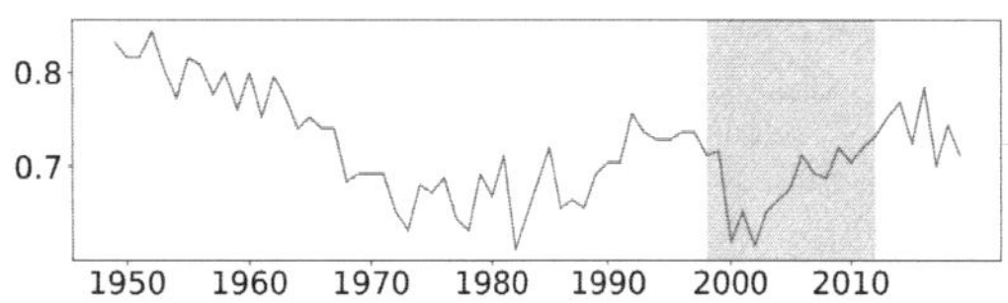

Figure 4: Proportion of the top 250 nouns that are newly prominent in a Palestinian context that have positive valence, by year. The time period shown in pink is the target period 1998-2012.

This confirms the impression that there is more positive sentiment among the newly prominent *Palestinian*-modified words of the 2010s, compared with those of earlier decades.[8]

Finally, we wished to move to an even finer temporal grain, so we re-ran the above analysis, but now targeting specific years rather than decades. For each year, we used Equation 1 to identify which words showed disproportionately greater relative frequency in that year, compared with all previous years since 1948 — that is, which words were newly prominent in a Palestinian context in that year. Space does not permit presenting the actual words retrieved, but Figure 4 shows the proportion of positive valence among the top 250 words per year; the graph for the top 50 is similar but noisier. As with the by-decades analysis above, the overall timeline seems broadly consistent with the historical record. We see a decline in positivity, from a Western standpoint, with the rise of the PLO in the mid-1960s through the 1970s, at a time when Palestinians were most saliently associated in the West with guerilla activity. There is a clear rise in positive sentiment in the 1990s, perhaps reflecting the brief period of Palestinian quasi-respectability in the West that was associated with the Madrid and Oslo processes, and the hopes that this could lead to a resolution of the Palestine question. This positivity continues into the beginning of the target period (1998-2012), suggesting that the cultural shift we are interested in may have ridden on the coattails of the generally more positive sentiment of the 1990s. This is followed by an abrupt decrease in positive sentiment at the beginning of the Second Intifada in 2000 — followed by a recovery by the mid-2000s. Overall, this by-year profile is consistent with the by-decade analysis above, and in particular with the mixed picture for the 2000s seen in that analysis.

We take these results — especially the by-decade results above — to suggest that the cultural shift is historically novel.

Study 3: When did specific words first appear in a Palestinian context?

The above analyses concern increases in frequency, of the sort that we have seen for *Palestinian nakba*. But *Palestinian nakba* did not just increase in frequency — it increased from essentially zero (recall Figure 1). Are there other *Palestinian*-modified words that also increased from essentially zero during the same target period, and if so, do these words also suggest an openness to Palestinian perspectives? And to maintain a fine temporal grain: in which specific years did such words appear?

To answer these questions, we determined, for each *Palestinian*-modified noun in the lexicon (i.e. each noun preceded by the national adjective *Palestinian*, e.g. *Palestinian restaurants*), when that adjective-noun pair entered the lexicon. We did this by examining the raw frequency profile for that adjective-noun pair over time, and identifying the first year for which the frequency of that adjective-noun pair reached 10% of its maximum.[9] Figure 5 illustrates this for the noun *subjectivity* (i.e. the bigram *Palestinian subjectivity*). We were interested specifically in which bigrams entered during or after the period of interest, 1998-2012, although of course many bigrams entered before

[8]The DistilBERT-based sentiment analysis model returns the values positive and negative, but not neutral, and many words that intuitively appear to have neutral valence, e.g. *materials, comment*, are classified as positive by this model. For this reason, it may be helpful to think of positive classification from this model as meaning either positive or neutral, or equivalently non-negative.

[9]Regier and Khalidi (2024) used a different method, based on that of Xu et al. (2016, Supporting Information), which is in turn based on that of Kass et al. (2014, sections 14.2.1 and 14.2.2). We found that our simpler method yielded more satisfactory results. For example, the Regier and Khalidi (2024) method marks *Palestinian intifadeh* as entering the language in 1983 and *Palestinian intifada* in 1991, despite the similarity in the frequency profiles for the two bigrams. In contrast, the method we use here has both bigrams entering the language in the same plausible year, 1988.

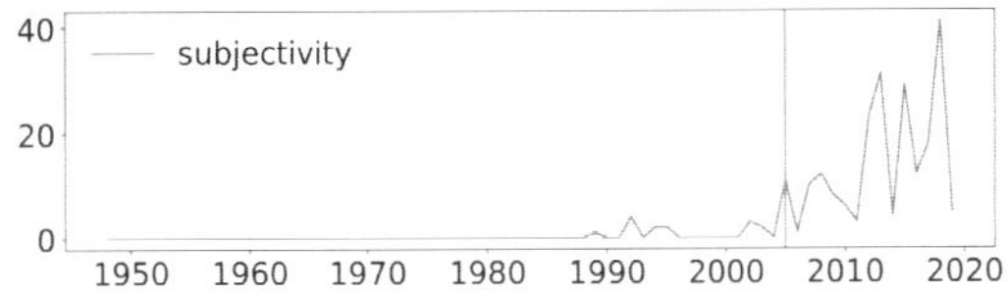

Figure 5: Frequency trace for the bigram *Palestinian subjectivity*, with its year of entry into the lexicon, 2005, marked by a vertical red line.

that time. For this reason, we focused on those *Palestinian*-modified nouns that entered the language between 1998 and the last year of the dataset, which is 2019. These are shown in Table 3, with the adjective *Palestinian* left implicit. It can be seen that there were *Palestinian*-modified nouns other than *nakba* that entered the lexicon during this period and that suggest openness to Palestinian perspectives. An early example is *sumud*, and the food theme appears again as well: *restaurants, dishes, food, kitchen*, along with other words that suggest a psychological closeness to Palestinians: *memory, testimonies, moms, filmmaking, subjectivity*. We saw earlier that many of these words increased in frequency in a *Palestinian*-modified context during the target period; now we see that the corresponding bigrams in fact entered the lexicon at that time. However this is interrupted by a sudden theme of violence around the year 2000, at the beginning of the Second Intifada: e.g. *mortar, homicide, clashes, sniper*. This is consistent with the mixed picture of the 2000s that we saw in the by-decade analysis above, and the by-year sentiment analysis, but now with specific words attached to specific years. By the mid-2000s, many of the newly entering words again suggest a psychological closeness to Palestinian experiences, e.g. *subjectivity* (2005), *food* (2007), *indigeneity* (2010) — but see also *jihadists, jihadi, jihadist*.[10] Overall, we see a shift from initial openness to Palestinian perspectives, to a theme of violence during early 2000s, then back to more openness later on — giving some temporal detail to the idea proposed earlier of the 2000s as a time of contestation and possible change.

We take these results, concerning when *Palestinian*-modified nouns first entered the English lexicon, to support the idea that a general cultural shift occurred during the period of interest, marked by greater openness to Palestinian perspectives. These results also help to characterize that

1998:	restaurants practitioners sumud imam livelihoods debts nakba photographers
1999:	edition gunfire bomber soccer plates print dishes noncompliance survey testimonies compilations lawmaker localities
2000:	facilitators mortar schoolbooks homicide airspace classrooms clashes telecommunications sniper con gays descendants victimhood hackers snipers medics
2001:	publics narratives football stakeholders teens intifadas apologists suicide auxiliaries textbooks corruption imams textbook toddler ceasefire
2002:	license symbol reform masculinity rapper presidency reforms website gatherings filmmaker landholder polling premier memories web moms patriation custodianship
2003:	rabbinic coordinator spouses mobility spaces space tanna compound memory cinema
2004:	cartoon internet jihadists noncitizens jihadi applications jihadist rappers
2005:	modernity cinemas queers filmmaking shahid cohort subjectivity interviewee rap
2006:	member confl commemoration
2007:	nonviolence movies food series
2008:	heathenism
2009:	hip
2010:	indigeneity
2011:	bid websites
2012:	accession st kitchen
2014:	plaintiffs

Table 3: Nouns *n* for which the bigram "Palestinian *n*" entered the lexicon, 1998-2019. Each noun is shown listed by its year of entry. The years 2013 and 2015-2019 are missing from the table because no *Palestinian*-noun bigrams entered the lexicon in those years.

shift at a finer temporal grain.

Conclusions

We have shown (1) that the period 1998-2012 witnessed a shift in English language use, marked by greater openness to Palestinian perspectives; (2) that that shift was historically unusual; and (3) that the date of entry of specific *Palestinian*-modified words into English is consistent with that cultural shift. Our findings are consistent with the U.S. polling results of Telhami (2018, 2020) and at the same time elaborate the picture in several respects. The polling results highlighted the 2010s as a period of change; our results confirm that but also underscore the importance of the precursors to that moment: the 1990s as a period of generally positive sentiment toward Palestinians, and the 2000s as a time of apparently conflicting portrayals, and change, eventually resulting in the consolidation, in the 2010s, of a view that is more open to Palestinian

[10]Recall that the *jihadist* and *indigeneity* themes were shared with the American prototypicality analysis.

perspectives. Our results also help to characterize that recently-emerging view, highlighting in particular the element of psychological closeness to, and implicitly the humanity of, Palestinians.

Some aspects of the cultural shift we have discussed are specific to Palestinians (e.g. *nakba*), while other aspects appear to reflect a broader recent cultural emphasis on previously marginalized perspectives more generally, not just with respect to Palestine (e.g. *indigeneity*). Finally, some other aspects are even more general (e.g. *internet*).

None of this should be allowed to obscure the fact that to a large extent the Anglophone world and the West more generally remain a hostile informational environment with respect to the Palestine question, especially in the context of the ongoing war on Gaza. The Palestine-sympathetic element of language use that we have identified, although real and increasingly influential, remains a countercultural element, and is opposed by standard governmental and elite opinion in much of the West. Still, we think it is significant that the support for Palestine that can be seen in the West today has a relatively long history, dating back to the late 1990s — because that long history suggests that this support has a degree of momentum and is therefore unlikely to be easily halted or reversed.

We have suggested that this cultural shift may help to explain the increase in prominence of the Nakba in the West — but what explains the occurrence of the cultural shift itself? The evidence we have seen does not allow us to pinpoint a specific cause with any certainty, but does allow informed speculation. We have seen that the 1990s generally were a period of more positive sentiment toward Palestinians, likely because of the Madrid and Oslo processes and the hope that these might lead to a resolution of the Palestine question. The 1990s also saw the advent of the internet, as reflected in some of our analyses, and this new medium allowed wide access to a range of ideas and perspectives that previously had not been as easily accessible. This context may help to explain why mention of the Nakba in English began in the late 1990s, an entire half century after the event itself, and not before. This initial period of apparent openness to Palestinian perspectives was then abruptly challenged by the events of the Second Intifada (2000), also reflected in our analyses, and by the attacks of September 11 2001. Mansour (2002) has argued that the September 11 attacks led some in the West to "lump together indiscriminately" (p. 13) those attacks and the Second Intifada, resulting in a worldview in which the U.S. and Israel were confronting a single opponent. At the same time, those attacks also motivated a number of U.S. scholars to examine the Israel/Palestine question closely, in some cases leading to a critique of U.S. policy toward Israel (e.g. Mearsheimer and Walt, 2007). It appears that there eventually grew out of that contested period a set of linguistic usages that were substantially more open to Palestinian perspectives than those that had preceded them — an initially quiet but tangible precursor to today's still-contested environment.

Limitations

The subset of the Google Books dataset that we use may exhibit some change in composition over time (Pechenick et al., 2015; Schmidt et al., 2021), despite our best efforts to mitigate this issue. Moreover, the dataset only covers years through 2019, and thus misses the period of cultural change connected with the ongoing war in Gaza. The restriction to (national adjective, noun) bigrams misses cultural trends that may be reflected elsewhere in language. Finally, the data are drawn from books and are thus skewed toward the language of the cultural elite. These limitations could be addressed by attempting to replicate using a different data source that avoids these issues. The overall argument could be strengthened by more thoroughly probing the robustness of our results to changes in specific methods used for e.g. sentiment analysis, prototypicality for a given time period, and the like.

Acknowledgments

We thank Dan Jurafsky, Charles Kemp, and 3 anonymous reviewers for helpful comments on an earlier draft of this paper. Any errors are our own.

References

Nahla Abdo and Nur Masalha. 2018. *An oral history of the Palestinian Nakba*. Zed Books, London.

Wael F. Al-Sarraj and Heba M. Lubbad. 2018. Bias detection of Palestinian/Israeli conflict in Western media: A sentiment analysis experimental study. In *2018 International Conference on Promising Electronic Technologies (ICPET)*, pages 98–103.

Diana Allan. 2021. *Voices of the Nakba: A Living History of Palestine*. Pluto Press, London.

Jaya Caporusso, Damar Hoogland, Mojca Brglez, Boshko Koloski, Matthew Purver, and Senja Pollak. 2024. A computational analysis of the dehumanisation of migrants from Syria and Ukraine in Slovene news media. In *Proceedings of the 2024 Joint International Conference on Computational Linguistics, Language Resources and Evaluation (LREC-COLING 2024)*, pages 199–210.

Kathleen Christison. 1999. *Perceptions of Palestine: Their influence on U.S. Middle East policy*. University of California Press, Berkeley and Los Angeles, CA.

Felix Hamborg, Anastasia Zhukova, and Bela Gipp. 2019. Automated identification of media bias by word choice and labeling in news articles. In *2019 ACM/IEEE Joint Conference on Digital Libraries (JCDL)*, pages 196–205.

Nick Haslam. 2006. Dehumanization: An integrative review. *Personality and Social Psychology Review*, 10(3):252–264.

Robert E. Kass, Uri T. Eden, and Emery N. Brown. 2014. *Analysis of Neural Data*. Springer, New York.

Camille Mansour. 2002. The impact of 11 September on the Israeli-Palestinian conflict. *Journal of Palestine Studies*, 31(2):5–18.

Nur Masalha. 2012. *The Palestine Nakba: Decolonising History, Narrating the Subaltern, Reclaiming Memory*. Zed Books, London.

John J. Mearsheimer and Stephen M. Walt. 2007. *The Israel Lobby and U.S. Foreign Policy*. Farrar, Straus and Giroux, New York.

Julia Mendelsohn, Yulia Tsvetkov, and Dan Jurafsky. 2020. A framework for the computational linguistic analysis of dehumanization. *Frontiers in Artificial Intelligence*, 3.

Jean-Baptiste Michel, Yuan Kui Shen, Aviva Presser Aiden, Adrian Veres, Matthew K. Gray, The Google Books Team, Joseph P. Pickett, Dale Hoiberg, Dan Clancy, Peter Norvig, Jon Orwant, Steven Pinker, Martin A. Nowak, and Erez Lieberman Aiden. 2011. Quantitative analysis of culture using millions of digitized books. *Science*, 331(6014):176–182.

Saif Mohammad. 2018. Obtaining reliable human ratings of valence, arousal, and dominance for 20,000 English words. In *Proceedings of The Annual Conference of the Association for Computational Linguistics (ACL)*, Melbourne, Australia.

Saif Mohammad and Peter Turney. 2013. Crowdsourcing a word-emotion association lexicon. *Computational Intelligence*, 29:436–465.

Burt L. Monroe, Michael P. Colaresi, and Kevin M. Quinn. 2008. Fightin' words: Lexical feature selection and evaluation for identifying the content of political conflict. *Political Analysis*, 16:372–403.

Susan Opotow. 1990. Moral exclusion and injustice: An introduction. *Journal of Social Issues*, 46(1):1–20.

Eitan A. Pechenick, Christopher M. Danforth, and Peter S. Dodds. 2015. Characterizing the Google Books corpus: Strong limits to inferences of socio-cultural and linguistic evolution. *PLoS ONE*, 10:e0137041.

Terry Regier. 2016. Perceptions of Palestine: The view from large linguistic datasets. *Journal of Palestine Studies*, XLV:41–54.

Terry Regier and Muhammad Ali Khalidi. 2024. Palestine and the Western "street". *Security in Context*. Policy Paper 24-06.

Ahmad H. Sa'di and Lila Abu-Lughod. 2007. *Nakba: Palestine, 1948, and the Claims of Memory*. Columbia University Press, New York.

Victor Sanh, Lysandre Debut, Julien Chaumond, and Thomas Wolf. 2019. DistilBERT, a distilled version of BERT: Smaller, faster, cheaper and lighter. In *5th Workshop on Energy Efficient Machine Learning and Cognitive Computing - NeurIPS 2019*.

Benjamin Schmidt, Steven T. Piantadosi, and Kyle Mahowald. 2021. Uncontrolled corpus composition drives an apparent surge in cognitive distortions. *Proceedings of the National Academy of Sciences*, 118(45):e2115010118.

Yasmeen Serhan. 2023. The American public's views on Israel are undergoing a profound shift. Washington hasn't caught up. *Time*. July 19, 2023.

Shibley Telhami. 2018. Americans are increasingly critical of Israel. *Foreign Policy*. December 11, 2018.

Shibley Telhami. 2020. Changing American public attitudes on Israel/Palestine: Does it matter for politics? In *Israel/Palestine: Exploring A One State Reality — POMEPS Studies 41*, pages 76–82.

Joshua Tenenbaum and Thomas Griffiths. 2001. The rational basis of representativeness. In *Proceedings of the 23th Annual Conference of the Cognitive Science Society*, pages 1036–1041.

Yang Xu, Terry Regier, and Barbara C. Malt. 2016. Historical semantic chaining and efficient communication: The case of container names. *Cognitive Science*, 40(8):2081–2094.

Wajdi Zaghouani, Mustafa Jarrar, Nizar Habash, Houda Bouamor, Imed Zitouni, Mona Diab, Samhaa El-Beltagy, and Muhammed AbuOdeh. 2024. The FIGNEWS shared task on news media narratives. In *Proceedings of The Second Arabic Natural Language Processing Conference*, pages 530–547. Association for Computational Linguistics.

Constantin Zureiq. 1948. *Ma'na al-nakba [The meaning of the catastrophe]*. Dar al-'ilm lil-malayin, Beirut.

Cognitive Geographies of Catastrophe Narratives: Georeferenced Interview Transcriptions as Language Resource for Models of Forced Displacement

Annie K. Lamar[1,2*], Rick Castle[1,2*], Carissa Chappell[1,2*], Emmanouela Schoinoplokaki[1,2*], Allene M. Seet[1,2*], Amit Shilo[1*], Chloe Nahas[3]
[1]Department of Classics, University of California, Santa Barbara
[2]Low-Resource Language (LOREL) Lab, University of California, Santa Barbara
[3]Department of Psychology, University of Montreal
Correspondence: aklamar@ucsb.edu

Abstract

We present a machine-understandable geotagged dataset of translated interviews from the Nakba Archive alongside a complete georeferenced dataset of named locations mentioned in the interviews. In a preliminary analysis of this dataset, we find that the cognitive relationship of interviewees to place and spatiality is significantly correlated with gender. Our data also shows that interviewees with birthplaces depopulated in the 1948 Nakba incorporate references to named places in their interviews in substantially different ways than other interviewees. This suggests that the status of the interviewee's birthplace may impact the way they narrate their experiences. Our work serves as a foundation for continued and expanded statistical and cognitive models of Palestinian forced displacement.

1 Introduction

The Nakba Archive (The Nakba Archive, 2002), a grassroots oral history collective, conducts and archives interviews with Palestinians forcibly displaced during the 1948 Palestinian Nakba. Only thirty of the over five hundred interviews in the Archive have been transcribed and translated into English. In this paper, we present a new language resource to enable semantic and cognitive geospatial analysis of the translated portion of the Nakba Archive.

We provide a georeferenced, machine-understandable dataset of the translated interviews from the Nakba Archive. Due to the limits of current named entity recognition (NER) models for multilingual datasets, we performed the georeferencing manually. We also offer a preliminary analysis of the interviews through the lens of cognitive geography and computational corpus linguistics.

We observe two significant outcomes in our preliminary analysis. First, we find that interviewees' linguistic usage of named places and types of places is significantly correlated to gender (see 4.1). Second, we find that interviews with people whose birthplaces were depopulated in the 1948 Nakba contain references to fewer named places, places in a smaller geographic range, and places, on average, farther from the interviewee's birthplace than other interviews. This suggests that the status of the interviewee's hometown may impact the way they narrate their experiences (see 4.3-4).

2 Background

2.1 The Palestinian Nakba of 1948

The Nakba marks the mass exodus of more than 700,000 Palestinians in 1948, the destruction of more than five-hundred Palestinian villages, and the erasure of hundreds of years of history and local culture after the creation of the state of Israel (Khalidi, 1992; Pappé, 2006). The Nakba had a long-standing impact on the population, creating a massive ongoing refugee crisis (Masalha, 2003). These refugees were refused the right to return to Palestine and to their homes despite United Nations Resolution 194 (United Nations General Assembly, 1948).

The cultural memory of the Nakba is a central element in Palestinian identity and motivates the pursuit of justice and return (Sa'di, 2007; Morris, 2004). This event has left Palestinians with intergenerational trauma that continues to have an impact on mental health and collective identity (Kassem, 2011; Pappé, 2006). The Nakba is both a historical event and a symbol for the ongoing process of colonization and displacement of the Palestinian people (Finkelstein, 2003). Official archives and documents from government sources reveal military plans, such as the Dalet plan, to gain control of Palestinian territories and to displace Palestinians (Pappé, 2006). Every year the Nakba is commemorated on May 15 as a reaffir-

Proceedings of the Proceedings of the 1st International Workshop on Nakba Narratives as Language Resources, pages 18–29
January 20, 2025.

mation of Palestinian rights and remembrance of the injustices endured by the population (Sayigh, 1994).

2.2 Cognitive and Semantic Geography

Cognitive geography is a set of methods and approaches to understanding human thought and behavior as it pertains to space, place, and environment (Mark et al., 1999; Montello, 2018). The field uses geographic features and references to infer how people perceive, conceptualize, and respond to their environments.

Cognitive geography approaches include methods from geospatial semantics, a subfield that focuses on understanding the meaning of geographic entities (Hu, 2018). Such approaches are not necessarily limited to coordinate-based geography, especially when considering regions with vague or changing geographic boundaries (Montello et al., 2014).

In our preliminary analysis, we consider both coordinate and non-coordinate characteristics of named places. We annotate and analyze, for example, the categories of named places an interviewee mentions and the density of references to named places within the transcribed text. Our approach is limited by the amount, quality, and language of the available data (see Limitations).

We do not draw conclusions about the cognition or emotions of the interviewees, but rather we offer a framework for future research into the relationship of displaced peoples and their geographic environments.

3 Data and Language Resource Creation

The Nakba Archive (The Nakba Archive, 2002) is a digital collection of interviews with Palestinians forcibly displaced during the 1948 Palestinian Nakba. Of the over five-hundred oral histories currently preserved in the Nakba Archive, only thirty have been transcribed and translated from Arabic to English. Our structured, geotagged, and georeferenced dataset created from the interviews presented by the Nakba Archive is a significant new language resource for computational historians, linguists, and activists. The dataset has been published in the Harvard Dataverse (Lamar et al., 2024).

3.1 Data Structuring and Annotation

For each of the thirty translated interviews, we construct a dataset that partitions interviewer prompts and their respective interviewee responses. We record separately all the metadata about the interview that is provided by the Nakba Archive, including the interviewee name(s), place and date of birth, place and date of interview, interviewer name, and permalink.[1,2] We also add metadata that includes the language of the original oral interview[3] and the presumed gender[4] of both the interviewee and interviewer. Interview text and metadata are correlated by unique identifiers.

3.2 Geotagging and Georeferencing

For each of the thirty translated interviews, we manually tag every named geographic location mentioned in the text of the interview. Note that locations mentioned by interviewers and in footnotes are tagged, but not considered in our analysis. We consider a "location" to be any instance of a named place for which we reasonably expected to find geographic coordinates. For example, in the phrase "my home" we do not tag a location, but in the phrase "my home in Haifa," we tag "Haifa" as a location.

We then create a set of all tagged named locations from the interviewee responses. There are a total of 331 unique locations in the dataset. For each named location, we manually locate the latitude and longitude. Many places in the dataset have the same names and their physical location must be determined through context; in addition, some places were only able to be located relative to other places or landmarks and by the use of historical resources and scanned maps. If the location exists as an entity on Wikipedia (Wikimedia Foundation, 2012), we use the coordinates presented there. If not, we use other mapping tools and context clues to assign a likely latitude and longitude. If such resources are used, they are cited in the *notes* variable of the dataset containing georeferenced places.

[1] For the sake of data stability, we preserve the PDF files of the translated interviews as they were available through the Nakba Archive in September 2024.

[2] Most of the interview transcripts also include additional information and definitions relevant to the interview content in numbered footnotes. We annotated and recorded each of the footnotes in a separate data table, which is available alongside the other components of our dataset.

[3] Although all the interviews currently in the Nakba Archive are in Arabic, we preserve this variable to make it easier for future researchers to join this dataset with others.

[4] One interview contains responses by two interviewees, Jabr Muhammad Yunis and Khalidiya Muhammad Yunis. Because Jabr Muhammad Yunis does a large portion of the speaking in this interview, we consider the interviewee to be 'male' for the purpose of metadata.

Category	Description	Example	Count	Frequency
Camp	Refugee camp.	Shatila Camp	11	3.32%
City	Large inhabited settlement.	Nablus	65	19.64%
Continent	Name of a continent or portion that mentions continent.	Eastern Europe	8	2.42%
Country	Name of a country.	Syria	26	7.85%
Feature	Specific, named locations such as landmarks, shops, bridges, etc.	Qasmiya Bridge	50	15.11%
Moshav	Jewish agricultural settlement.	Meiron	5	1.51%
Neighborhood	A named neighborhood or district within a city.	Burj al-Barajneh	18	5.44%
Region	Large portion of a country or countries.	Upper Galilee	12	3.63%
School	School of any level, including universities.	Birzeit University	23	6.95%
Town	Inhabited settlement larger than a village, smaller than a city.	al-Nasirah	29	8.76%
Village (-1948)	Village depopulated in 1948.	al-Kabri	55	16.62%
Village (current)	Currently inhabited village.	Yirka	29	8.76%

Table 1: Location categories used in our dataset with descriptions and distribution of categories throughout the dataset of georeferenced places. The **Count** column includes the number of unique places in each category. Note that **Frequency** is the number of places within a particular category out of the list of unique places. For frequencies within the interview text, see Results and Analysis below.

3.3 Location Categorization

We also label each of the 331 locations with a location category. We include twelve possible categories. Whenever possible, we use the label provided by Wikipedia. Otherwise, we use context clues to infer the category to which a location belongs. More information about the location categories is available in Table 1.[5]

4 Results and Analysis

Of all the locations mentioned in these interviews, Palestine is by far the most frequent. Over 7% of geographic references are to Palestine. The next most common reference is to the large city of 'Akka (Acre), which represents 4.97% of references.

4.1 Named Geographic References by Interview

There are 1,168 references to 331 unique named geographic locations in the thirty translated interviews available in the Nakba Archive. The distribution of named geographic references across the interviews is shown in Figure 1.

There is a significant correlation between the gender of the interviewee and the frequency of references to named locations ($r(28) = -.49, p < .01$).[6] Men make 50% more references to named locations than women. The frequency of geographic references is not significantly correlated to the gender of the interviewer ($r(28) = -.14, p > .01$). Likewise, the interviewee's gender does not have a statistically significant correlation to the total length of the interview ($r(28) = -.13, p > .01$;

[5]Note that we code "Palestine" as a country for the purposes of this language resource.

[6]In this study, presumed gender was coded as binary; we use 0 to represent 'male' and 1 to represent 'female'.

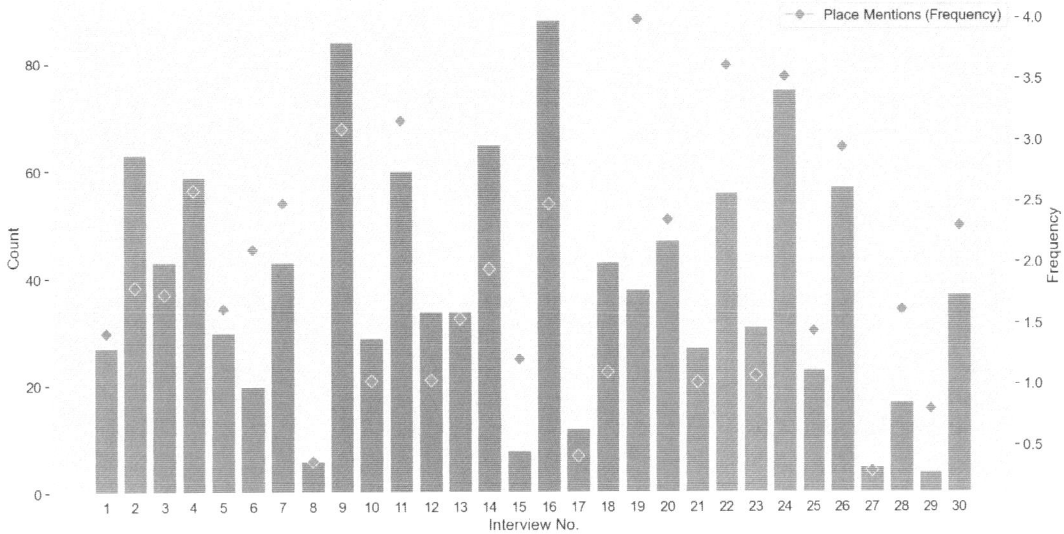

Figure 1: Distribution of named geographic references across all thirty interviews in our dataset. The distribution is presented both as **Count** (bars, left y-axis) and **Frequency** (diamonds, right y-axis). Interviews are represented as numbers on the x-axis for the sake of space; the map of interview numbers to interviewee names is included in Appendix A.

Place Type	Female	Male
Camp	-74.16	55.95
City	-32.87	24.8
Continent	-66.78	50.38
Country	-27.33	20.61
Feature	-16.13	12.17
Moshav	45.35	-34.21
Neighborhood	-64.22	48.45
Region	-41.86	31.58
School	-75.94	57.29
Town	-3.1	2.34
Village (-1948)	8.35	-6.3
Village (current)	47.06	-35.5

Table 2: Percent difference between the expected number of references to **Place Type** and the true number of references, grouped by interviewee gender. Men comprise 57% of the dataset, so the expected number of references to, for example, cities is (0.57 * total number of references to cities=485). Men are thus expected to make 277 references to cities, but in fact make 345: a 24.80% difference.

length computed as word count).

It is therefore unsurprising that when we consider named references grouped by location category, men make more than the statistically expected number of references (i.e. 57%) in almost all categories (Table 2). Male interviewees make, for example, 345 references to cities, a number about 25% higher than we would expect for a dataset comprised of 57% men (expected: 277).

There are three types of locations that women reference with a frequency greater than is expected. The first of these categories, moshavs, has an extremely limited representation in the dataset. The second category, villages depopulated in 1948, shows only a slight over-representation among female interviewees. The third category, however, is well-represented. Women make nearly 50% more references to currently inhabited named villages than is expected based on the gender demographics of the dataset. In fact, of the total 244 references to named villages, women make 125 of them.

4.2 Named Geographic References by Interview Time

We use the concept of interview time in our analysis. Interview time is based on the concept of narrative time, the time it takes the narrator to tell a story in text (Genette, 1980). We define interview time as the percent of total interview progress based on word count.[7] This allows us to examine at what stage of the interview participants mention

[7]Note that many transcripts appear to not include the entirety of the interview. We base interview time on the transcripts provided by the Nakba Archive without consideration of video timestamps.

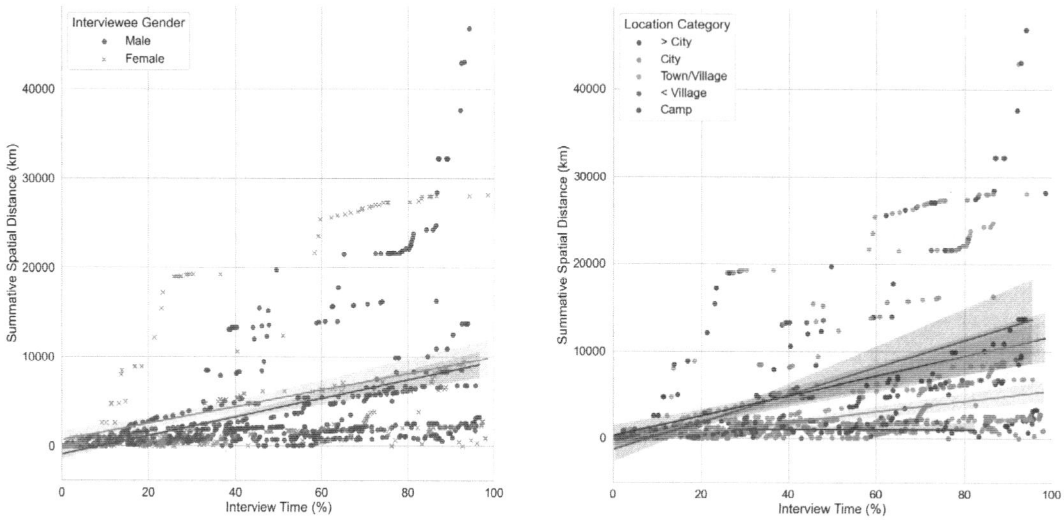

Figure 2: Scatter plots showing summative distance vs. interview time, grouped by gender of interviewee (left) and location category (right). Each dot represents the total summative distance at a specific time in the interview.

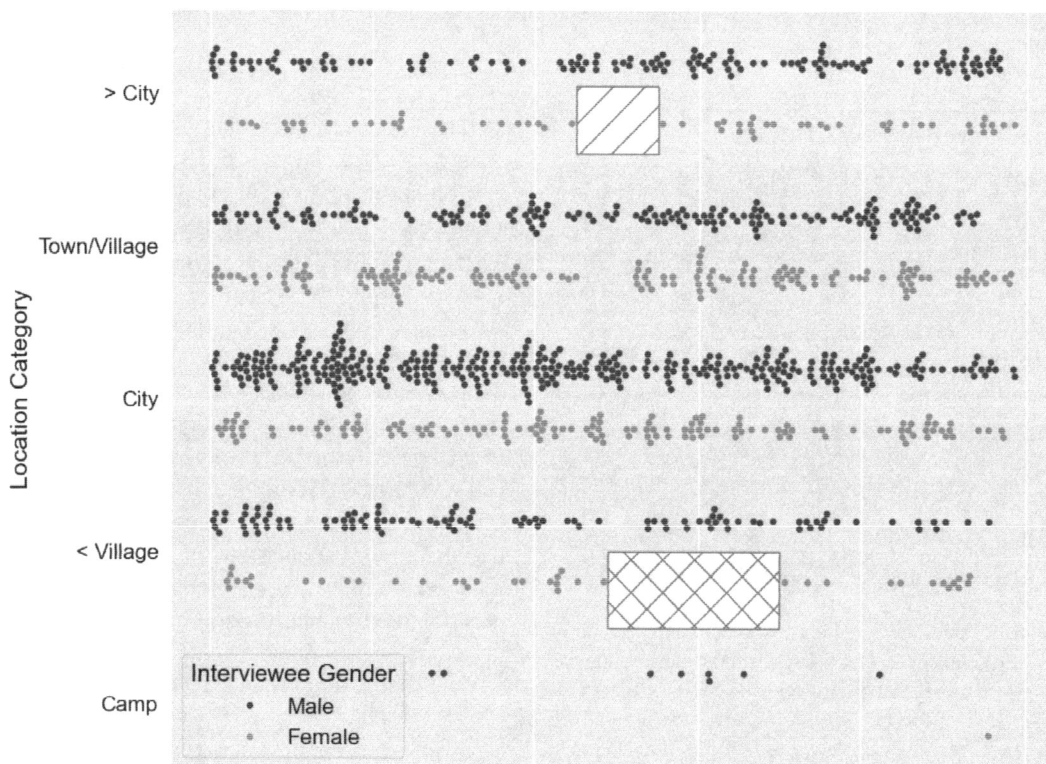

Figure 3: Swarmplot showing references to places in five broad location categories vs. interview time, grouped by gender. $> City$ includes continents, countries, and regions. $Town/Village$ includes towns, currently inhabited villages, and depopulated villages. $< Village$ includes features, schools, neighborhoods and moshavs. The red-hatched boxes highlight two spans of interview time in which women made zero references to cities (upper box) and villages, features, and schools (lower box).

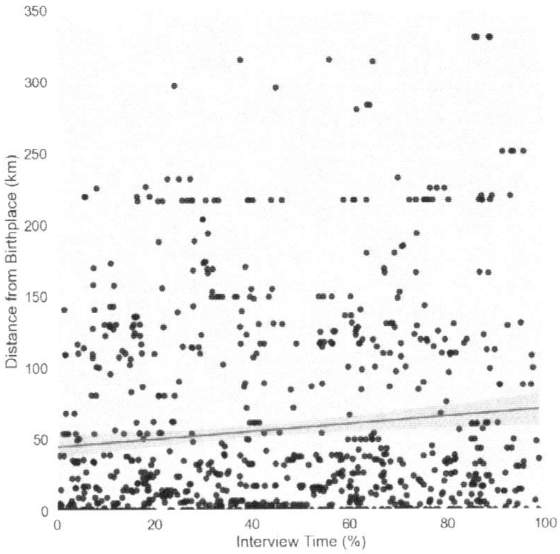

Figure 4: Scatter plot showing **Distance from Birthplace** vs. **Interview Time**. Each dot represents a single reference to a named location. The red line is a linear trend line. For readability, this scatter plot only shows references to locations with a distance from interviewee's birthplace within 0.1 standard deviations. The complete dataset is published in the Harvard Dataverse (Lamar et al., 2024).

certain named places or categories of places while controlling for the length of the interview.

Figure 3 shows the distribution of named references to places within five broad categories. For male interviewees, we observe a slightly higher frequency of overall named geographic references earlier in the interview.

For female interviewees, we observe a fairly consistent frequency of overall named geographic references throughout the interview, with some exceptions. Near the middle of the interview, at about 45%-55% of interview time, women make no references to named geographic entities larger than cities. From 55% to 70% of interview time, women make zero references to named features, schools, or neighborhoods. During this same span of interview time, men make most of their references to refugee camps.[8]

4.3 Spatial Distance and Geographic Range

We use two metrics to evaluate the georeferenced dataset in terms of coordinate-based spatial distance: distance from birthplace and summative distance. Whenever the distance between two pairs of coordinates is computed, we use haversine distance (de Mendoza y Rios, 1795). Haversine distance uses the haversine trigonometric function (Equation 1).

$$haversin(\theta) = sin^2\left(\frac{\theta}{2}\right) \tag{1}$$

Let d be the spherical distance between two points and let r be the radius of Earth. Given two pairs of coordinates for those points (ϕ_1, ϕ_2) and (λ_1, λ_2), we compute haversine distance as in Equation 2. We implement the Haversine Python package (Rouberol and Deniau, 2024).

$$\begin{aligned} haversin\left(\frac{d}{r}\right) = \; & haversin(\phi_2 - \phi_1) \\ & + cos(\phi_1)cos(\phi_2) \\ & \times haversin(\lambda_2 - \lambda_1) \end{aligned} \tag{2}$$

4.3.1 Distance from Birthplace

We first investigate the distance between named locations and an interviewee's birthplace over interview time. As shown in Figure 4, when we consider the named locations with a distance from interviewee's birthplace within 0.1 standard deviations, we observe only a slight upward trend across interview time. Further investigation with a larger dataset is required to determine if this trend is an artifact of the limited size of our dataset (see Conclusion).

4.3.2 Summative Distance

We define summative distance as the total distance between all points in the interview, in the order they are mentioned. For example, if an interviewee consecutively mentions Place A, Place B, Place A, and Place C, we sum $haversin(A - B)$, $haversin(B - A)$, $haversin(A - C)$. Therefore, summative distance will *always* increase over interview time; our analysis depends on the relative rate of increase.

We find very minimal difference in the rate of summative distance growth between male and female interviewees (Figure 2, left). It is notable that at approximately 80% through the interview, some interviewees name locations that are a relatively greater distance away than previously named locations. This result is primarily influenced by the interviews of Nicola Ziadeh and Renee Kutih, represented by interviews nine and twenty-three, respectively. Nicola Ziadeh mentions locations in England and Russia in the context of education, dramatically increasing the summative distance. Renee Kutih mentions a number of cities relatively

[8]There is only one reference to a refugee camp made by a female interviewee.

distant from each other in Israel and Palestine, and recalls a maid from Jizin in Saudi Arabia.

We also find that further into the interview, smaller, more specific named locations have a greater impact on summative distance (Figure 2, right). $City$ has a slow rate of increase while $< Village$ (including features, schools, and neighborhoods) has the highest rate of increase. This might suggest that even though interviewees continue to mention a variety of distant places, they name increasingly specific locations (e.g. a specific neighborhood, rather than a city) nearer to the end of the interview. One possible explanation for this is an established vocabulary between the interviewer and interviewee; since the interviewee has provided ample context for their story by the end of the interview, the specific names of places make sense to the interviewer.

4.4 Named Geographic References by Status of Birthplace

Of the thirty interviewees,[9] exactly half provide a birthplace that was one of the villages depopulated in 1948. We find a significant correlation between status of birthplace and distance from birthplace across all named location references ($r(1163) = .18, p < .01$) (Figure 5, left). The mean distance from birthplace mentioned by the group of interviewees with birthplaces depopulated in 1948 is 1,485.24 km vs. a mean distance from birthplace of 1,057.73 km for the other interviewees.

We also observe, however, a much slower rate of increase of summative distance for interviewees with birthplaces depopulated in 1948. This is largely due to two factors. First, interviewees with birthplaces depopulated in 1948 mention named places far less than the other interviewees. Although representing half the dataset, the former set of interviewees only make 37.8% of references to named places.

Second, interviewees with birthplaces depopulated in 1948 reference a much smaller geographic range of named places overall. We compute geographic range as the maximum distance between any two places named in a single interview. The mean geographic range for interviewees with birthplaces depopulated in 1948 is 28% smaller than that for the other interviewees.

[9]Jabr Muhammad Yunis and Khalidiya Muhammad Yunis, who are interviewed together, list the same birthplace.

Interviewees from depopulated birthplaces verbalize geographies in their narratives that are simultaneously farther from their birthplaces and closer to their birth region.

5 Conclusion

We present a geotagged machine-understandable dataset of the translated interviews from the Nakba Archive alongside a complete georeferenced dataset of named locations mentioned in the interviews. Our structured, geotagged, and georeferenced dataset created from the interviews presented by the Nakba Archive is a significant new language resource for computational historians, linguists, and activists.

We also offer a preliminary analysis as an exemplum of how this data can be used in the future. We find 1,168 references to 331 unique named geographic locations in the thirty translated interviews available in the Nakba Archive. We find a significant correlation between the gender of the interviewee and the frequency of references to geographic locations. By considering spatial distance, we find that interviewees mention places slightly farther from their birthplace the farther they are into the interview and that smaller, more specific locations have a greater impact on summative distance near the end of the interviews.

Finally, we also observe a much slower rate of increase of summative distance for interviewees with birthplaces depopulated in 1948. Investigation into the underlying data reveals that such interviewees mention fewer named places overall and present narratives with smaller geographic ranges.

We intend for these results to serve as a model for continued work and to allow for work towards a cognitive model of geospatial displacement. Information about how displaced peoples understand place and their role in it is invaluable for those working to promote peace and create opportunities for healing connections between homelands and forcibly displaced peoples.

6 Limitations

The two most significant limitations of our work are (1) our inability to work with data in the original language of Arabic and (2) our annotation of only named locations rather than all locations ("my home," "the river") in the interviews. Our analysis is therefore limited to those interviews made available by the Nakba Archive in English and to

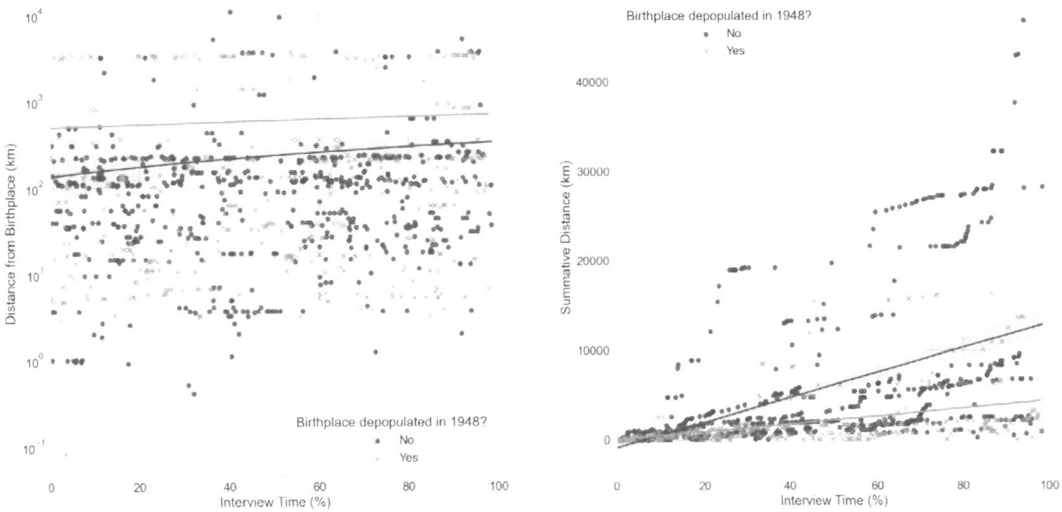

Figure 5: Scatter plots showing distance from birthplace vs. interview time (left) and summative distance vs. interview time (right), each grouped by categorization of birthplace (depopulated in 1948 or not). Note the logarithmic y-axis for the left plot.

consideration of named geographic locations. It is our hope that our method and open-source code can be used by researchers with linguistic and cultural expertise in Arabic.

Other limitations also include the availability of data, especially for small villages and towns that do not have coordinates available through WikiData or other major mapping services like Google Maps. In these cases, we relied on context clues from the interviews (e.g. "five kilometers south of Yaffa") to assign coordinates. Still, we were unable to locate coordinates for fourteen locations in the dataset, which represent 4% of the dataset of named places.

Acknowledgments

We express gratitude to the interviewees whose stories comprise the language resource presented above. We also thank the creators of the Nakba Archive and the interview translators, without whom this project would not have been possible.

References

J. de Mendoza y Rios. 1795. *Memoria sobre algunos Métodos nuevos de calcular la Longitud por las distancias lunares: y aplicacion de su teórica á la solucion de otras problemas de navegacion.* Imprenta Real.

Norman Finkelstein. 2003. *Image and Reality of the Israel-Palestine Conflict.* Verso Books.

Gérard Genette. 1980. *Narrative Discourse: An Essay in Method.* Cornell University Press.

Yingjie Hu. 2018. Geospatial semantics. *Comprehensive Geographic Information Systems*, page 80–94.

Fatma Kassem. 2011. *Palestinian Women: Narrative Histories and Gendered Memory.* Zed Books.

Walid Khalidi. 1992. *All that Remains: The Palestinian Villages Occupied and Depopulated by Israel in 1948.* Institute for Palestine Studies.

Annie K. Lamar, Emmanouela Schoinoplokaki, Rick Castle, Carissa Chappell, and Allene M. Seet. 2024. Georeferenced Interview Transcriptions from the Nakba Archive.

David M. Mark, Christian Freksa, Stephen C. Hirtle, Robert Lloyd, and Barbara Tversky. 1999. Cognitive models of geographical space. *International Journal of Geographical Information Science*, 13(8):747–774.

Nur-eldeen Masalha. 2003. *The Politics of Denial: Israel and the Palestinian Refugee Problem.* Pluto Press.

Daniel Montello, Alinda Friedman, and Daniel Phillips. 2014. Vague cognitive regions in geography and geographic information science. *International Journal of Geographical Information Science*, 28:1802–1820.

Daniel R. Montello. 2018. *Handbook of Behavioral and Cognitive Geography.* Edward Elgar Publishing.

Benny Morris. 2004. *The Birth of the Palestinian Refugee Problem Revisited.* Cambridge University Press.

National Information Standards Organization (NISO). 2022. *CRediT, Contributor Roles Taxonomy*. National Information Standards Organization.

Ilan Pappé. 2006. *The Ethnic Cleansing of Palestine*. Oneworld Publications.

Balthazar Rouberol and Julien Deniau. 2024. Haversine. `https://pypi.org/project/haversine`. Version 2.8.1.

Lila Sa'di, Ahmad H.; Abu-Lughod, editor. 2007. *Nakba: Palestine, 1948, and the Claims of Memory*. Columbia University Press.

Rosemary Sayigh. 1994. *Too Many Enemies: The Palestinian Experience in Lebanon*. Zed Books.

The Nakba Archive. 2002. Nakba Archive.

United Nations General Assembly. 1948. *Resolution 194 (III), Article 11*.

Wikimedia Foundation. 2012. Wikidata.

A Appendix: Interviewee Names and Metadata

Interview ID	Interviewee	Gender	Birthyear	Birthplace
1	Ibrahim Mahmoud Blaybil	Male	1920	Taytabah, Palestine
2	Fifi Khouri	Female	1922	Yafa, Palestine
3	Hasna Mana	Female	1931	al-Manshiyya, Palestine
4	Hamda Jumaa	Female	NA	Arab al-Zubayd, Palestine
5	Ahmad Agha	Male	1930	Tarshiha, Palestine
6	Rifaat al-Nimir	Male	1918	Nablus, Palestine
7	Husayn Mustafa Taha	Male	1921	Miar, Palestine
8	Jabr Muhammad Yunis	Male	1924	Safsaf, Palestine
8	Khalidiya Muhammad Yunis	Female	1922	Safsaf, Palestine
9	Nicola Ziadeh	Male	1907	Damascus, Syria
10	Muhammad Jamil Arabi	Male	1923	Haifa, Palestine
11	Mahmud Abu al-Hayja	Male	1928	Haifa, Palestine
12	Umar Shihada	Male	1922	Qabbaa, Palestine
13	Abd al-Rahman Saad al-Din	Male	1915	al-Zib, Palestine
14	Taliba Muhammad Fuda	Female	1929	Suhmata, Palestine
15	Amina Abd al-Karim al-Wakid	Female	NA	Aylut, Palestine
16	Ismail Shammout	Male	1930	Lydda, Palestine
17	Fatima Shaaban	Female	1928	al-Zib, Palestine
18	Amina Hasan banat	Female	1931	Shaykh Dannun, Palestine
19	Salih al-Nasir	Male	1912	Saffuriyya, Palestine
20	Husayn Lubani	Male	1937	al-Damun, Palestine
21	Kamila al-Abd Tahir	Female	1933	Saliha, Palestine
22	Kamil Ahmad Balawi	Male	1928	Shafa Amr, Palestine
23	Renee Kutih	Female	1925	Ramla, Palestine
24	Muhammad Abu Raqaba	Male	1929	Akka, Palestine
25	Subhiya Salama	Female	NA	al-Zahiriyya, Palestine
26	Anis Sayigh	Male	1931	Tabariyya, Palestine
27	Maryam Uthman	Female	1937	al-Husayniyya, Palestine
28	Fatima Abdallah	Female	NA	Sasaa, Palestine
29	Maryam Mahmud Sabha	Female	1920	al-Zib, Palestine
30	Hasan al-Husayni	Male	1925	al-Quds, Palestine

Table 3: Interviewee metadata, including name, presumed gender, birthyear and birthplace.

B Appendix: Interview Metadata

Interview ID	Location	Date	Interviewer
1	Ayn al-Hilweh camp, Sayda	2004-02-07	Mahmoud Zeidan
2	Hamra, Beirut	2004-07-06	Bushra Mughrabi
3	Ayn al-Hilweh camp, Sayda	2003-01-01	Mahmoud Zeidan
4	Qasmiya gathering north of Sur	2003-01-01	Bushra Mughrabi
5	Burj al-Barajneh, Beirut	2004-03-14	Bushra Mughrabi
6	Beirut	2003-12-11	Mahmoud Zeidan
7	Miye wa Miye, Sayda	2003-04-25	Mahmoud Zeidan
8	Ayn al-Hilweh camp, Sayda	2003-01-01	Mahmoud Zeidan
9	Beirut	2004-01-29	Mahmoud Zeidan
10	Mazbud, Iqlim al-Kharub	2003-10-12	Mahmoud Zeidan
11	Burj al-Barajneh, Beirut	2003-01-01	Mahmoud Zeidan
12	Taalabaya, al-Biqaa	2004-05-29	Mahmoud Zeidan
13	Beirut	2003-01-02	Mahmoud Zeidan
14	Not provided.	2003-10-05	Amira Ahmad Alwan
15	al-Bus camp, Sur	2003-10-15	Bushra Mughrabi
16	Malaab al-Baladi, Beirut	2003-10-11	Mahmoud Zeidan
17	al-Bus camp, Sur	2003-05-15	Jihad al-'Ali
18	Burj al-Barajneh, Beirut	2003-01-01	Bushra Mughrabi
18	Burj al-Barajneh, Beirut	2003-01-01	Mahmoud Zeidan
19	Ayn al-Hilweh camp, Sayda	2003-01-01	Mahmoud Zeidan
20	Trablus, Lebanon	2004-02-08	Mahmoud Zeidan
21	al-Murayja, Beirut	2004-07-09	Bushra Mughrabi
22	Badawi camp, North Lebanon	2003-01-01	Amira Ahmad Alwan
23	Verdun, Beirut	2011-08-17	Mahmoud Zeidan
24	Beirut	2003-11-12	Mahmoud Zeidan
25	Ayn al-Hilweh camp, Sayda	2006-04-29	Bushra Mughrabi
26	Beirut	2003-01-01	Mahmoud Zeidan
27	Burj al-Shamali, Sur	2004-05-09	Bushra Mughrabi
28	Mar Elias camp	2004-03-25	Muhammad al-Masri
29	al-Maashuq, Sur	2003-10-23	Mahmoud Zeidan
30	Verdun, Beirut	2003-12-19	Mahmoud Zeidan

Table 4: Interview metadata, including date and location of interview and name of interviewer. If only a year was provided, we supplied January 1 as the month and day.

C Contributor Roles

We use the CRediT framework to provide detailed information about the contributions of each of this paper's authors (National Information Standards Organization (NISO), 2022).

Author	A	B	C	D	E	F	G	H	I	J	K	L	M	N
Lamar	◆	●	◆	◆	◆	◆	◆	◆	◆	◆	◆	◆	◆	◆
Castle	●	◆	-	-	●	●	●	-	-	-	-	-	●	●
Chappell	●	●	-	-	●	●	-	-	-	-	-	●	●	●
Schoinoplokaki	●	●	-	-	●	●	-	-	-	-	-	-	◆	●
Seet	●	●	-	-	●	●	-	-	-	-	-	-	●	●
Shilo	◆	-	-	-	-	●	-	-	-	-	◆	-	●	◆
Nahas	-	-	-	-	-	-	-	-	-	-	-	-	●	-

Table 5: The ◆ symbol indicates (co-)lead role in category; ● indicates contribution in category. **A: Conceptualization** (Ideas; formulation or evolution of overarching research goals and aims), **B: Data Curation** (Management activities to annotate (produce metadata), scrub data and maintain research data (including software code, where it is necessary for interpreting the data itself) for initial use and later re-use), **C: Formal Analysis** (Application of statistical, mathematical, computational, or other formal techniques to analyze or synthesize study data), **D: Funding Acquisition** (Acquisition of the financial support for the project leading to this publication), **E: Investigation** (Conducting a research and investigation process, specifically performing the experiments, or data/evidence collection), **F: Methodology** (Development or design of methodology; creation of models), **G: Project Administration** (Management and coordination responsibility for the research activity planning and execution), **H: Resources** (Provision of study materials, reagents, materials, patients, laboratory samples, animals, instrumentation, computing resources, or other analysis tools), **I: Software** (Programming, software development; designing computer programs; implementation of the computer code and supporting algorithms; testing of existing code components), **J: Supervision** (Oversight and leadership responsibility for the research activity planning and execution, including mentorship external to the core team), **K: Validation** (Verification, whether as a part of the activity or separate, of the overall replication/reproducibility of results/experiments and other research outputs), **L: Visualization** (Preparation, creation and/or presentation of the published work, specifically visualization/data presentation), **M: Writing - Original Draft** (Preparation, creation and/or presentation of the published work, specifically writing the initial draft), **N: Writing - Review & Editing** (Preparation, creation and/or presentation of the published work by those from the original research group, specifically critical review, commentary or revision – including pre- or post-publication stages)

Sentiment Analysis of Nakba Oral Histories: A Critical Study of Large Language Models

Huthaifa I. Ashqar
Arab American University, Jenin P.O. Box 240, Palestine
Huthaifa.ashqar@aaup.edu

Abstract

This study explores the use of Large Language Models (LLMs), specifically ChatGPT, for sentiment analysis of Nakba oral histories, which document the experiences of Palestinian refugees. The study compares sentiment analysis results from full testimonies (average 2500 words) and their summarized versions (300 words). The findings reveal that summarization increased positive sentiment and decreased negative sentiment, suggesting that the process may highlight more hopeful themes while oversimplifying emotional complexities. The study highlights both the potential and limitations of using LLMs for analyzing sensitive, trauma-based narratives and calls for further research to improve sentiment analysis in such contexts.

1 Introduction

The Nakba, meaning "catastrophe" in Arabic, refers to the forced displacement and dispossession of Palestinians during the 1948 occupation by the Israeli colonial power, a pivotal moment that reshaped the social, cultural, and political landscape of Palestine and the Middle East (Gluck, 2008). Narratives surrounding the Nakba are deeply embedded in the collective memory of Palestinian communities, transmitted through generations via oral histories, personal testimonies, and cultural expressions (Nur, 2008). These narratives, rich in emotional depth, political significance, and historical context, have become essential language resources for understanding the human impact of this traumatic event (Sa'di & Abu-Lughod, 2007). However, the challenge of interpreting, preserving, and analyzing such complex narratives has intensified in the age of artificial intelligence (AI) and large language models (LLMs), which have emerged as powerful tools for analyzing text at scale (Jaradat et al., 2024; Radwan et al., 2024).

Sentiment analysis, a key subfield of natural language processing (NLP), offers the potential to systematically evaluate the emotional content of texts (Assiri et al., 2024; H. Yang et al., 2024), thereby providing insights into the emotional and psychological dimensions of the Nakba narratives. By applying sentiment analysis to Nakba oral histories, we gain the ability to quantify and explore emotions like grief, loss, resistance, and resilience within these stories (Bhattacharjee et al., 2024; Q. Yang et al., 2024). However, while LLMs have demonstrated exceptional capabilities in processing and analyzing vast datasets, they are not without their limitations, particularly when applied to sensitive, culturally charged, and historically complex narratives such as those related to the Nakba (Coeckelbergh, 2023; Tian et al., 2024). These models often struggle with the subtleties of language, historical context, and the lived experiences embedded in oral histories, raising questions about their adequacy in capturing the full emotional and cultural resonance of such narratives (Shi et al., 2023; Zhang et al., 2023).

This paper critically examines the application of sentiment analysis to Nakba oral histories, exploring both the potential and the pitfalls of using LLMs to analyze such narratives. It argues that while LLMs can offer valuable insights into the emotional tone of texts, they must be used with caution, considering the unique cultural and historical context of the Nakba. The study positions Nakba narratives as crucial language resources, emphasizing their role in shaping collective memory and identity, while also critiquing the limitations of AI tools in fully capturing the intricacies of human experience and emotion. By doing so, the paper highlights the importance of interdisciplinary approaches—combining computational methods with cultural sensitivity—when applying AI-driven tools to historically significant and emotionally complex language resources such as Nakba oral histories.

Proceedings of the Proceedings of the 1st International Workshop on Nakba Narratives as Language Resources, pages 30–36
January 20, 2025.

2 Methods

2.1 Dataset

For this study, we utilized the Nakba Archive, a grassroots oral history collective established in 2002 with the aim of documenting the experiences of Palestinian refugees in Lebanon who lived through the 1948 Nakba (Allan, 2005; Hawari, 2023). This dataset is particularly valuable as it includes about 30 video interviews with first-generation Palestinian refugees from different Palestinian villages and towns that were displaced or destroyed during the creation of the Israeli colonial state. The interviews, recorded by refugees in camps in Lebanon, provide firsthand accounts of the mass displacement, dispossession, and violence experienced by Palestinian communities during the Nakba (Allan, 2005; Hawari, 2023).

The Nakba Archive offers a comprehensive and personal account of the Nakba (Fu, n.d.; Regan, 2022), which displaced approximately one million Palestinians, leaving them homeless and dispossessed of their lands. The destruction of Palestinian villages is detailed in these interviews, and the narratives offer vivid depictions of life before 1948 in Palestine. These oral histories serve as primary sources that document not only the traumatic events of the Nakba but also the emotional and psychological impacts that have shaped Palestinian collective identity across generations (Allan, 2005; Fu, n.d.; Hawari, 2023).

The dataset contains a wide range of emotional expressions and personal reflections, which are essential for the sentiment analysis conducted in this study . The interviews capture the depth of grief, loss, resilience, and resistance, reflecting the ongoing struggle for Palestinian liberation, self-determination, and the right of return. The richness and diversity of the testimonies are key to understanding the long-lasting effects of dispossession on the lives of Palestinian refugees and their descendants.

Given its depth and significance, the Nakba Archive offers a unique and invaluable resource for studying how sentiment is embedded in oral histories, especially those related to traumatic historical events (Manna', 2013; Saadah, 2021). The sentiments expressed in these interviews not only shed light on the individual and collective emotional responses to displacement but also provide insight into the broader cultural and political implications of the Nakba on Palestinian identity and memory (Allan, 2005). This dataset, therefore, serves as a critical tool in understanding the role of Nakba narratives as language resources, facilitating an initial and empirical exploration of sentiment within the context of historical trauma and its ongoing repercussions in Palestinian collective mind.

2.2 Proposed Framework

This study proposes a comprehensive framework for analyzing the sentiments embedded in the oral testimonies of Palestinian refugees from the Nakba Archive, utilizing ChatGPT as the primary tool for sentiment analysis. The framework involves a step-by-step approach that first processes the full-length testimonies and then compares the sentiment analysis results from both the original and summarized versions of the testimonies as shown in Figure 1. The framework consists of four main steps.

The first step of the framework involves using ChatGPT to perform sentiment analysis on the complete oral testimonies. For each experiment, we ran ChatGPT five times to ensure consistency, and we took the average. Each testimony, on average, contains 2,500 words, providing rich, detailed accounts of personal experiences and reflections. ChatGPT, as a language model trained on vast datasets, is employed to analyze the emotional tone, sentiment polarity (positive, negative, neutral), and emotional intensity expressed in each full testimony (Havaldar et al., 2023; Kumar et al., 2024; Patel & Fan, 2023). The sentiment analysis in this study aims to capture the emotional responses related to themes of displacement, trauma, loss, resilience, and hope that are central to the Nakba narratives (Allan, 2005; Regan, 2022). This analysis allows for an in-depth understanding of the emotions conveyed across different aspects of the refugees' experiences.

In the next step, ChatGPT is used to summarize each full testimony into approximately 300 words. This step involves distilling the key points, themes, and emotional expressions from the original testimonies while preserving their core messages. Summarization is a critical component, as it enables the analysis of more concise versions of the testimonies, making it easier to compare the sentiments without losing the essence of the original accounts (Kabadjov et al., 2009; Krugmann & Hartmann, 2024). By focusing on the most relevant parts of each narrative, the summarized version facilitates a more streamlined analysis, which can be crucial for examining large datasets of oral histories.

Following the summarization process, ChatGPT is again used to conduct sentiment analysis on the new, condensed versions of the testimonies. This second round of sentiment analysis aims to examine how the emotional tone and sentiment evolve when the testimonies are reduced to their essential elements. By comparing the sentiment expressed in these shorter summaries with the results from the full testimonies, the study can evaluate whether the sentiment is captured effectively and if any emotional nuances are lost during the summarization process (Kabadjov et al., 2009).

The final step in the framework involves comparing the sentiment analysis results from the full testimonies with those from the summarized versions. This comparison is central to understanding the impact of summarization on sentiment expression and whether important emotional nuances are preserved or altered. The study will assess key metrics such as sentiment polarity (positive, negative, neutral) and the intensity of emotional responses in both the original and summarized texts. This comparison will provide valuable insights into the relationship between text length, content condensation, and the retention of emotional depth, highlighting the potential trade-offs when working with condensed versions of oral histories.

The proposed framework allows for a structured and systematic approach to sentiment analysis, leveraging ChatGPT's natural language processing capabilities to process large amounts of qualitative data efficiently. The study investigates the ability of LLMs to understand the narrative sentiments of Nakba testimonies and to what extent it exposes bias towards the emotional nuances that are preserved in this oral history. By comparing the sentiment analysis results across both full and summarized versions of the testimonies, the study also aims to provide a deeper understanding of how different formats of narrative influence the emotional tone and content of the Nakba oral histories.

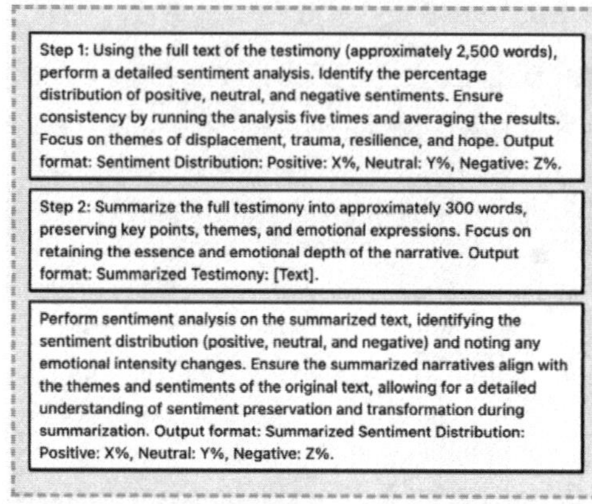

Figure 1: Prompt template for Sentiment Analysis and Summarization of Nakba Oral Histories Using ChatGPT.

3 Analysis and Results

In this study, sentiment analysis was conducted on both the full and summarized versions of ten Nakba oral testimonies, with the results broken down into positive, neutral, and negative sentiment categories for each individual testimony. The following analysis provides a comparison between the sentiment distribution of the full testimonies and their corresponding summaries, along with a critical assessment of the findings.

3.1 Sentiment Results

The sentiment analysis of the full testimonies and the summarized ones are shown in Table 2. The results suggest that the overall emotional tone of the testimonies is predominantly neutral, with a smaller portion reflecting negative sentiments. For the summarized, when compared to the full testimonies, the summarized versions show a slight increase in positive sentiment (31% vs. 26.3%) and a decrease in negative sentiment (19.5% vs. 28.7%). The neutral sentiment remains relatively consistent in both the full and summarized versions, with a small increase from 45% to 49.5%.

Sentiment	Full	Summarized
Positive	26.3%	31.0%
Neutral	45.0%	49.5%
Negative	28.7%	19.5%

Table 1: Sentiment analysis results.

3.2 Key Observations and Assessment

Increase in Positive Sentiment in Summarized Versions: One notable change between the full and summarized versions is the increase in positive sentiment. The average positive sentiment increased by 4.7 percentage points from the full testimonies (26.3%) to the summarized versions (31%). This shift suggests that the summarization process may have inadvertently emphasized more hopeful or resilient aspects of the testimonies, potentially glossing over the more negative or traumatic details in order to condense the narrative.

Decrease in Negative Sentiment in Summarized Versions: Conversely, the negative sentiment decreased significantly from 28.7% in the full testimonies to 19.5% in the summaries. This reduction may reflect the simplification of complex emotional expressions during the summarization process. It is possible that the summarized versions, by omitting certain contextual details and emotional depth, downplayed the intensity of negative sentiments such as grief, anger, and despair, which are prominent themes in the full testimonies. This reduction may not necessarily indicate a shift in the refugees' emotional experience but rather a result of truncating or neglecting the emotional complexity of the narratives.

Individual Variations: There are also notable variations across individual testimonies. For example, Testimony 10 shows a dramatic shift from a relatively balanced sentiment distribution (25% positive, 55% neutral, 20% negative) in the full version to almost completely neutral testimony (95% neutral) in the summary. This stark contrast suggests that the summarization might have completely neutralized the emotional tone of this specific testimony, possibly omitting key emotional elements or reframing the narrative in a more detached manner. In other cases, such as Testimony 3, positive sentiment increased significantly from 35% to 55%, indicating that the summarized version may have emphasized more hopeful aspects of the testimony. These variations highlight the complexity of summarization and the subjective nature of sentiment analysis using LLMs.

The comparison between the sentiment analysis of full and summarized testimonies reveals important insights into how narrative condensation affects emotional expression using LLMs. While the summarized versions exhibited an increase in positive sentiment and a decrease in negative sentiment, the neutral sentiment remained relatively stable. These changes underscore the potential risks of summarizing emotionally complex narratives using LLMs and how LLMs might not be suitable to fully understand such oral history. It seems that the summarization process may unintentionally obscure the full emotional depth of the testimonies, particularly with regard to the more negative sentiments.

4 Discussion

The results of the sentiment analysis on the full and summarized Nakba oral histories offer valuable insights into the capabilities and limitations of LLMs such as ChatGPT. Specifically, the observed shifts in sentiment—particularly the increase in positive sentiment and decrease in negative sentiment in the summarized versions—raise important questions about how LLMs process, condense, and represent emotional content in complex narratives. This discussion will explore what these shifts reveal about the behavior of LLMs in sentiment analysis and summarization tasks.

The increase in positive sentiment in the summarized testimonies, compared to the full versions, can be attributed to several factors inherent in the summarization process. In the context of the Nakba testimonies, this shift could reflect the LLM's tendency to neglect aspects such as fear, sad, or grief. Instead, LLMs emphasized positive emotions and hope, which are central to the Palestinian refugee experience but may not be as prominent in the more traumatic or sorrowful details of the longer narratives. Since summarization inherently involves reducing the complexity of emotional expression, LLMs might emphasize elements that allow for a more coherent and cohesive portrayal, possibly skewing the sentiment toward the positive end of the spectrum.

Moreover, LLMs like ChatGPT are trained on vast datasets with a significant amount of positive, optimistic language. This bias could influence the model to unintentionally highlight positive aspects of the narrative, even if those sentiments are less central in the full testimony. The summarization process could amplify this tendency, resulting in summaries that appear more positive in sentiment, even when the original narrative is emotionally complex or predominantly negative.

The reduction in negative sentiment observed in the summarized testimonies can also be understood through the lens of LLM behavior. Negative emotions, particularly those related to trauma, grief, and loss, are often more nuanced and detailed in the full testimonies. When tasked with summarizing these narratives, the LLM might omit or condense the detailed expressions of pain, anger, or sorrow to meet the constraints of brevity and focus on key events or themes.

In some cases, the model may unintentionally downplay the intensity of negative emotions by rephrasing or generalizing painful experiences. This could occur due to the model's propensity to avoid overly dramatic language or its tendency to reduce emotional complexity due to low resources of the Nakba and Palestinian narrative in the training dataset of LLMs. Furthermore, negative sentiments that are less immediately apparent or require more context might be excluded from summaries, leading to a shift in sentiment toward the neutral or positive end of the spectrum.

It is important to note that while the summarization process may reduce the explicit negativity in the text, this does not necessarily reflect a change in the underlying emotional experience of the refugees. Instead, it highlights the limitations of LLMs in capturing the full emotional depth of complex, traumatic narratives. In reducing the complexity of the text, the model may inadvertently present a version of the testimony that appears less negative, even if the full testimony conveys a much more emotionally charged story.

4.1 LLMs Behavior in Sentiment Analysis

The shifts in sentiment observed in this study provide several key insights into the behavior of LLMs, particularly in their application to sentiment analysis of sensitive, complex narratives:

Bias Toward Simplification: LLMs, when tasked with summarizing lengthy narratives, tend to simplify and condense emotional expressions. This simplification can lead to a distortion of the emotional tone of the original text. In the case of the Nakba testimonies, the reduced complexity in the summarized version may have skewed the sentiment analysis toward more positive and neutral expressions, obscuring the depth of negative emotional experiences.

Inability to Fully Capture Emotional Complexity: While LLMs are highly effective at processing and analyzing language, they often struggle with capturing the full emotional complexity of human experience, particularly in narratives shaped by trauma and historical injustice as well as experiences with low-resource data. These models are adept at identifying clear emotional signals (e.g., happiness, sadness, anger), but they may fail to fully grasp the subtleties of human emotions, especially in long, complex, and multi-faceted narratives.

Potential Bias in Summarization: In the case of Palestinian Nakba testimonies, the model may inadvertently introduce bias by favoring positive or neutral expressions that align more closely with the type of language typically found in general-purpose datasets. This could result in summaries that do not fully capture the lived realities of refugees, potentially diminishing the perceived severity of their experiences.

Context Sensitivity and Narrative Construction: LLMs may not fully understand the historical, cultural, or emotional contexts in which the Nakba testimonies were given. As a result, the summaries produced by the model may reflect a construction of the narrative that is less true to the original testimony, impacting the sentiment analysis. In other words, the emotional tone of a narrative can be shaped by the way the story is framed, and LLMs may inadvertently alter this framing during summarization.

5 Conclusion

This study aimed to evaluate the performance and behavior of LLMs in performing sentiment analysis on Nakba oral histories, with a particular focus on how summarization of complex, emotionally charged narratives influences sentiment results. The primary objective was to examine whether LLMs, specifically ChatGPT, could accurately capture and analyze the emotional tone of testimonies from Palestinian refugees, and how summarization might affect the representation of these sentiments. The contribution of this work lies in its novel application of LLMs to sensitive historical narratives, providing valuable insights into the potential and limitations of these models for sentiment analysis in emotionally complex contexts.

The study highlights several limitations. First, the sentiment analysis conducted by ChatGPT may have been influenced by biases in the model's training data, leading to a misrepresentation of the emotional tone in the Palestinian refugee testimonies. Additionally, the summarization process itself likely oversimplified the complexity of the full narratives, which may have distorted the sentiment analysis results. These limitations point to the need for more specialized models capable of understanding the cultural and historical contexts of sensitive narratives like the Nakba. The future work will also compare different LLMs to see if the conclusions hold across them.

References

Allan, D. (2005). Mythologising al-nakba: Narratives, collective identity and cultural practice among Palestinian refugees in Lebanon. *Oral History*, 47–56.

Assiri, A., Gumaei, A., Mehmood, F., Abbas, T., & Ullah, S. (2024). DeBERTa-GRU: Sentiment Analysis for Large Language Model. *Computers, Materials & Continua*, *79*(3).

Bhattacharjee, A., Xu, S. Y., Rao, P., Zeng, Y., Meyerhoff, J., Ahmed, S. I., Mohr, D. C., Liut, M., Mariakakis, A., & Kornfield, R. (2024). " It Explains What I am Currently Going Through Perfectly to a Tee": Understanding User Perceptions on LLM-Enhanced Narrative Interventions. *ArXiv Preprint ArXiv:2409.16732*.

Coeckelbergh, M. (2023). Narrative responsibility and artificial intelligence: How AI challenges human responsibility and sense-making. *AI & SOCIETY*, *38*(6), 2437–2450.

Fu, M. (n.d.). Catastrophe and Reincarnation: Nakba and Memory in Diana Allan's Voices of the Nakba and Kamal Aljafari's Port of Memory. *Managing Editors*, 19.

Gluck, S. B. (2008). *Oral History and al-Nakbah*. Taylor & Francis.

Havaldar, S., Rai, S., Singhal, B., Liu, L., Guntuku, S. C., & Ungar, L. (2023). Multilingual language models are not multicultural: A case study in emotion. *ArXiv Preprint ArXiv:2307.01370*.

Hawari, Y. (2023). *Voices of the Nakba: A Living History of Palestine: edited by Diana Allan. London: Pluto Press, 2021. 368 pages. 23.00paper, 12.00 e-book*. Taylor & Francis.

Jaradat, S., Nayak, R., Paz, A., Ashqar, H. I., & Elhenawy, M. (2024). Multitask Learning for Crash Analysis: A Fine-Tuned LLM Framework Using Twitter Data. *Smart Cities*, *7*(5), 2422–2465. https://doi.org/10.3390/smartcities7050095

Kabadjov, M., Balahur, A., & Boldrini, E. (2009). Sentiment intensity: Is it a good summary indicator? *Language and Technology Conference*, 203–212.

Krugmann, J. O., & Hartmann, J. (2024). Sentiment Analysis in the Age of Generative AI. *Customer Needs and Solutions*, *11*(1), 3.

Kumar, C. U. O., Gowtham, N., Zakariah, M., & Almazyad, A. (2024). Multimodal Emotion Recognition Using Feature Fusion: An LLM-Based Approach. *IEEE Access*.

Manna', A. (2013). The Palestinian Nakba and its continuous repercussions. *Israel Studies*, *18*(2), 86–99.

Nur, M. (2008). Remembering the Palestinian Nakba: Commemoration, oral history and narratives of memory. *Holy Land Studies*, *7*(2), 123–156.

Patel, S. C., & Fan, J. (2023). Identification and description of emotions by current large language models. *BioRxiv*, 2023–2027.

Radwan, A., Amarneh, M., Alawneh, H., Ashqar, H. I., AlSobeh, A., & Magableh, A. A. A. R. (2024). Predictive Analytics in Mental Health Leveraging LLM Embeddings and Machine Learning Models for Social Media Analysis. *International Journal of Web Services Research (IJWSR)*, *21*(1), 1–22.

Regan, B. (2022). *Diana Allan (ed.) Voices of the Nakba: A Living History of Palestine*. Edinburgh University Press The Tun-Holyrood Road, 12 (2f) Jackson's Entry ….

Saadah, M. J. (2021). The Palestinian perspective: Understanding the legacy of al-Nakba through the Palestinian narrative. *Berkeley Undergraduate Journal*, *35*(2).

Sa'di, A. H., & Abu-Lughod, L. (2007). *Nakba: Palestine, 1948, and the claims of memory*. Columbia University Press.

Shi, F., Chen, X., Misra, K., Scales, N., Dohan, D., Chi, E. H., Schärli, N., & Zhou, D. (2023). Large language models can be easily distracted by irrelevant context. *International Conference on Machine Learning*, 31210–31227.

Tian, Y., Huang, T., Liu, M., Jiang, D., Spangher, A., Chen, M., May, J., & Peng, N. (2024). Are Large Language Models Capable of Generating Human-Level Narratives? *ArXiv Preprint ArXiv:2407.13248*.

Yang, H., Zhao, Y., Wu, Y., Wang, S., Zheng, T., Zhang, H., Ma, Z., Che, W., & Qin, B. (2024). Large Language Models Meet Text-Centric Multimodal Sentiment Analysis: A Survey. *ArXiv Preprint ArXiv:2406.08068*.

Yang, Q., Ye, M., & Du, B. (2024). Emollm: Multimodal emotional understanding meets large language models. *ArXiv Preprint ArXiv:2406.16442*.

Zhang, W., Deng, Y., Liu, B., Pan, S. J., & Bing, L. (2023). Sentiment analysis in the era of large language models: A reality check. *ArXiv Preprint ArXiv:2305.15005*.

The Nakba Lexicon: Building a Comprehensive Dataset from Palestinian Literature

Izza Abu Haija[1], Salim Almandhari[2], Mo El-Haj[2], Jonas Sibony[3], Paul Rayson[2]

[1]Freie Universität Berlin, Berlin, Germany
[2]UCREL NLP Group, Lancaster University, Lancaster, UK
[3]Department of Arabic and Hebrew Studies, Sorbonne Université, Paris, France - CERMOM

Correspondence: izza.abuhaija@gmail.com

Abstract

This paper introduces the Nakba Lexicon, a comprehensive dataset derived from the poetry collection *Asifa 'Ala al-Iz'aj* (Sorry for the Disturbance) by Istiqlal Eid, a Palestinian poet from El-Birweh. Eid's work poignantly reflects on themes of Palestinian identity, displacement, and resilience, serving as a resource for preserving linguistic and cultural heritage in the context of post-Nakba literature. The dataset is structured into ten thematic domains, including political terminology, memory and preservation, sensory and emotional lexicon, toponyms, nature, and external linguistic influences such as Hebrew, French, and English, thereby capturing the socio-political, emotional, and cultural dimensions of the Nakba. The Nakba Lexicon uniquely emphasises the contributions of women to Palestinian literary traditions, shedding light on often-overlooked narratives of resilience and cultural continuity. Advanced Natural Language Processing (NLP) techniques were employed to analyse the dataset, with fine-tuned pre-trained models such as ARABERT and MARBERT achieving F1-scores of 0.87 and 0.68 in language and lexical classification tasks, respectively, significantly outperforming traditional machine learning models. These results highlight the potential of domain-specific computational models to effectively analyse complex datasets, facilitating the preservation of marginalised voices. By bridging computational methods with cultural preservation, this study enhances the understanding of Palestinian linguistic heritage and contributes to broader efforts in documenting and analysing endangered narratives. The Nakba Lexicon paves the way for future interdisciplinary research, showcasing the role of NLP in addressing historical trauma, resilience, and cultural identity.

1 Introduction

The Nakba, meaning "catastrophe" in Arabic, marks a significant chapter in Palestinian history, signifying the mass displacement and loss of homeland that followed the establishment of the State of Israel in 1948. This event not only reshaped Palestinian society but also deeply affected its linguistic, cultural, and political landscapes. Palestinian literature has since played a vital role in documenting and preserving the memory, identity, and collective experiences of Palestinians across generations. Within this literary tradition, the works of poets such as Istiqlal Eid serve as essential records of the Palestinian narrative, capturing the nuanced emotional and socio-political complexities faced by Palestinian communities (Sa'di and Abu-Lughod, 2007).

Istiqlal Eid (?[1]), a Palestinian poet from El-Birweh[2], uses her poetry to convey a powerful perspective on identity, exile, and resistance. Her collection, *Asifa 'Ala al-Iz'aj* (Sorry for the Disturbance), weaves a tapestry of themes central to the Palestinian experience, from cultural memory to the impact of displacement. As a female poet writing in both Modern Standard Arabic and Palestinian dialect, Eid's work provides a unique vantage point into the resilience of Palestinian identity, amplified by her familial connection to the iconic poet Mahmoud Darwish. This connection grounds her in the cultural and historical heritage of her homeland while navigating the challenges of being a refugee within her own country (Eid, 2017).

This study builds on Eid's poetry to cre-

[1]The author refuses to disclose her birthdate or age, and thus it is represented as "?" in respect of her wishes

[2]El-Birweh, also spelled as Al-Birwa, was a Palestinian village, located 10.5 kilometres (6.5 miles) east of Acre (Akka). The village was depopulated during the 1948 Arab-Israeli conflict and subsequent wars.

Proceedings of the Proceedings of the 1st International Workshop on Nakba Narratives as Language Resources, pages 37–47
January 20, 2025.

ate a Nakba Lexicon, a structured dataset of terms relevant to the Palestinian experience post-1948. By categorising terms from Eid's poetry into thematic domains—such as political terminology, memory and preservation, sensory and emotional lexicon, toponyms, and Hebrew linguistic influence—we aim to provide a comprehensive resource for Natural Language Processing (NLP) applications. This lexicon not only preserves a record of Palestinian linguistic and cultural heritage but also offers a framework for computational analysis of post-Nakba literature.

Through this project, we highlight the significant yet often overlooked contributions of female voices in Palestinian literature, emphasising the importance of diverse perspectives in documenting historical trauma and resilience. The Nakba Lexicon stands as a resource for analysing the linguistic, emotional, and cultural dimensions of Palestinian literary works, enabling a more nuanced understanding of the lasting impact of the Nakba on Palestinian identity and memory.

2 Related Work

Research on the linguistic and cultural preservation within Palestinian literature has gained traction in recent years, particularly as scholars explore the ways in which language and literature document and sustain collective memory. Palestinian authors and poets have frequently employed their work as a form of resistance and preservation, capturing the personal and collective traumas associated with displacement and cultural erasure (McDonald, 2013). Much of this research underscores the role of poetry and narrative in retaining pre-Nakba identities, toponyms, and cultural references, emphasising literature as a safeguard against the loss of heritage (Uebel, 2014; El-Ghadban and Strohm, 1900).

The influence of Mahmoud Darwish is central to studies on Palestinian poetry, with his works providing foundational insights into themes of exile, memory, and identity. Darwish's poetry is widely cited as a significant source of inspiration for Palestinian authors, including Istiqlal Eid, who not only shares Darwish's geographic roots but also his commitment to documenting Palestinian heritage (Mattawa, 2014). Scholars have examined Darwish's impact on modern Palestinian literature and how his style of prose poetry has been adapted by subsequent generations of Palestinian poets who seek to articulate their own experiences of statelessness and longing (Eid, 2016).

In the field of Natural Language Processing (NLP), efforts to develop language models and datasets for low-resource languages, particularly dialects, are also relevant to this study (Magueresse et al., 2020; El-Haj et al., 2015). Research on Arabic dialects and low-resource NLP applications provides insights into the complexities of handling linguistic diversity within Palestinian literature, especially given the mixture of Modern Standard Arabic and Palestinian dialect in Eid's work (Kwaik et al., 2018; Darwish et al., 2021). Projects focusing on the creation of lexicons and domain-specific terminologies have demonstrated the potential for computational approaches to capture unique linguistic and cultural expressions, facilitating further analysis and preservation of marginalised narratives (Sonn et al., 2013).

Work on thematic and emotional lexicons has also been explored in NLP, particularly in the context of trauma and cultural resilience (Kirmayer et al., 2009). Studies have shown that by structuring lexicons around themes such as political terminology, sensory language, and cultural references, researchers can gain a more profound understanding of how language embodies historical events and communal identity (Kenter et al., 2012; Schmidt and Burghardt, 2018). The categorisation approach proposed in this study builds on these foundations by organising terms specific to the Nakba within distinct domains, enabling a targeted NLP analysis that respects the cultural context of the lexicon.

This work contributes to these existing efforts by developing a Nakba-focused lexicon within Palestinian literature, which aims to support both linguistic preservation and nuanced computational analysis. Through a female poet's perspective, our research not only enhances existing NLP applications but also addresses the gendered aspects of cultural documentation, highlighting the significant yet often underrepresented contributions of women in post-Nakba literary production.

3 Overview of the Author

Istiqlal Eid (?-), a poet originally from El-Birweh, incorporates the term "Biladna" (meaning "Our Country") into her identity, referring to herself as "Bint el-Birweh" (the Daughter of El-Birweh). Currently residing in Tamra and working as an English teacher, her name, meaning "independence," was chosen by her father in hope of Palestinian autonomy after the Nakba of 1948. Later, Eid added "Biladna" to signify her desire for freedom from oppression and corruption in Arab lands. El-Birweh, her birthplace, is also significant as it is the hometown of celebrated poet Mahmoud Darwish, her maternal uncle.

Eid identifies as a refugee in her own homeland. Her family, despite remaining in what is now Israel's 1948 territories, cannot reside in El-Birweh, which has since become a Jewish settlement. Eid's main publication, a poetry collection titled *ʾĀsifa ʿAlā el-ʾIzʿāj* (آسفة على الإزعاج, *Sorry for the Disturbance*), was released in 2017. She is also working on a collection of short stories titled *Šḥār wimšaḥāra* (شحار و مشحّرة, *Smears and a Smeared Woman*).

Our research analyses selections from Eid's 2017 *Diwan*, rooted in the cultural and geographical exile reminiscent of Darwish. Her family's displacement to Tamra left them labelled as "present absentees[3]" (Makhoul, 2012), indicating their presence in the state yet denial of access to ancestral lands.

Eid's prose poetry style often adopts a sarcastic tone, written in a blend of Modern Standard Arabic and Palestinian dialect. Her work reflects an effort to safeguard the Palestinian narrative, documenting pre-Nakba names, figures, and places, and preserving Palestinian history and Nakba memories.

Arabic Language

The Arab world has long experienced a state of *diglossia*, defined as the simultaneous presence of two distinct levels of language, or even two different languages, within the same society, each occupying distinct communicative domains (Ferguson, 1959; Fishman, 1967). In the Arabic-speaking world, this results in the coexistence of vernacular Arabic, or *dialectal Arabic*—a collection of localized, often mutually unintelligible varieties—and *Modern Standard Arabic* (MSA), the standardized, literary form used in formal settings such as media, education, and interregional communication. MSA is taught in schools and represents the unifying linguistic thread across Arabic-speaking regions, though it remains separate from daily spoken varieties (Owens, 2001; Versteegh, 1997).

These dialectal forms of Arabic vary significantly across regions, with a sort of linguistic continuum existing along geographical lines. Generally, dialects become more divergent as geographical distance increases; for instance, the Arabic spoken in Galilee closely resembles the dialect of southern Lebanon, while eastern Moroccan Arabic is more akin to western Algerian varieties. Yet dialect similarity also depends on historical, social, and religious factors, which create distinct links between urban and rural varieties. The Arabic spoken in Jerusalem, for instance, shares specific features with that of Beirut, as both are urban dialects with complex social histories (Rosenhouse, 2007). Additionally, many dialects in the Arab world are influenced by contact with other languages, which further diversifies the linguistic landscape. In Iraq, Arabic dialects have absorbed elements from Aramaic, Kurdish, and Farsi, while in North Africa, Tamazight influences are prominent (Al-Wer and de Jong, 2009).

4 The Linguistic Context of Palestinians in Israel

The declaration of Israel in 1948 reshaped not only the territorial but also the linguistic landscape, transforming Palestinian citizens from a majority into a minority with a marginalized language. The shift placed Arabic in a subordinate position relative to Hebrew, reflecting the asymmetrical political and social power dynamics between the Palestinian minority and the Jewish Israeli majority (Henkin-Roitfarb, 2011). After 1948, Arabic was increasingly perceived within Israel as a language of opposition,

[3] According to Makhoul (2012) in their Survey of Palestinian Refugees and Internally Displaced Persons 2013-2015 (p. 8), internally displaced persons (IDPs) in Mandate Palestine fall into two main categories. The first group includes approximately 384,200 Palestinians who have been displaced within Israel since 1948, while the second group comprises around 334,600 Palestinians displaced within the territories occupied since 1967

while Hebrew was elevated as the cornerstone of the nation-building process (Spolsky and Shohamy, 1999).

For Palestinian citizens of Israel, proficiency in Hebrew became essential for navigating official and social settings, while Arabic faced reduced support in public institutions. In Jewish Israeli schools, Arabic instruction was often limited to military contexts, highlighting the asymmetrical status of the two languages (Spolsky and Shohamy, 1999; Amara, 2002). This bilingual reality reflects a linguistic hierarchy, where Arabic serves as both a practical language and a symbol of cultural resilience. In literature and cultural expression, language plays a critical role in maintaining and asserting Palestinian identity. Despite its marginalized status, Arabic serves as a medium for exploring themes of identity, resistance, and cultural continuity.

Given these influences, the Arabic of the '48 Palestinians occupies a distinct position in the landscape of Palestinian dialectology. The continuous interaction with Hebrew and the isolation from other Palestinian dialects contribute to a rich, hybrid linguistic identity that reflects the historical and social complexities of Palestinian communities within Israel (Horesh, 2021).

5 Methodology and Dataset Classification

Eid's work provides a rich source of Nakba-related terminology, facilitating the creation of a comprehensive dataset for Natural Language Processing (NLP) applications. By focusing on a female voice, we aim to create an inclusive dataset that captures diverse experiences in Palestinian literature, while emphasising the significant yet often overlooked contributions of women. This approach enables nuanced NLP analyses of language and themes in post-Nakba literary works.

The dataset is structured into thematic categories, capturing linguistic adaptations to evolving Palestinian identity and socio-political realities:

1. Political Terminology

Terms in this category describe new political realities post-Nakba, such as "peace,", "war," "occupation," and "resistance," as well as names of displaced communities, refugee camps, and geopolitical terms resulting from the conflict.

2. Memory and Preservation

This category encompasses literary efforts to preserve the pre-Nakba past, highlighting key events, significant dates, and collective tragedies. It includes terms commemorating losses, displacement, and destruction of Palestinian communities, documenting shared trauma and the struggle for remembrance of pre-1948 Palestine.

3. Sensory and Emotional Lexicon

Words conveying sensory experiences and emotions such as pain, loss, displacement, and longing, evoke the physical and psychological impact of the Nakba on individuals and communities.

4. Toponyms and Place Names

This category records Palestinian names of cities, villages, and regions from both pre-1948 and post-Nakba periods. It reflects the geographical and cultural evolution caused by conflict and occupation.

5. Names of People

Palestinian activists resist the reduction of their identities to numbers—whether as war casualties or UNRWA[4] ration card recipients. Palestinian authors counteract this by recording names of those who died, thus our dataset compiles names from Eid's *Diwan*, both of well-known figures and ordinary people.

6. Social and Cultural Lexicon

Terms here relate to traditional customs, songs, proverbs, and cultural practices that embody Palestinian identity. The lexicon reflects the continuity and transformation of cultural expressions from pre- to post-Nakba.

[4]UNRWA stands for the United Nations Relief and Works Agency for Palestine Refugees in the Near East. It was established in 1949 to provide assistance and protection to Palestinian refugees displaced during the 1948 Arab-Israeli conflict and subsequent wars. UNRWA offers services such as education, healthcare, social services, and emergency aid in its areas of operation, which include the West Bank, Gaza Strip, Jordan, Lebanon, and Syria.

7. Natural World

This category includes names of plants, trees, herbs, and animals significant to the Palestinian landscape, often symbolising resilience and rootedness. Some plants were uprooted post-Nakba, with names changing due to dialectal influences in Lebanon, Syria, and Jordan. Eid preserves these terms in the Palestinian memory archive.

8. Hebrew and Linguistic Influence

Addressing the forced incorporation of Hebrew terminology in Palestinian literature due to occupation, this category includes terms borrowed from Hebrew or used to describe life under occupation.

This classification structure illustrates the diversity of linguistic responses to historical, cultural, and political shifts surrounding the Nakba. It underscores the efforts to preserve cultural memory, adapt to new realities, and articulate experiences of displacement and resistance. For specific examples of expressions and their classifications, see Appendix A.

6 Experiments

Building upon the methodology and thematic classification discussed earlier, we conducted experiments to analyse the linguistic and cultural nuances embedded in the dataset. The dataset comprises 222 sentences, each carefully annotated with a word or phrase that reflects its language type and lexical class. These annotations aim to capture the complex interplay of linguistic elements present in Istiqlal Eid's work, including Modern Standard Arabic, Palestinian dialect, and Hebrew influences.

The annotated data is categorised into ten distinct lexical classes, as illustrated in Figure 1. The distribution highlights the diversity of terms used in post-Nakba literature, with notable proportions allocated to categories such as Toponyms (27.5%), Names of People (21.7%), and Politics (18.3%). Smaller but significant categories include Culture (9.2%), Nature (7.9%), Memory (7.9%), and Sensory and Emotional Lexicon (5.0%). External linguistic influences, including Hebrew (1.3%), French (0.8%), and English (0.8%), reflect the historical and sociopolitical interactions shaping the linguistic landscape.

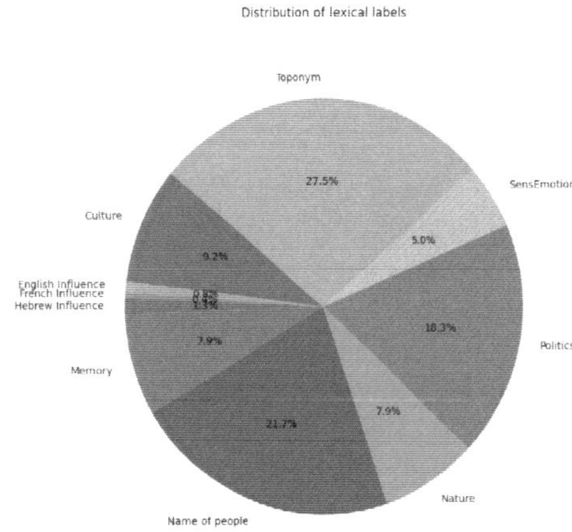

Figure 1: Lexical labels

These classifications provide insight into the thematic emphasis of the Nakba Lexicon, illustrating how language is used to articulate identity, resistance, and memory. To complement this analysis, each sentence has also been identified in terms of its language type, classified into six categories, as detailed in Table 1. This dual classification highlights the dynamic interaction of standardised and dialectal forms, alongside the incorporation of external linguistic influences, offering a holistic view of the dataset's linguistic diversity.

This experiment provides a foundation for exploring how language is used in Palestinian literature to articulate themes of displacement, memory, and resilience, while also enabling computational analysis of these themes within Natural Language Processing applications.

Label	Count	Percentage
Dialect	35	15.77%
Hebrew (translitterated)	2	0.90%
Neologism - Standard	1	0.45%
Standard	185	83.33%
Standard DialectStandard	1	0.45%
Standardized neologism(means being Israelised)	1	0.45%

Table 1: Language type distribution

7 Lexical Classification

To further investigate the linguistic richness and thematic organisation of the dataset, we applied machine learning techniques for lexical classification. The goal of this step was to assess how effectively computational models can identify and categorise the nuanced linguistic elements present in Istiqlal Eid's work, particularly across Modern Standard Arabic, Palestinian dialect, and Hebrew influences.

The primary technique employed for this task was the Term Frequency-Inverse Document Frequency (TF-IDF) embedding approach, which represents texts as numerical vectors based on their significance within the dataset. These vectors were used as input to train four traditional machine learning models: Support Vector Machines (SVM), Logistic Regression, Random Forest, and Naïve Bayes. These models were selected for their proven effectiveness in text classification tasks, where SVM excels at finding optimal hyperplanes for classification, Logistic Regression provides interpretability, Random Forest is robust against overfitting, and Naïve Bayes is efficient for small datasets. To address the limited size of the dataset, bigram features were incorporated (`ngram_range=(1, 2)`) to enhance representation by capturing contextual relationships between words.

In addition to these traditional approaches, two state-of-the-art pre-trained language models, ARABERT (Antoun et al., 2020) and MARBERT (Abdul-Mageed et al., 2021), were utilised to classify the lexical classes. These models were chosen for their specialised design, which caters to the unique linguistic characteristics of Arabic, including morphology, syntax, and dialectal variations. ARABERT is tailored for Modern Standard Arabic tasks, while MARBERT focuses on Arabic dialects, making both models well-suited to handle the mix of Standard Arabic, Palestinian dialect, and Hebrew influences present in the dataset. Both models were evaluated in two settings: first, as-is without additional training, to assess their generalisation capabilities, and second, fine-tuned on our dataset to adapt them to the specific nuances of post-Nakba literature. Fine-tuning was conducted with early stopping criteria to prevent overfitting, halting training after three consecutive evaluation epochs without validation loss improvement. Model checkpoints were saved after each epoch to ensure the best possible performance.

Preprocessing was applied to standardise the input data, including steps such as diacritisation removal, extra space trimming, stop word elimination, symbol cleaning, and character normalisation. These steps ensured the dataset was consistent and suitable for effective computational analysis.

This classification effort not only provides insights into the dataset's linguistic diversity but also highlights the potential of machine learning and large language models in analysing post-Nakba literature. By bridging traditional and modern NLP techniques, the experiments showcase a comprehensive approach to understanding and preserving Palestinian linguistic and cultural heritage.

8 Results and Discussion

The experimental results highlight the linguistic diversity captured in the Nakba Lexicon dataset, which is essential for understanding the interplay of language types in post-Nakba literature. Table 1 provides a breakdown of the language types annotated within the dataset. Standard Arabic constitutes the majority (83.33%), reflecting its role as the primary medium for formal literary expression. Dialectal Arabic, accounting for 15.77% of the dataset, highlights the significance of regional vernaculars in conveying personal and cultural narratives. Smaller contributions, such as transliterated Hebrew (0.90%), illustrate the linguistic influence of socio-political contexts, particularly the interaction between Palestinian Arabic and Hebrew. This distribution demonstrates the dataset's potential for analysing both the standardised and dialectal aspects of Arabic, as well as cross-linguistic interactions in Palestinian literature.

The lexical classification task assesses the ability of models to categorise words and phrases into predefined lexical classes, reflecting the diverse linguistic elements of the Nakba Lexicon. Table 2 summarises the performance of various machine learning models on this task. Traditional models, such as SVM and Random Forest, yielded moderate results, with F1-scores ranging from 0.09 to 0.19, indicating limitations in capturing the complexity of the dataset. In contrast, large language models (LLMs) such as ARABERT and MARBERT demonstrated significant improvements. Fine-tuned MARBERT achieved the highest F1-score of 0.68, showcasing its ability to effectively capture and classify the nuanced lexical features present in Arabic literature. These results highlight the importance of domain-specific pre-trained models for processing culturally and linguistically rich datasets like the Nakba Lexicon.

The language classification task evaluates the ability of models to identify the language type of each sentence within the dataset, reflecting its multilingual and dialectal diversity. Table 3 presents the performance of various models in this task. Traditional machine learning models, including SVM, Logistic Regression, and Random Forest, provided consistent and reasonable results, achieving F1-scores in the range of 0.76 to 0.77. These models, however, lacked the sophistication needed to fully capture the complexity of multi-class classification in Arabic datasets. Fine-tuned ARABERT outperformed all other models, achieving the highest F1-score of 0.87, demonstrating its capability to handle intricate linguistic variations and multi-class tasks effectively. MARBERT closely followed with an F1-score of 0.84, further validating the efficacy of pre-trained language models in addressing the challenges posed by diverse linguistic datasets like the Nakba Lexicon.

Models	Precision	Recall	F1-score
SVM	0.36	0.13	0.19
Logistic Regression	0.27	0.05	0.09
Random Forest	0.34	0.11	0.17
Naive Bayes	0.41	0.11	0.17
AraBERT (10 epoch)	0.70	0.42	0.53
MARBERT (7 epoch)	**0.88**	**0.56**	**0.68**

Table 2: Performance of Machine Learning and Pre-trained Models in Lexical Classification Tasks

These results underscore the profound challenges posed by the linguistic diversity and nuanced language use in post-Nakba literature. The Nakba Lexicon, as reflected in the dataset's composition and classification tasks, captures a unique confluence of standardised, dialectal, and externally influenced linguistic features. This complexity mirrors the fragmented identities and cultural resilience of Palestinians, as expressed in their literary and linguistic heritage. The moderate performance of traditional machine learning models highlights the difficulty of computationally analysing such a linguistically rich and context-dependent dataset. These models, while capable of providing baseline insights, struggle to fully grasp the intricate layers of meaning and cultural references embedded in post-Nakba narratives.

Conversely, the superior performance of fine-tuned large language models, such as ARABERT and MARBERT, illustrates their capacity to bridge computational methods with cultural and historical contexts. By leveraging domain-specific pre-trained models, this study demonstrates how advanced NLP techniques can contribute to preserving and analysing Palestinian narratives in a way that respects their linguistic and cultural particularities. The high F1-scores achieved by ARABERT and MARBERT, particularly in language classification, underscore their potential to capture the interplay of Modern Standard Arabic, Palestinian dialects, and Hebrew influences within Nakba-related literature. This capability is crucial for understanding how language has been used as a medium of resistance, memory preservation, and identity formation in the face of displacement and marginalisation.

Furthermore, these findings highlight the value of computational approaches in elevating underrepresented narratives in global discourses. By enabling the analysis of low-resource languages and culturally rich datasets, NLP offers a pathway to amplify marginalised voices and ensure their stories are preserved for future generations. In the case of the Nakba Lexicon, this study not only contributes to the documentation of Palestinian heritage but also lays the groundwork for applying similar methods to other marginalised linguistic communities.

Models	Precision	Recall	F1-score
SVM	0.71	0.82	0.76
Logistic Regression	0.71	0.84	0.77
Random Forest	0.71	0.84	0.77
Naive Bayes	0.71	0.84	0.77
AraBERT (7 epoch)	**0.87**	**0.87**	**0.87**
MARBERT (8 epoch)	0.84	0.84	0.84

Table 3: Performance of Machine Learning and Pre-trained Models in Language Classification Tasks

Ultimately, this research illustrates the potential of integrating computational tools with literary and cultural studies to address historical traumas and support cultural resilience. The challenges faced in classifying such a nuanced dataset reflect broader issues in preserving endangered narratives, while the successes achieved with advanced models point to a future where technology can play a vital role in safeguarding cultural memory. The Nakba Lexicon serves as both a technical achievement and a testament to the enduring power of language in articulating collective experiences of resistance, loss, and hope.

9 Conclusion and Future Work

This study introduced the Nakba Lexicon, a comprehensive dataset derived from the poetic works of Istiqlal Eid, capturing the linguistic, cultural, and emotional dimensions of Palestinian post-Nakba literature. By categorising the dataset into thematic domains and leveraging computational methods, we demonstrated how advanced Natural Language Processing (NLP) techniques can preserve and analyse marginalised linguistic and cultural narratives. The lexicon serves as a bridge between computational tools and cultural studies, offering a resource for exploring the nuanced interplay of identity, memory, and resilience in the face of historical trauma.

The experimental results underline the challenges inherent in processing such a linguistically rich and contextually complex dataset. Traditional machine learning models, while providing baseline insights, struggled to fully capture the intricate dynamics of Palestinian literature, especially the interplay of Modern Standard Arabic, Palestinian dialects, and Hebrew influences. In contrast, pre-trained language models like ARABERT and MARBERT significantly outperformed these models, with MARBERT excelling in lexical classification and ARABERT achieving state-of-the-art results in language classification. These findings highlight the potential of domain-specific models to address the unique demands of datasets that blend linguistic, cultural, and historical layers.

The Nakba Lexicon is more than a computational dataset; it is a testament to the enduring power of language as a medium for resistance, memory preservation, and cultural continuity. By amplifying the voices embedded in Palestinian literature, this research not only contributes to the documentation of Palestinian heritage but also underscores the role of NLP in safeguarding endangered narratives. These efforts align with a broader vision of using technology to amplify the stories of marginalised communities and preserve their cultural identities for future generations.

Future work will expand the Nakba Lexicon to include additional texts from Palestinian authors and poets, aiming to enhance its representativeness and robustness. We also intend to explore cross-dialectal adaptations, capturing the linguistic diversity across Arabic-speaking regions affected by the Nakba. Integrating context-aware models, such as transformer-based architectures, will enable deeper analysis of the interplay between language, culture, and history. Furthermore, collaborative efforts with historians, linguists, and cultural preservationists will enrich the lexicon's applications, fostering interdisciplinary approaches to understanding and preserving cultural heritage.

Once this paper is accepted, the Nakba Lexicon will be released publicly, providing researchers and practitioners with a valuable resource for computational analysis and a meaningful contribution to preserving the narratives of resilience and resistance within Palestinian literature.

10 Limitations

While this study highlights the potential of the Nakba Lexicon for preserving and analysing linguistic and cultural narratives, several limitations must be acknowledged. First, the dataset size is relatively small, consisting of 222 annotated sentences, which limits the generalisability of the experimental results. While the inclusion of fine-tuned models like ARABERT and MARBERT significantly improved performance, a larger and more diverse dataset is required to ensure broader applicability and robust generalisation across different contexts and linguistic variations.

Second, the dataset primarily focuses on the works of a single poet, Istiqlal Eid, which, while rich and representative of certain aspects of Palestinian literature, may not fully capture the breadth of linguistic and cultural diversity present in the wider corpus of Palestinian writing. Expanding the dataset to include other authors, genres, and dialects would provide a more comprehensive representation of the post-Nakba narrative.

Third, the reliance on pre-trained models like ARABERT and MARBERT, while beneficial, highlights challenges in adapting NLP tools to datasets that mix standardised and dialectal Arabic, as well as incorporating influences from Hebrew and other languages. Future work should address these challenges by developing more targeted models that can better accommodate such linguistic complexities.

Lastly, the dataset's cultural and historical sensitivity requires careful handling to ensure its appropriate use in research and applications. Collaborative efforts with cultural preservationists and community stakeholders are essential to ensure that the dataset is used responsibly and meaningfully.

Despite these limitations, the Nakba Lexicon represents a significant step forward in combining computational tools with cultural preservation, offering valuable insights into the intersections of language, identity, and historical trauma. Addressing these limitations in future work will further enhance its value as a resource for interdisciplinary research.

References

Muhammad Abdul-Mageed, AbdelRahim Elmadany, and El Moatez Billah Nagoudi. 2021. ARBERT & MARBERT: Deep bidirectional transformers for Arabic. In *Proceedings of the 59th Annual Meeting of the Association for Computational Linguistics and the 11th International Joint Conference on Natural Language Processing (Volume 1: Long Papers)*, pages 7088–7105, Online. Association for Computational Linguistics.

Enam Al-Wer and Rudolf de Jong. 2009. *Arabic Dialectology: In Honour of Clive Holes on the Occasion of his Sixtieth Birthday*. BRILL.

Muhammad Amara. 2002. The place of arabic in israel.

Wissam Antoun, Fady Baly, and Hazem Hajj. 2020. AraBERT: Transformer-based model for Arabic language understanding. In *Proceedings of the 4th Workshop on Open-Source Arabic Corpora and Processing Tools, with a Shared Task on Offensive Language Detection*, pages 9–15, Marseille, France. European Language Resource Association.

Kareem Darwish, Nizar Habash, Mourad Abbas, Hend Al-Khalifa, Huseein T Al-Natsheh, Houda Bouamor, Karim Bouzoubaa, Violetta Cavalli-Sforza, Samhaa R El-Beltagy, Wassim El-Hajj, et al. 2021. A panoramic survey of natural language processing in the arab world. *Communications of the ACM*, 64(4):72–81.

Istiqlal Eid. 2017. *Asifa 'Ala al-Iz'aj [Sorry for the Disturbance]*. Dar al-Arkan lil-Intaj wa al-Nashr, Israel.

Muna Abu Eid. 2016. *Mahmoud Darwish: literature and the politics of Palestinian identity*. Bloomsbury Publishing.

Yara El-Ghadban and Kiven Strohm. 1900. The ghosts of resistance: dispatches from palestinian art and music. *Palestinian music and song expression and resistance since*, pages 175–200.

Mahmoud El-Haj, Udo Kruschwitz, and Chris Fox. 2015. Creating language resources for under-resourced languages: methodologies, and experiments with arabic. *Language Resources and Evaluation*, 49:549–580.

Charles A. Ferguson. 1959. Diglossia. *Word*, 15(2):325–340.

Joshua A. Fishman. 1967. Bilingualism with and without diglossia; diglossia with and without bilingualism. *Journal of Social Issues*, 23(2):29–38.

Roni Henkin-Roitfarb. 2011. Hebrew and arabic in asymmetric contact in israel. *Lodz Papers in Pragmatics*, 7(1):61–100.

Uri Horesh. 2021. Palestinian dialects and identities shifting across physical and virtual borders. *Multilingua: Journal of Cross-Cultural and Interlanguage Communication*, 40(5):647–673.

Tom Kenter, Tomaž Erjavec, Maja Žorga Dulmin, and Darja Fišer. 2012. Lexicon construction and corpus annotation of historical language with the CoBaLT editor. In *Proceedings of the 6th Workshop on Language Technology for Cultural Heritage, Social Sciences, and Humanities*, pages 1–6, Avignon, France. Association for Computational Linguistics.

Laurence J Kirmayer, Megha Sehdev, Rob Whitley, Stéphane F Dandeneau, and Colette Isaac. 2009. Community resilience: Models, metaphors and measures. *International Journal of Indigenous Health*, 5(1):62–117.

Kathrein Abu Kwaik, Motaz Saad, Stergios Chatzikyriakidis, and Simon Dobnik. 2018. Shami: A corpus of levantine arabic dialects. In *Proceedings of the eleventh international conference on language resources and evaluation (LREC 2018)*.

Alexandre Magueresse, Vincent Carles, and Evan Heetderks. 2020. Low-resource languages: A review of past work and future challenges. *arXiv preprint arXiv:2006.07264*.

Manar H Makhoul. 2012. The forces of presence and absence: Aspects of palestinian identity transformation in israel between 1967-1987. *Journal of Levantine Studies*, 2(1):135–159.

Khaled Mattawa. 2014. *Mahmoud Darwish: The poet's art and his nation.* Syracuse University Press.

David A McDonald. 2013. *My voice is my weapon: Music, nationalism and the poetics of palestinian resistance.* Duke University Press.

Jonathan Owens. 2001. *Arabic as a Minority Language.* Walter de Gruyter.

Judith Rosenhouse. 2007. The arabic dialects in the north of israel. *Bulletin of the School of Oriental and African Studies, University of London*, 55(1):19–41.

Ahmad H Sa'di and Lila Abu-Lughod. 2007. *Nakba: Palestine, 1948, and the claims of memory.* Columbia University Press.

Thomas Schmidt and Manuel Burghardt. 2018. An evaluation of lexicon-based sentiment analysis techniques for the plays of Gotthold Ephraim Lessing. In *Proceedings of the Second Joint SIGHUM Workshop on Computational Linguistics for Cultural Heritage, Social Sciences, Humanities and Literature*, pages 139–149, Santa Fe, New Mexico. Association for Computational Linguistics.

Christopher C Sonn, Garth Stevens, and Norman Duncan. 2013. Decolonisation, critical methodologies and why stories matter. In *Race, memory and the apartheid archive: Towards a transformative psychosocial praxis*, pages 295–314. Springer.

Bernard Spolsky and Elana Shohamy. 1999. *The Languages of Israel: Policy, Ideology, and Practice.* Multilingual Matters.

Carly M Uebel. 2014. *Carrying Palestine: Preserving the" Postmemory" Palestinian Identity and Consolidating Collective Experience in Contemporary Poetic Narratives.* Ph.D. thesis, University of Oregon.

Kees Versteegh. 1997. *The Arabic Language.* Edinburgh University Press.

A Appendix: Expressions and Lexical Examples

This appendix provides detailed examples of expressions and lexical terms from the Nakba Lexicon, including linguistic and cultural explanations.

1. **16 / 1 / Dialect / Sensory Name of Place: أحمرالفاير**
   aḥmar al-fayir "blazing red" A dialectal expression composed of أحمر aḥmar 'red' and the participle فاير fayir 'burning, raging'. Fayir is a local dialectal pronunciation related to Standard Arabic (SA) فائر fā ir. The Palestinian Arabic (PA) has dropped the hamza and replaced it by the consonant /y/, aligning it with the vowel /i/. Comparison: SA فائر fā ir - PA فاير fayir.

2. **19 / 1 / Dialect / Hebrew Influence: السيكوباتية**
   Sikopatiya "Psychopathy" The form *sikopatiya* may derive from SA سيكوباتية sīkūbātiyya / saykūbātiyya or from English "psychopathy," with phonological influence from Modern Hebrew (MH). The Palestinian Jordanian variant seems to retain English features such as the diphthong /ay/ and interdental /ṯ/.

3. **21 / 2 / Dialect / Cultural (Dialect): إحنا بخير**
   iḥna bxer "We're all right" Common PA form إحنا بخير iḥna b-xer compared with SA نحن بخير naḥnu bi-xayr. PA features include the dropping of short vowels (ب b-, cp. SA ب bi-), diphthong reduction (خير xer, SA خير xayr), and a specific form for the first-person personal pronoun إحنا iḥna (SA نحن naḥnu).

4. **28 / 2 / Dialect / Hebrew Influence: هلولويا هلّولويا**
   Halluluya halluluya "Hallelujah, hallelujah" Originates from Hebrew *halelu yah* "praise God," although it is difficult to determine when it was borrowed. Possibly through Christianity, making it a very ancient legacy, but it might have been updated through contact with MH.

5. **32 / 1 / Dialect / Hebrew Influence: فنطازيا**
   Fanṭazya "fantasy" A local adaptation of the international word "fantasy." Unlike usual SA فانتازيا fāntāzya, the PA form includes an emphatic /ṭ/, i.e., *fanṭazya*, which might be an internal evolution or, less probably, an orthographic influence from MH.

6. **36 / 5 / Dialect / Cultural: Proverb: على أد فراشك مدّ اجريك**
   ala ədd frašak mid ižrik "Cut your coat according to your cloth." This PA proverb contrasts with SA: PA على أد ala ədd vs. SA على قد alā qadd. Additionally, metathesis is seen: PA اجر ižr vs. SA رجل rižl.

7. **140 / 2 / Dialect / Toponym: صباح الخير على مخيّم شاتيلا**
   Ṣabaḥ al-xer ala muxayyam šātīlā "Good morning Shatila refugee camp" The word شاتيلا Šātīlā might be related to the Aramaic root $\sqrt{\check{s}.t.l.}$ related to "plants," as seen in the Syriac words *štilta* 'plantation' and *štala* 'to plant.'

8. **130 / 1 / Standardised Neologism / Political Register (and Cultural): Post-Nakba: أسرلتنا**
   Asralatna A verb indirectly derived from the name 'Israel,' from which the consonant root $\sqrt{s.r.l.}$ has been extracted. This neologism demonstrates the ability of Semitic linguistic structures to create roots from foreign words.

Arabic Topic Classification Corpus of the Nakba Short Stories

Osama Hamed[1,*] and Nadeem Zaidkilani[2,3,*]

[1]Department of Computer Systems Engineering, Palestine Technical University - Kadoorie, Palestine
osama.hamed@ptuk.edu.ps, sam.hamed@gmail.com
[2]Department of Computer Engineering and Security Mathematics, University Rovira i Virgili, Spain
[3] Department of Engineering and Technology, Al-Zaytona University of Science and Technology, Palestine
nadeem.zaidkilani@estudiants.urv.cat, nadeem.kilani@zust.edu.ps,nadimkilani@gmail.com

[*]These authors contributed equally to this work.

Abstract

In this paper, we enrich Arabic Natural Language Processing (NLP) resources by introducing the "Nakba Topic Classification Corpus (NTCC)," a novel annotated Arabic corpus derived from narratives about the Nakba. The NTCC comprises approximately 470 sentences extracted from eight short stories and captures the thematic depth of the Nakba narratives, providing insights into both historical and personal dimensions. The corpus was annotated in a two-step process. One third of the dataset was manually annotated, achieving an IAA of 87% (later resolved to 100%), while the rest was annotated using a rule-based system based on thematic patterns. This approach ensures consistency and reproducibility, enhancing the corpus's reliability for NLP research. The NTCC contributes to the preservation of the Palestinian cultural heritage while addressing key challenges in Arabic NLP, such as data scarcity and linguistic complexity. By like topic modeling and classification tasks, the NTCC offers a valuable resource for advancing Arabic NLP research and fostering a deeper understanding of the Nakba narratives

1 Introduction

Automatic document categorization has gained significant importance due to the continuous influx of textual documents on the web. The rise of the Internet and Web 2.0 has led to an unprecedented increase in unstructured data generated from various sources, particularly social media. This vast array of unstructured information presents both a challenge and an opportunity for data processing and management, enabling researchers to extract meaningful insights. One of the key tasks in this realm is text classification, which has witnessed substantial advancements recently, particularly with the advent of machine learning (ML) techniques (Elnagar et al., 2020).

Text categorization, often referred to interchangeably as text classification, involves predicting predefined categories or domains for a given document. This automated process can either identify the most relevant single category or multiple closely related categories. Given the enormous volume of available documents online, manual classification is impractical, necessitating automated classifiers that transform unstructured text into machine-readable formats (Elnagar et al., 2020).

While text categorization has been well-studied in several languages, including English, the Arabic language remains underrepresented in this research area. Despite Arabic being the fourth most widely used language on the Internet and the sixth official language recognized by the United Nations (Wahdan et al., 2024), there are few studies focusing on Arabic text classification (Alyafeai et al., 2022). The scarcity of comprehensive and accessible Arabic corpora presents significant obstacles for researchers. Most existing datasets are small, lack predefined classes, or require extensive modifications before use. This limitation complicates the validation and comparison of proposed methods, hindering progress in Arabic text categorization (Elnagar et al., 2020).

In this paper, we introduce the NTCC, a new Arabic dataset specifically designed for emotion detection in narratives surrounding the Nakba—a pivotal event in Palestinian history characterized by displacement and loss. These stories are crucial for preserving the historical events and documenting the suffering of the Palestinian people since 1948. Our dataset encompasses five distinct categories: (i) historical events and politics, (ii) emotions and spirituality, (iii) nature and daily life, (iv) homesickness and war/conflict, and (v) others. "Others" is dedicated to sentences that do not belong to any of the defined categories. This structure aims to provide researchers with flexibility in annotation and a more nuanced understanding of the narratives.

Proceedings of the Proceedings of the 1st International Workshop on Nakba Narratives as Language Resources, pages 48–55
January 20, 2025.

By releasing this dataset, which consists of approximately 470 sentences extracted from eight stories, we aim to facilitate the application of various NLP and machine learning related tasks. Our Arabic annotated corpus will pave the way for researchers in machine learning and NLP to conduct numerous studies, potentially leading to advancements in sentiment analysis, topic modeling, and other classification tasks. Notable works in this area include the use of deep learning models for text classification, sentiment analysis using recurrent neural networks (RNNs), and transformer-based architectures such as BERT for enhanced context understanding.

This work contributes to preserving Palestinian heritage and the Palestinian issue by documenting these experiences. Our objective is to enhance the predictive capabilities for semantic analysis on future unseen data, while contributing to the growing body of research in Arabic corpora and text classification.

This paper is organized as follows. In Section 2, we present prior and recent research on Arabic topic classification. Section 3 provides a comprehensive analysis of the data handling. Section 4 summarizes the steps followed, and describes the proposed approach for corpus construction. In Section 5, we conclude and point out ideas for future search.

2 Related Work

The construction and utilization of structured Arabic corpora are essential for advancing Arabic text classification and Natural Language Processing (NLP). Due to the unique challenges posed by Arabic—including its complex morphology, rich dialectal variations, and limited open-source resources—the development of specialized corpora has become a focal point in recent studies.

Albared et al. (2023) propose an approach to Arabic topic classification using generative and AutoML techniques, demonstrating how the success of classification models is heavily dependent on high-quality, diverse datasets. This study underscores the necessity of large, labeled corpora that allow models to generalize effectively, addressing Arabic's unique linguistic challenges. In a similar direction, the OSAC (Open-Source Arabic Corpora) initiative (Saad and Ashour, 2010) tackles resource scarcity by providing open-access corpora to improve classification and clustering. OSAC compiles a wide range of Arabic texts, including social media and news articles, thereby supporting the development of more robust classification models.

In line with OSAC, the Ahmed and Ahmed (2021) study on Arabic news classification develops a specialized corpus that enhances machine learning algorithms for news categorization. It stresses the importance of balanced data across categories to mitigate classification biases. Likewise, systematic reviews such as (Elnagar et al., 2020) identify trends across Arabic NLP resources, noting that existing corpora often suffer from domain specificity and dialectal homogeneity. These studies collectively advocate for more diversified corpora that cover both Modern Standard Arabic (MSA) and regional dialects to bolster model robustness across different language forms.

Addressing specific NLP challenges, AL-Sarayreh et al. (2023) discuss data augmentation and annotation techniques as solutions to enrich Arabic corpora, especially in low-resource contexts. They suggest that creative approaches to annotation and corpus expansion are essential for capturing Arabic's linguistic diversity. Furthermore, Wahdan et al. (2024) emphasizes the importance of domain-specific corpora and advocates for expanding corpus types to represent the broader spectrum of Arabic content. This work argues that larger and more varied datasets can yield substantial improvements in classification accuracy and task transferability.

In summary, as Arabic NLP research progresses, the development of specialized, open-source, and diverse Arabic corpora remains critical. The aforementioned studies contribute to this goal by offering resources that not only enhance classification accuracy, but also address broader challenges related to language variation, resource availability, and domain-specific needs in Arabic NLP.

3 Data Handling

We want to construct a new Arabic topic classification corpus based on the Nakba narratives. The raw data represents a set of Nakba short stories that contains the narratives of Nakba, e.g. the suffering, memories, ... etc. as they were told by refugees. The stories were taken from the Nakba Archive website[1].

[1] https://www.nakba-archive.org

3.1 Raw Data Gathering

On the Nakba Archive website, in the project section, we have extracted a collection of eight Nakba stories, written by different authors, which are in PDF format. Each of these stories needs a special attention to become suitable for NLP related tasks.

3.2 Data Cleaning

In addition to the Arabic diacritics that rarely appear in the text. We noticed that the stories contain some special characters, a few English texts, and web references as uniform resource locators (URLs). The diacritics were removed using the PyArabic (Zerrouki, 2023) Python library. Whereas, the remaining noise was removed using regular expressions.

3.3 Data Preprocessing

We want to create/construct an annotated dataset for topic classification that is taken from Nakba stories. We started this task by data preprocessing, which falls into three main steps:

Convert PDF to Structured Format Although the PDF is primarily a format for visual presentation, it contains unstructured data. Instead, we decided to convert to a structured format like CSV or Excel. This not only makes it easy to work with NLP tools/libraries such as Pandas and NLTK (Bird et al., 2009), but also allows any additional metadata to be stored alongside the text.

Text Normalization With the help of PyArabic, we normalized the Arabic text by removing the extra white spaces and the Tatweel.

Paragraph to Sentences Each paragraph was split into sentences based on appropriate sentence ending using the **NLTK** Python library. This will enable us to annotate the sentences easily, and add the corresponding labels in the future. The eight stories result in a set of 605 sentences. As part of the preprocessing stage, meaningless sentences—such as incomplete phrases, non-informative lines (e.g., "etc."), or formatting artifacts—were manually identified and removed by annotators. This process ensured that the dataset, which ultimately consisted of 473 contextually relevant sentences, was clean and ready for further analysis.

3.4 Topic Categorization

To categorize the topics covered in each story found on the Nakba archive website, two experts analyzed the text and listened to the interviews made with refugees. The experts were able to classify the Nakba stories' topics into four main categories. We also added the "Other" category to avoid mismatch in classification.

- Historical Events and Politics: This category includes key historical and political events of the Nakba, including key events, political decisions, and their implications on Palestinian society.
- Emotions and Spirituality: This category includes narratives that express deep emotional experiences such as grief, loss, and hope, alongside spiritual reflections.
- Nature and Daily Life: This category merges the depiction of the natural Palestinian landscape with the rhythms of everyday life.
- Homesickness and War/Conflict: This category covers the emotional longing for a lost homeland and the harsh realities of war and conflict. It combines narratives that express a deep sense of nostalgia and displacement with stories that highlight the struggles and violence experienced during the Nakba, emphasizing the enduring impact of conflict on individuals and communities.

Table 1 contains relevant examples of those five categories. We are going to use these categories as a basis for creating and annotating the Nakba Arabic topic classification corpus.

3.5 Corpus Category-Based Stats and Visualization

This work contributes to preserving Palestinian heritage by documenting these experiences, aligning with recent efforts in NLP for cultural preservation (Cabezas et al., 2022).

Nakba Stories Stats We are working with a relatively small dataset of stories. Table 2 shows the "No. of Tokens" for the eight Nakba stories.

Nakba Stories Word-Cloud The word-cloud in Figure 1 visually represents the most frequent terms

Category	Arabic Keywords Examples	Translation
Historical Event & Politics	سياسات قمعية، النكبة	Nakba, Repressive Policies
Emotions & Spirituality	مشاعر الحزن، الإيمان	Faith, Sadness Feelings
Nature & Daily Life	شروق الشمس، العمل في الحقول	Working in the Fields, Sunrise
Homesickness & War-Conflict	حلم العودة، قصف	Bombing, Dream of Return

Table 1: The topic categories found in Nakba stories.

ID	Arabic Title	English Title	No. of Tokens
1	افتتاحية	Introduction	556
2	ذاكرة لا تفنى	An Enduring Memory	1472
3	طوابير	Queues	2082
4	أبو عادل الفاتح	Abu Adel, The Opener	2069
5	حنين	Longing	1113
6	الدخان فالخبز فالأسلاك الشائكة	Smoke, bread, & Barbed Wire	1479
7	أم الشهيد	The Martyr's Mother	1700
8	كيف لي أن أغفر	How Can I Forgive?	1817

Table 2: The statistics of the Nakba stories.

Figure 1: The Nakba stories presented as word-cloud.

in the dataset, with the size of each word corresponding to its frequency of occurrence. It can be clearly seen that the Arabic word طوابير /TwAbyr/, (Eng: Queues) is among the most frequent words in the Nakba stories. TwAbyr represents suffering in the daily life activities at refugee camps.

Being done with data handling steps, which are depicted using flowchart in Figure 2. We are ready for the next steps that relate to corpus construction.

4 Corpus Construction

This section presents our approach to developing a topic-classification dataset derived from Nakba narratives. Given that Arabic NLP research has historically received less attention than research on Western languages (Darwish et al., 2020), our work aims to enrich Arabic NLP resources with this specialized Nakba corpus.

4.1 Data Annotation

The topics covered in the Nakba stories were classified into five categories (including "Others"), as shown in Table 1. Annotating the corpus involved labeling the content of all stories, sentence by sentence, using one of the five categories. To achieve this, we employed a two-phase process that combined manual and automated annotation approaches.

In the first phase, a random sample of 33.33% of the dataset was manually annotated by two experts to establish a ground truth. This subset was carefully reviewed and refined over two iterative rounds, achieving an inter-annotator agreement (IAA) of 87%, which increased to 100% after resolving disagreements. The resulting ground truth subset served as the benchmark for evaluating various automated annotation methods.

In the second phase, the remaining two-thirds of the corpus were annotated using a rule-based classification system, which leveraged thematic

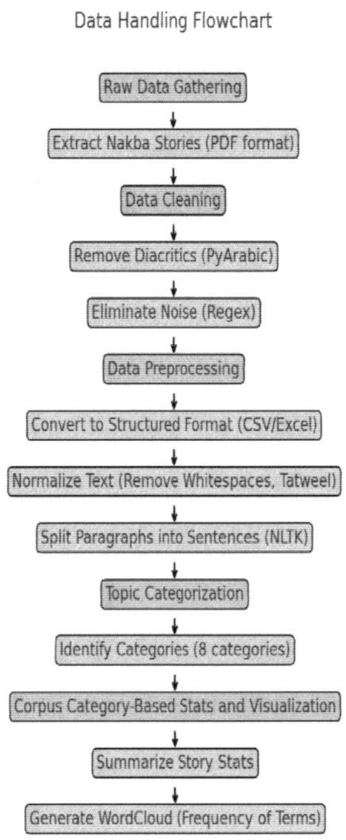

Figure 2: Data handling for Nakba stories.

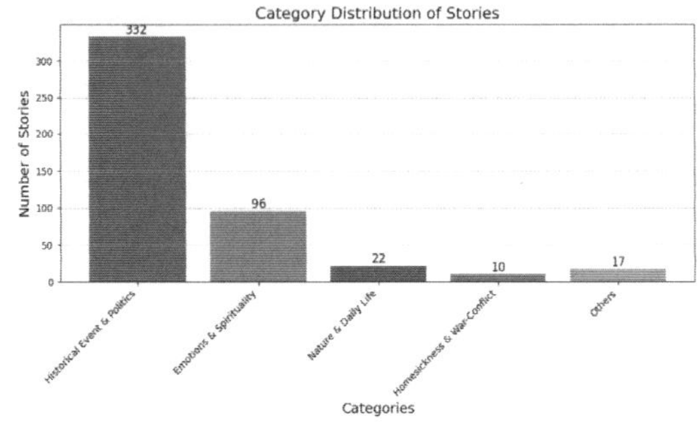

Figure 3: The category distributions in all stories.

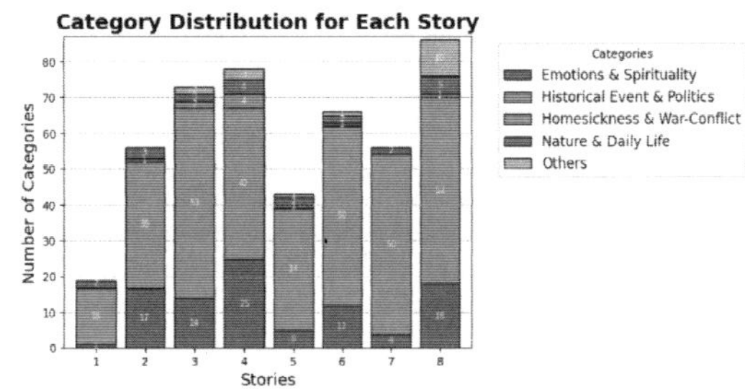

Figure 4: The category distributions for each story.

keywords and linguistic patterns identified from the manually annotated subset. For example, sentences mentioning terms such as *"diaspora"* or *"exile"* were categorized under *Homesickness & War/Conflict*, while sentences referencing political events were classified as *Historical Events & Politics*. This rule-based method, refined iteratively, demonstrated the highest accuracy compared to other methods such as KMeans clustering (Lloyd, 1982), TFIDF (Bafna et al., 2016), and AraBERT (Antoun et al., 2020).

The evaluation of these models focused on their ability to replicate expert annotations without additional training or fine-tuning. The aim was not to replace expert annotations for this relatively small dataset of 470 sentences but to assess the feasibility of using these models as scalable tools for annotating larger datasets in the future. By combining manual annotations with the rule-based system, we ensured consistency and reproducibility, creating a reliable corpus for advancing Arabic NLP studies.

These results are obtained using the rule-based (RB) classifier. Figure 3 presents the distribution of stories across five categories: Historical Event & Politics (HEP), Emotions & Spirituality (ES), Nature & Daily Life (NDL), Homesickness & War-Conflict (HWC), and Others. The "HEP" category dominates with 332 entries, followed by "ES" with 96 entries. Categories such as "NDL," "HWC," and "Others" are represented by fewer entries, with 22, 10, and 17 entries, respectively.This distribution suggests a strong emphasis on political and emotional themes in the dataset, while other topics, such as daily life and conflict-related stories, are less prevalent. The imbalance in category distribution points to the dataset's thematic concentration on historical and political narratives, highlighting potential gaps in diversity regarding more personal or nature-related themes.

Figure 4 illustrates the distribution of categories across eight stories, as obtained using the rule-based classifier. "HEP" appears most frequently, followed by "HWC." "ES" and "NDL" are represented less frequently, while the "Others" category is rarely mentioned. Story 8 stands out with the highest number of categories, with "HEP" and "HWC" being the dominant themes. This chart highlights the varying thematic focus of the stories, with political and emotional topics being more prevalent in the dataset.

4.2 Inter-Annotator Agreement

It is important to review the resulting topic classification labels obtained using the different three approaches. With assistance from two experts, the

ID	Type/ Approaches	Arabic Text
195	Agreement/ Expert 1 vs. Expert 2	إنه ملكي، إنها حريّتي وهذه أرضي
332	Disagreement/ Expert 1 vs. Expert 2	فلسطيني لبناني المهم ما في فلسطيني سادة
341	Agreement/ RB vs. Experts	لم أ صدق أن الله كرمني وجعلني ألتقي بأم شهيد
361	Disagreement/ RB vs. Experts	يا ريتني قدرت

Table 3: Examples of agreement and disagreement encountered during annotation.

inclusion of human factor allows not only for measuring Inter-Annotator Agreement (IAA), but also for helping to quantify the subjectivity of the task and refine the category definitions.

To assess the reliability and consistency of the three approaches, we calculated the IAA using Cohen's Kappa (Cohen, 1960) as shown in Equation 1. This follows Artstein and Poesio (2008), who applied Cohen's Kappa in computational linguistics.

$$\kappa = \frac{p_o - p_e}{1 - p_e} \tag{1}$$

where

p_o = the observed agreement,

p_e = the expected agreement by chance.

We computed the IAA using Equation 1 and got an initial rate of 87%, which indicates substantial agreement. Discrepancies in annotation were often due to the complexity and interference of topic expressions. To resolve these differences, we organized a post-annotation step where annotators discussed and clarified difficult cases. Through these discussions, we updated our annotation guidelines and conducted a second round of annotation, yielding an improved Kappa score of 100%.

Table 3 shows examples of agreement and disagreement that were encountered during annotation. For example, the sentence 195 (Eng: It's mine, it's my freedom and this is my land) belongs to "Emotions & Spirituality" was annotated correctly by both experts. Whereas, the sentence 332 (Eng: Palestinian Lebanese, the important thing is that there are no pure Palestinians) belongs to "Historical Event & Politics" was annotated correctly by only one expert, the other annotated it as "Emotions & Spirituality". Another example – among rule-based (RB) and the experts, the sentence 341 (Eng: I could not believe that God had honored me and made me meet the mother of a martyr.) belongs to "Emotions & Spirituality" was annotated correctly by both the experts and RB. Whereas, the sentence 361 (Eng: I wish I could) belongs to "Emotions & Spirituality" was annotated correctly by the experts, and annotated wrongly by the RB, namely as "Historical Event & Politics".

4.3 Evaluation Metrics

The evaluation focused on the ability of different automated methods to replicate expert annotations without additional training or fine-tuning. The models tested included:

- **Rule-based system:** Using thematic keywords and contextual patterns derived from the ground truth data.
- **KMeans clustering:** Applied directly to the dataset to group similar sentences.
- **TFIDF:** Used to extract features for classification based on term importance.
- **AraBERT:** A pre-trained Arabic language model used for sentence classification.

The performance of each model was compared against the manually annotated ground truth. The rule-based system achieved the highest accuracy, demonstrating its effectiveness in capturing thematic categories. This evaluation highlights the potential of automated models for annotating large-scale datasets, even without further training or fine-tuning.

For this task, two experts were recruited to review and annotate a sample of 159 sentences (i.e. one third) of the data independently. As inspired by Artstein and Poesio (2008), this iterative process helped ensure that the final corpus annotations are consistent and reliable.

We are utilizing accuracy, calculated as in Equation 2, to evaluate the different classification approaches. The accuracy of each classification approach (on the one-third of the data) is calculated by comparing it to the manually annotated sample.

The confusion matrix (CM) in Figure 5 illustrates the performance of the rule-based approach in classifying Arabic text into five categories: Historical Event & Politics, Emotions & Spirituality, Homesickness & War-Conflict, Nature & Daily Life, and Others. The matrix shows correct and incorrect predictions per class. Notably, the rule-based model performs best in classifying Historical Event & Politics, with 59 correct predictions. However, it struggles in distinguishing between more similar categories, such as Emotions & Spirituality and Homesickness & War-Conflict, as evidenced by misclassifications.

When comparing this rule-based model to other approaches, such as TFIDF and AraBERT, the rule-based model outperforms them with a higher accuracy of 61.33%. In contrast, the TFIDF and AraBERT models achieve significantly lower accuracy rates of 25% and 34%, respectively. This analysis demonstrates that the rule-based approach, despite its limitations in handling nuanced category distinctions, outperformed other methods by leveraging thematic keywords and contextual rules, as detailed in Section 4.1. In contrast, the lower accuracy of TFIDF and AraBERT underscores the challenges these methods face when applied to domain-specific datasets without fine-tuning.

This confusion matrix, therefore, represents the performance of the rule-based approach and highlights areas where improvement is needed, especially in distinguishing between certain categories. It is important to note that while the rule-based approach shows the highest accuracy, further research into hybrid models or the application of more sophisticated methods like AraBERT or TFIDF could lead to improvements in classification performance.

$$\text{Accuracy} = \frac{\text{Number of True Predictions}}{\text{Total Number of Predictions}} \qquad (2)$$

4.4 Discussion

This study evaluated the feasibility of using automated models to annotate Arabic narratives, focusing on scalability for larger datasets. While manually annotating 470 sentences is straightforward, the aim was to test these models as tools for automating the annotation of thousands or millions of sentences in future research.

The rule-based classifier outperformed other approaches, leveraging thematic keywords and patterns to achieve the best accuracy. This suggests that carefully designed rule-based systems

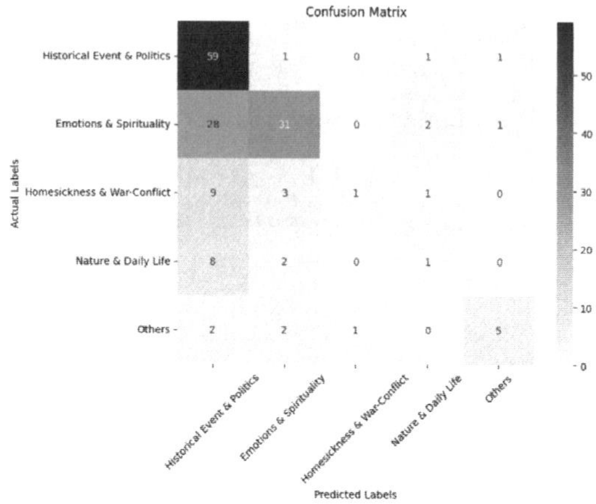

Figure 5: The confusion matrix (CM).

can effectively handle datasets with well-defined categories. However, pre-trained models like AraBERT exhibited lower accuracy due to the domain-specific nature of the Nakba narratives, highlighting the need for fine-tuning or specialized training for such contexts.

The low accuracy of ML models reflects Arabic NLP challenges, such as linguistic complexity and limited annotated datasets. The high inter-annotator agreement (87%, later 100%) highlights the reliability of manual annotations.

An essential aspect of this study was the grouping of categories, such as *"Emotions and Spirituality"* and *"Conflict and Homesickness."* This decision was informed by the natural co-occurrence of these themes in Nakba narratives. Emotional expressions are often intertwined with spiritual reflections, and narratives of conflict frequently evoke sentiments of homesickness. For instance, a sentence like *"My prayers keep me strong even as I endure exile"* captures both emotional and spiritual dimensions. Grouping these categories simplifies annotation, reduces ambiguity, and enhances the dataset's ability to capture intertwined themes.

However, this approach introduces limitations, as some sentences may lean more toward one aspect of a paired category. Future work should explore multi-label annotation schemes to better reflect the nuanced overlap between themes and provide more precise annotations.

These findings underscore the challenges of classifying Nakba narratives with existing models and emphasize the importance of expanding the dataset to address category imbalances. Future research should focus on fine-tuning transformer models and exploring advanced annotation schemes to overcome the limitations of small and specialized datasets. These enhancements will enable more robust analyses of Nakba narratives and contribute to advancing Arabic NLP research.

5 Conclusion

We presented the Nakba Topic Classification Corpus[2], an Arabic annotated dataset developed to support research in Arabic NLP, particularly in topic classification and emotion detection. Through careful preprocessing, annotation, and validation, we achieved good topic labels across five categories. This corpus is expected to bridge gaps in Arabic NLP resources and provide a foundation for future applications, including sentiment analysis and other machine learning classification tasks. By preserving and categorizing Nakba narratives, our work not only contributes to advancing Arabic NLP, but also serves as a vital resource for preserving and analyzing cultural narratives, offering a more in-depth understanding of the Nakba's historical and emotional dimensions.

Future research could expand the corpus by adding Nakba stories from diverse regions, Arabic dialects, and leveraging pre-trained models like GPT.

Acknowledgments

The authors would like to thank *Palestine Technical University - Kadoorie* in Tulkarm, Palestine for providing support.

References

Jeelani Ahmed and Muqeem Ahmed. 2021. Online news classification using machine learning techniques. *IIUM Engineering Journal*, 22(2):210–225.

Sallam AL-Sarayreh, Azza Mohamed, and Khaled Shaalan. 2023. Challenges and solutions for arabic natural language processing in social media. In *International conference on Variability of the Sun and sun-like stars: from asteroseismology to space weather*, pages 293–302. Springer.

Doha Albared, Hadi Hamoud, and Fadi Zaraket. 2023. Arabic topic classification in the generative and automl era. In *Proceedings of ArabicNLP 2023*. Association for Computational Linguistics.

Zaid Alyafeai, Mona Alshahrani, Maram Alenazi, Hesham Altwaijry, and Tayyaba Iqbal. 2022. A survey on arabic nlp: Where we are and where we are heading. *Journal of King Saud University-Computer and Information Sciences*, 34(6):2406–2423.

Wissam Antoun, Fady Baly, and Hazem Hajj. 2020. Arabert: Transformer-based model for arabic language understanding. *arXiv preprint arXiv:2003.00104*.

Ron Artstein and Massimo Poesio. 2008. Inter-coder agreement for computational linguistics. *Computational Linguistics*, 34(4):555–596.

Prafulla Bafna, Dhanya Pramod, and Anagha Vaidya. 2016. Document clustering: Tf-idf approach. In *2016 International Conference on Electrical, Electronics, and Optimization Techniques (ICEEOT)*, pages 61–66. IEEE.

Steven Bird, Ewan Klein, and Edward Loper. 2009. *Natural Language Processing with Python*. O'Reilly Media Inc.

José Cabezas, Thomas Loiseau, and Juan Villena-Román. 2022. Cultural heritage preservation in the digital age: Challenges and approaches in natural language processing. *Journal of Cultural Heritage*, 57:105–118.

Jacob Cohen. 1960. A coefficient of agreement for nominal scales. *Educational and Psychological Measurement*, 20(1):37–46.

Kareem Darwish, Hamdy Mubarak, Ahmed Abdelali, Mohamed Eldesouki, and Sabit Hassan. 2020. A panoramic survey of natural language processing in the arab world. *arXiv preprint arXiv:2011.12631*.

Ashraf Elnagar, Ridhwan Al-Debsi, and Omar Einea. 2020. Arabic text classification using deep learning models. *Information Processing Management*, 57(1):102121.

Stuart Lloyd. 1982. Least squares quantization in pcm. *IEEE Transactions on Information Theory*, 28(2):129–137.

Motaz K Saad and Wesam Ashour. 2010. Osac: Open source arabic corpora. In *6th ArchEng Int. Symposiums, EEECS*, volume 10, page 55.

Ahlam Wahdan, Mostafa Al-Emran, and Khaled Shaalan. 2024. A systematic review of arabic text classification: areas, applications, and future directions. *Soft Computing*, 28(2):1545–1566.

Taha Zerrouki. 2023. Pyarabic: A python package for arabic text. *Journal of Open Source Software*, 8(84):4886.

[2]https://github.com/PsArNLP/Nakba

Exploring Author Style in Nakba Short Stories: A Comparative Study of Transformer-Based Models

Osama Hamed[1] and Nadeem Zaidkilani[2,3]

[1]Department of Computer Systems Engineering, Palestine Technical University - Kadoorie, Palestine
osama.hamed@ptuk.edu.ps, sam.hamed@gmail.com
[2]Department of Computer Engineering and Security Mathematics, University Rovira i Virgili, Spain
[3] Department of Engineering and Technology, Al-Zaytona University of Science and Technology, Palestine
nadeem.zaidkilani@estudiants.urv.cat, nadeem.kilani@zust.edu.ps,nadimkilani@gmail.com

Abstract

Measuring semantic similarity and analyzing authorial style are fundamental tasks in Natural Language Processing (NLP), with applications in text classification, cultural analysis, and literary studies. This paper investigates the semantic similarity and stylistic features of Nakba short stories, a key component of Palestinian literature, using transformer-based models, AraBERT, BERT, and RoBERTa. The models effectively capture nuanced linguistic structures, cultural contexts, and stylistic variations in Arabic narratives, outperforming the traditional TF-IDF baseline. By comparing stories of similar length, we minimize biases and ensure a fair evaluation of both semantic and stylistic relationships. Experimental results indicate that RoBERTa achieves slightly higher performance, highlighting its ability to distinguish subtle stylistic patterns. This study demonstrates the potential of AI-driven tools to provide more in-depth insights into Arabic literature, and contributes to the systematic analysis of both semantic and stylistic elements in Nakba narratives.

1 Introduction

A very useful Natural Language Processing (NLP) tool is text similarity. It has many practical applications and allows us to find text that is similar to another text. The recent advancements in NLP have significantly improved the ability to analyze literary and cultural texts, offering new opportunities for exploring the richness of literary traditions. The development of deep learning models such as BERT and RoBERTa has made it possible to accurately capture the complexities of Arabic texts, a challenge that previous methodologies struggled to address (Devlin et al., 2019; Liu et al., 2019).

Nakba short stories, which depict the collective experiences and historical trauma of the Palestinian people, are an essential component of Palestinian literature and culture. However, analyzing Arabic literary texts computationally remains challenging due to the rich morphology, varied dialects, and cultural nuances of the language (Elmadany et al., 2020). Recent studies have shown the efficacy of transformer-based models in capturing these linguistic complexities, making them invaluable tools for semantic analysis (Antoun et al., 2020; Reimers and Gurevych, 2019). Furthermore, efforts to integrate cultural and historical context into text analysis have underscored the importance of domain-specific datasets and tailored pretraining strategies for effective semantic representation (Zaghouani et al., 2018; Saidi et al., 2024).

This research leverages deep learning models to measure semantic similarity and analyze authorial styles in Nakba narratives, aiming to uncover shared themes and stylistic variations among authors in this culturally significant genre. By applying advanced computational techniques, we investigate how well modern NLP models can grasp the nuanced linguistic structures and cultural context embedded within Arabic literary works. This study contributes to a more profound understanding of how these narratives convey social and political messages and demonstrates the potential of AI-driven tools to objectively and systematically analyze Arabic literature. This work sets a foundation for future research in using AI for cultural and literary studies. This work presents a framework and a database to discover whether new Nakba stories are similar to existing ones. To benchmark our results, we utilize TF-IDF (Bafna et al., 2016) as a baseline method, allowing for comparative analysis with advanced transformer-based models.

This paper is organized as follows. In Section 2, we present prior and recent research on Arabic text similarity. Section 3 provides a comprehensive analysis of the dataset, our analysis is enriched with visualization. Section 4 presents the experimental settings, describes the proposed approach and discusses our reported results. In Section 5, we

Proceedings of the Proceedings of the 1st International Workshop on Nakba Narratives as Language Resources, pages 56–62

conclude and point out ideas for future search.

2 Related Work

Semantic similarity measures the extent to which two pieces of text share meaning, a vital task in various NLP applications, such as text classification, information retrieval, and machine translation. Arabic, with its complex morphology and diverse genres, presents unique challenges for semantic similarity tasks. This literature review focuses on recent machine learning-based approaches for measuring semantic similarity in Arabic text, emphasizing studies by Antoun et al. (2020), Reimers and Gurevych (2019), Saidi et al. (2024) and Ismail et al. (2022) respectively.

Antoun et al. (2020) introduced AraBERT, a transformer model pre-trained on large Arabic corpora, which has shown effectiveness in various Arabic NLP tasks, including semantic similarity. Its domain-specific adaptations make it well-suited for handling the morphological complexity of Arabic text.

Author style detection has gained attention in NLP as a means of exploring linguistic patterns unique to individual authors. Transformer-based models such as BERT and RoBERTa have demonstrated their ability to capture stylistic nuances, as seen in studies such as Reimers and Gurevych (2019) that explore sentence embeddings for stylistic comparisons. These methods are particularly relevant for Nakba short stories, where narrative styles vary from author to author.

Saidi et al. (2024) introduced a hybrid model combining BERT and a Gated Recurrent Unit (GRU) network for capturing semantic similarity in Arabic texts. Their model exploits BERT's powerful contextual embeddings to represent words in their specific contexts, which are then passed through a GRU layer to capture sequential dependencies. The study highlights the model's efficacy in handling various Arabic genres, demonstrating significant improvements over traditional methods. However, the reliance on large annotated datasets for fine-tuning remains a limitation, particularly given the scarcity of genre-specific Arabic corpora.

Ismail et al. (2022) proposed a semantic-based similarity approach using pre-trained word embeddings and a deep neural network architecture. Their model integrates multiple linguistic features, including morphological and syntactic information, to enhance the understanding of semantic relationships between Arabic texts. This approach has shown promising results in capturing subtle semantic nuances, especially in formal and classical Arabic genres. Nevertheless, the model struggles with informal and dialectal variations, which are prevalent in contemporary Arabic literature.

3 Data

Our data represents Nakba stories, which were taken from the Nakba Archive website[1]. These narratives have been previously explored in the context of topic classification, as introduced by Hamed and Zaidkilani (2025), providing a complementary resource for analyzing Arabic texts.

3.1 Raw Data Gathering

From the project section in the Nakba Archive website, we extracted a collection of eight Nakba stories that are in PDF format. Each of these stories needs a special attention to become suitable for NLP related tasks.

3.2 Data Cleaning

In addition to the Arabic diacritics that rarely appear in the text. We noticed that the Nakba short stories contain English alphabets, special characters, URLs ... etc. The diacritics were removed using the PyArabic (Zerrouki, 2023) Python library[2]. We removed the remaining noise using regular expressions.

3.3 Data Preprocessing

We want to have a dataset suitable for NLP tasks. We did so using three main preprocessing steps:

Convert to a Structured Format Although the PDF is primarily a format for visual presentation, it contains unstructured data. Instead, we decided to convert to a structured format like CSV or Excel. This not only makes it easy to work with NLP tools/libraries such as Pandas and NLTK (Bird et al., 2009), but also allows any additional metadata to be stored alongside the text. Among others, this includes data labeling or annotation for specific NLP tasks such as Named Entity Recognition (NER) or Sentiment Analysis.

Text Normalization With the help of PyArabic (Zerrouki, 2023), we normalized the Arabic text by removing the extra white spaces and the Tatweel.

[1] `https://www.nakba-archive.org`

[2] `https://pypi.org/project/PyArabic/`

Paragraph to Sentences Each paragraph was split into sentences based on the appropriate sentence ending and using the **NLTK** Python library. As a result, we had a CSV/Excel file with about 470 rows. This will enable us to annotate the sentences easily, and add the corresponding labels in the future.

3.4 Data Stats and Visualization

Here, we shed the light on data stats and provide a sort of text visualization with the help of WordCloud library (Mueller, 2022).

Nakba Stories Stats We are working with a dataset that comprises eight Nakba short stories (473 sentences), totaling approximately 12,288 tokens, making it relatively small but sufficient for exploring semantic and stylistic features within a focused literary genre. Table 1 summarizes the stats of the eight Nakba stories. It is important to notice that the eight stories were written by different authors, making the dataset well-suited for analyzing authorial styles alongside semantic similarity.

Nakba Stories as WordCloud To produce a meaningful wordcloud, (i) we removed the Arabic stopwords using NLTK, and (ii) we removed the word suffixes and prefixes using PyArabic library. The WordCloud in Figure 1 provides a visual representation of the most frequent words/terms in the dataset, with the size of each word corresponding to its frequency of occurrence. As shown in the bottom-right-corner, it can be clearly seen that the Arabic word /TwAbyr/[3], also in Table 2, (Eng: Queues), and transliterated as /TwAbyr/ is among the most frequent words in the Nakba stories. TwAbyr are very common at refugee camps, and represent the suffering faced during the daily life activities. The dataset used in this study, which includes Nakba short stories and their associated preprocessing steps, is publicly available on GitHub [4].

4 Experimental Settings

In this study, we aim to measure semantic text similarity (STS) and analyze authorial styles in Arabic, focusing on Nakba short stories. Semantic similarity plays a crucial role in various NLP applications, such as text classification, information retrieval,

Figure 1: The Nakba stories presented as word-cloud.

and sentiment analysis, where understanding nuanced linguistic relationships is essential (Ismail et al., 2022). Recent advancements in transformer-based models like BERT (Devlin et al., 2019) and RoBERTa (Liu et al., 2019) have improved the ability to capture complex linguistic patterns, especially in underrepresented languages like Arabic. Our methodology leverages these pre-trained models to evaluate the semantic similarity across Nakba narratives, aiming to uncover recurring themes and patterns embedded within the cultural context of the stories. In addition to semantic similarity, we evaluate authorial style by analyzing linguistic features such as sentence complexity, word usage patterns, and lexical diversity. These features are extracted using embeddings from transformer-based models, enabling a detailed comparison of stylistic elements.

To benchmark these models, we use TF-IDF as a baseline, allowing for a comparative analysis of traditional versus deep learning approaches. TF-IDF was chosen as a baseline method for its traditional approach to measuring semantic similarity through term frequency and inverse document frequency. Despite its simplicity, TF-IDF provides a foundational perspective for evaluating the performance of more advanced models like BERT and RoBERTa.

4.1 System Description

BERT and RoBERTa were chosen due to their effectiveness in capturing intricate semantic relationships through deep bidirectional attention, an approach that excels in understanding context-sensitive word meanings (Devlin et al., 2019; Liu et al., 2019). This characteristic is particularly valuable for our study, as Nakba narratives often in-

[3] Broken Plural

[4] `https://github.com/PsArNLP/Nakba`

ID	Arabic Name	English Name	Author	No. of Tokens
1	افتتاحية	Introduction	Ihab Kilani	556
2	ذاكرة لا تفنى	An Enduring Memory	Munira Al-Shehabi	1472
3	طوابير	Queues	Sarah Daoud	2082
4	أبو عادل الفاتح	Abu Adel, The Opener	Oula Jomaa	2069
5	حنين	Longing	Alaa Sukari	1113
6	الدخان فالخبز فالأسلاك الشائكة	Smoke, bread, & Barbed Wire	Ahmad Sukari	1479
7	أم الشهيد	The Martyr's Mother	Rama Abu Naaseh	1700
8	كيف لي أن أغفر	How Can I Forgive?	Shaimaa Taha	1817

Table 1: Biographies of the authors and statistics of the Nakba stories.

Arabic Word	Meaning	Transliteration	Singular /Transliteration/
طوابير	Queues	TwAbyr	طابور /TAbur/

Table 2: The Arabic word /TwAbyr/.

clude historical, emotional, and cultural nuances that simpler models might overlook. Additionally, BERT's and RoBERTa's subword tokenization approach is well-suited to handle Arabic morphology, which features root-based word variations and complex inflection patterns (Antoun et al., 2020).

NLP Pipeline Our NLP Pipeline aims to evaluate the semantic similarity between Arabic texts by employing State-of-the-Art (SotA) Arabic NLP techniques and machine learning models, specifically BERT and RoBERTa. This NLP pipeline encompasses the following steps as depicted in Figure 2.

- Data Preprocessing: Preprocessing is a critical step to prepare our dataset for optimal performance with these models. The normalization and preprocessing of Arabic was ensured in a previous step. Additionally, we employed Arabic-specific tokenization techniques to manage script and morphological complexity, utilizing subword units that allow the model to process word roots effectively.

- Feature Extraction: We utilized BERT-based and RoBERTa-based models to generate contextualized embeddings for Arabic texts. We also ensured that embeddings capture nuanced semantic relationships between words and phrases.

- Similarity Calculation: We employed cosine similarity as the primary metric to quantify the semantic similarity between texts. We also compared the embeddings generated by TF-IDF, BERT, and RoBERTa models to assess text similarity.

4.2 Experimental Results

We aim to explore the degree of semantic similarity and variations in authorial styles among the Nakba short stories. As inspired by (Cer et al., 2018; Reimers and Gurevych, 2019), we didn't compare all pairs of stories, instead we only compared the stories of similar lengths. Doing that is not only necessary to avoid biases, but also to increase accuracy.

As shown in Figure 3, the heatmap provides a detailed view of the similarity scores for story pairs, highlighting RoBERTa's superior performance across all pairs.

Table 3 presents the reported results for the four models. The TF-IDF serves as a baseline comparison, offering insight into the improvements achieved by transformer-based models in capturing semantic relationships within Nakba stories.

Both BERT and RoBERTa achieve high semantic similarity scores for Nakba story pairs, with RoBERTa slightly outperforming BERT due to its optimized pretraining. AraBERT, a transformer model specifically fine-tuned for Arabic, also demonstrates strong semantic similarity performance, achieving scores comparable to BERT and RoBERTa. This highlights the effectiveness of

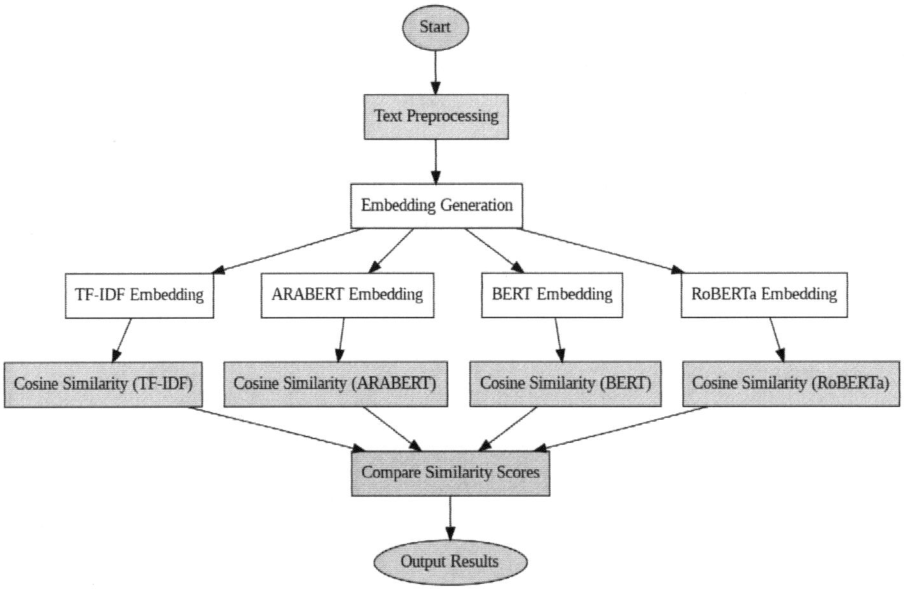

Figure 2: The Arabic text similarity analysis pipeline.

Criteria	Story 2 & 6	Story 7 & 8	Story 3 & 4
TF-IDF	54.40	42.16	**57.97**
AraBERT	**96.18**	93.87	95.23
BERT	**98.23**	97.89	97.77
RoBERTa	99.56	**99.77**	99.61

Table 3: Reported semantic similarity scores for Nakba short stories.

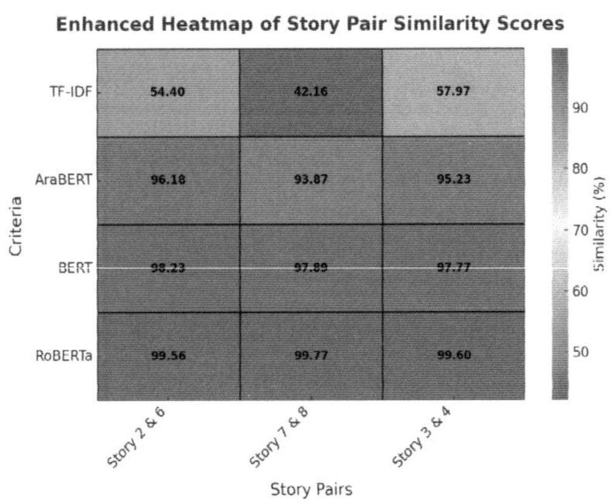

Figure 3: The heatmap of story pair similarities.

domain-specific adaptations in capturing Arabic linguistic and cultural nuances, despite slightly lower scores compared to RoBERTa. The results highlight shared cultural and historical themes, demonstrating the models' robustness. The results also indicate the ability of RoBERTa to capture subtle stylistic variations among authors, as reflected in differences in word choice and sentence construction. AraBERT, with its domain-specific pretraining, also performs well in identifying stylistic differences unique to Arabic.

4.3 Discussion

Table 3 reports the semantic similarity results for Nakba short stories using BERT and RoBERTa. Both models achieve high scores (above 97%), with RoBERTa slightly outperforming BERT, reflecting its superior contextual representation. Figure 4 illustrates the comparative performance of the models for each story pair, clearly demonstrating the gap between traditional TF-IDF and transformer-based models like BERT, RoBERTa, and AraBERT. These results highlight the models' ability to identify both shared cultural themes and distinct authorial styles in Nakba stories. For instance, RoBERTa excels in capturing stylistic variations, such as differences in sentence complexity and word usage patterns, which are critical for understanding individual narrative approaches. While the high scores demonstrate the models' robustness, they also high-

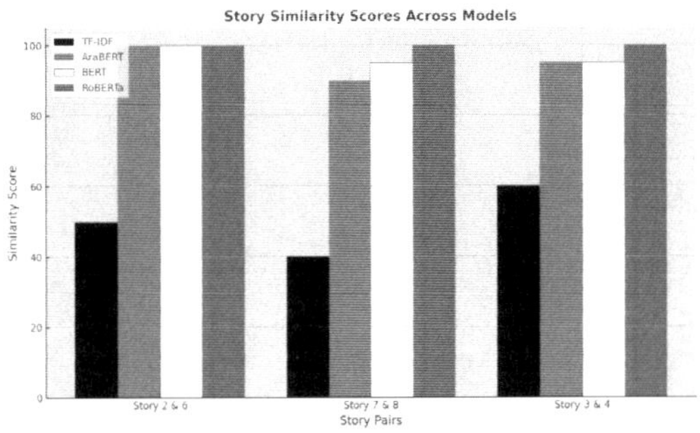

Figure 4: The stories similarities with different models.

light potential limitations in capturing subtle variations in stylistic or narrative details. Pairing stories of similar lengths ensures a fair evaluation by reducing bias.

The significant gap in performance between TF-IDF and transformer-based models like BERT and RoBERTa highlights the limitations of traditional approaches in capturing nuanced semantic relationships, particularly in linguistically complex narratives. These findings emphasize the potential of transformer models for broader literary analysis, including thematic clustering and pattern identification in Arabic texts.

5 Conclusion

In this paper, we investigated the semantic similarity and authorial styles of Nakba short stories using advanced transformer-based models, AraBERT, BERT, and RoBERTa. The high similarity scores achieved by all models underline their effectiveness in capturing nuanced linguistic structures, cultural contexts, and stylistic variations in Arabic texts. The slightly superior performance of RoBERTa highlights the impact of optimized pretraining on contextual representation and its ability to differentiate authorial styles within narratives. By comparing stories of similar length, we minimized bias and ensured a fair assessment of both semantic and stylistic relationships. This study demonstrates the potential of transformer-based models in the systematic analysis of Arabic literature, providing valuable insights into recurring themes, stylistic diversity, and shared cultural motifs.

Future work could focus on expanding the dataset to include a wider variety of Nakba narratives, allowing for more comprehensive analyses of semantic and stylistic variation. Incorporating additional stylistic features, such as syntactic complexity, lexical richness, and punctuation patterns, could provide more in-depth insights into authorial styles. Improving the models by fine-tuning on domain-specific corpora, adopting multitask learning approaches, or utilizing advanced architectures like SBERT for sentence-level embeddings could enhance their ability to capture subtle stylistic differences.

Acknowledgments

The authors would like to thank *Palestine Technical University - Kadoorie* in Tulkarm, Palestine for providing support.

References

Wissam Antoun, Fady Baly, and Hazem Hajj. 2020. Arabert: Transformer-based model for arabic language understanding. In *Proceedings of the 4th Workshop on Open-Source Arabic Corpora and Processing Tools*, pages 9–15.

Prafulla Bafna, Dhanya Pramod, and Anagha Vaidya. 2016. Document clustering: Tf-idf approach. In *2016 International Conference on Electrical, Electronics, and Optimization Techniques (ICEEOT)*, pages 61–66. IEEE.

Steven Bird, Ewan Klein, and Edward Loper. 2009. *Natural Language Processing with Python*. O'Reilly Media Inc.

Daniel Cer, Yinfei Yang, Sheng-yi Kong, Nan Hua, Nicole Limtiaco, Rhomni St. John, Noah Constant, Mario Guajardo-Cespedes, Steve Yuan, Chris Tar, et al. 2018. Universal sentence encoder. In *Proceedings of the 2018 Conference on Empirical Methods in Natural Language Processing: System Demonstrations*, pages 169–174.

Jacob Devlin, Ming-Wei Chang, Kenton Lee, and Kristina Toutanova. 2019. Bert: Pre-training of deep bidirectional transformers for language understanding. In *Proceedings of the 2019 Conference of the North American Chapter of the Association for Computational Linguistics: Human Language Technologies, Volume 1 (Long and Short Papers)*, pages 4171–4186.

AbdelRahim Elmadany, Hamdy Mubarak, Ahmed Kamal, Ahmed Eldin, Kareem Darwish, Tamer Elsayed, and Walid Magdy. 2020. Arabic offensive language detection with deep learning and text augmentation. In *Proceedings of the Fourth Workshop on Open-Source Arabic Corpora and Processing Tools, with a Shared Task on Offensive Language Detection*, pages 37–42.

Osama Hamed and Nadeem Zaidkilani. 2025. Arabic topic classification corpus of the nakba short stories. In *Proceedings of the Nakba and Natural Language Processing Workshop (Nakba-NLP)*. To appear.

S. Ismail, M. Hassan, and W. Aref. 2022. Arabic semantic-based textual similarity. In *Proceedings of the Third International Conference on Arabic Computational Linguistics*, pages 65–72.

Yinhan Liu, Myle Ott, Naman Goyal, Jingfei Du, Mandar Joshi, Danqi Chen, Omer Levy, Mike Lewis, Luke Zettlemoyer, and Veselin Stoyanov. 2019. Roberta: A robustly optimized bert pretraining approach. In *arXiv preprint arXiv:1907.11692*.

Andreas Mueller. 2022. Word cloud: A little word cloud generator in python.

Nils Reimers and Iryna Gurevych. 2019. Sentence-bert: Sentence embeddings using siamese bert-networks. In *Proceedings of the 2019 Conference on Empirical Methods in Natural Language Processing*.

A. Saidi, F. Al-Mousa, and H. Khalil. 2024. A bert-gru model for measuring the similarity of arabic text. In *Proceedings of the Second Arabic Natural Language Processing Conference*, pages 102–110.

Wajdi Zaghouani, Nizar Habash, Behrang Mohit, and Houda Bouamor. 2018. Arabic nlp tools for the processing of arabic heritage in the digital age. In *Proceedings of the Eleventh International Conference on Language Resources and Evaluation (LREC 2018)*.

Taha Zerrouki. 2023. Pyarabic: A python package for arabic text. *Journal of Open Source Software*, 8(84):4886.

Detecting Inconsistencies in Narrative Elements of Cross Lingual Nakba Texts

Nada Hamarsheh[1,a] **Zahia Elabour**[1,b] **Aya Murra**[1,c] **Adnan Yahya**[1,d]

[1] Electrical and Computer Engineering Department, Birzeit University, Birzeit, Palestine

a: hnada.edu@gmail.com
b: zahia-ali@hotmail.com
c: ayaibrahim065@gmail.com
d: yahya@birzeit.edu

Abstract

This paper proposes a methodology for contradiction detection in cross lingual texts about the Nakba. We outline a pipeline that includes text translation using Google's Gemini for context-aware translations, followed by a fact extraction task using either Gemini or the TextRank algorithm. We then apply Natural Language Inference (NLI) by using models trained for this task, such as XLM-RoBERTa and BART to detect contradictions from different texts about the Nakba. We also describe how the performance of such NLI models is affected by the complexity of some sentences as well as the unique syntactic and semantic characteristics of the Arabic language. Additionally, we suggest a method using cosine similarity of vector embeddings of facts for identifying missing or underrepresented topics in historical narrative texts. This work is a proof-of-concept, and the results are preliminary. However, they offer initial insights into biases, contradictions, and gaps in narratives surrounding the Nakba, providing a foundation for future research into contradictions in historical perspectives.

1 Introduction

Nakba (Arabic for catastrophe) refers to the displacement of hundreds of thousands of Palestinians from Palestine during the 1948 war between Arabs and Israel (United Nations, 2024). As a result of this catastrophe, approximately 750,000 Palestinians were forcefully displaced, 15,000 killed, and more than 531 towns and villages destroyed (Palestinian Central Bureau of Statistics (PCBS), 2008). With this catastrophe happening 76 years ago, the narratives that we have now surrounding it vary, with belief, denial, or skepticism.

Conflicting narratives regarding the history of the Nakba preceded it, and eventually led to it. A clear example that displays how a conflict in narratives contributed to the events leading up to Nakba is the famous phrase "A land without a people for a people without a land". This phrase, believed by many historical references to be a "Zionist slogan" (Muir, 2008), was in stark contrast to the 690,000 people who lived in Palestine in 1914 (Palestinian Central Bureau of Statistics (PCBS), 2021) before the Balfour Declaration and the waves of immigration to Palestine that followed.

By considering such examples of how a narrative can influence and be influenced by remarkable events of history, we establish the need for a systematic approach to review such narratives, and point to pieces of historical evidence that have been tampered with, dropped or manipulated.

In this paper, we propose a method that incorporates the use of Natural Language Processing (NLP) to review pieces of written text, compare texts from contrasting backgrounds, and lastly presents sentences where this contrast in facts happen, which in return indicates contradiction of information between the subject sources. The system also presents what statements have been left out in one source but mentioned in another. This highlighting of the contradictions found in the subject text, as well as some text failing to mention certain facts, can lead to better detect biases. By flagging such contradictions, historians and experts on the Nakba can make informed remedial decisions based on the approach outlined in this paper.

The system we propose begins by taking two input texts, the focus languages here are English and Arabic, and the texts are expected to reflect differing historical narratives about the Nakba. Since Arabic-speaking historians are the target, texts in English are first translated to Arabic. In a previous work of ours (Murra et al., 2024), we reached the conclusion that using Gemini for translation performed better than using machine translation models such as MarianMT. Therefore, we propose using Gemini to perform this step.

Then we extract facts that represent the ideas of

Proceedings of the Proceedings of the 1st International Workshop on Nakba Narratives as Language Resources, pages 63–74
January 20, 2025.

the texts. For this we suggest two methods of providing summaries, once by prompting Gemini, and the other by using the TextRank algorithm. The facts extracted by this step are assumed to reflect the contradictions and overlooked facts between the texts.

Lastly, we perform contradiction detection by utilizing the labels provided by NLI models such as XLM-RoBERTa (xlm-roberta-large-xnli) and BART (bart-large-mnli). This gives a score for the relationship between a pair of sentences, to indicate either an entailment, neutral, or contradiciton relationship.

For finding gaps in fact representation over the texts, we propose using embedding techniques on the facts extracted from the texts, then use similarity metrics, such as cosine similarity, to find unique sentences that are missing in the corresponding texts.

2 Background

In this paper, we suggest the use of automatic summarization of the subject texts. Automatic text summarization extracts the main ideas of a text document (Mallick et al., 2019). Summarization can happen in two types, extractive and abstractive summaries. An extractive summary produces a summary based on the sentences used in the text itself rather than producing a unique summary. It looks for identical information in documents and assigns a score to each statement based on how well it explains the other facts of the document. An abstractive summary, in contrast, generates a unique summary by rephrasing and restructuring the most important information from the original text (N. et al., 2022). However, summarization is a complex NLP problem influenced by text type, length, vocabulary level, and named entities. However, due to its abstract nature, it remains a longstanding issue (Bongale et al., 2022).

Google's Gemini is designed to improve automated text summarization by mimicking human-like sentence-level styles. It combines extractive and abstractive techniques, allowing for fine control over summary style and quality, which reduces risks like factual inaccuracies in summaries. Gemini introduces a "Fusion Index" to analyze and adjust sentence styles within new datasets, enhancing flexibility for different applications (Bao et al., 2023). While effective, this approach still lacks a clear way to measure its ability to generate fully abstracted summaries, marking an area for further exploration (Bao et al., 2023) .

TextRank is an unsupervised extractive text summarization algorithm that ranks sentences by extracting the main ideas from a document depending on their importance. It is related to Google's PageRank, which ranks web pages for online search results (Bongale et al., 2022).

With that said, it should be noted that research points to limitations in Arabic summarization techniques. This is linked to many reasons including the scarcity of annotated datasets in Arabic, the complexity of Arabic linguistics, morphology, and syntax. All these reasons lead to difficulties in obtaining a coherent summary that does not change the intended tone and meaning of the original text (Souri et al., 2023)

A notable technique in relationship inference from texts is the Natural Language Inference (NLI) task. NLI classifies the relationship between a pair of premise and hypothesis as either entailment, contradiction, or neutral. It forms the basis for higher-level NLP tasks like question-answering and summarization (Nie et al., 2019). In Arabic however, NLI is a challenging task because of the lexical ambiguity of the language, lack of large entailment datasets, etc. (Jallad and Ghneim, 2022)

3 System Implementation

3.1 Data Collection

To ensure the capability of achieving the aim of this paper, the text data collected employs samples of different and oftentimes contradicting perspectives on topics related to the Nakba, sourcing Arabic and/or English texts on the issue.

The texts used originate from different sources, such as articles from Wikipedia, academic journals by Arabs, Israeli, or others writing on the Nakba and the events of 1948, official reports of historians, governmental figures, or organization like the United Nations (UN), and lastly some articles from websites discussing the topic.

3.2 Translation

As our focus is mainly texts in Arabic or English, a translation task is crucial. We are particularly interested in presenting findings to Arabic readers, including historians and field experts. Therefore, English texts are translated to Arabic to ensure the results are relevant to the specific audience.

The process begins by detecting the language of

the text, ensuring that only content in English is processed for translation. Once identified, the English text is split into smaller chunks for translation using the Gemini-pro model.

The model is prompted to provide a translation in Arabic that preserves the tone and meaning of the original article. The model then translates each chunk from English to Arabic, removing unnecessary elements. This translation will be the source of the information and factual statements that will be processed for any contradictions.

To illustrate the process further, we referenced two articles to explain the proof-of-concept: , "The Nakba: Something That Did Not Occur (Although It Had to Occur)" (Bronstein, 2009), and "The Nakba: More than just a historical event" (Original: النكبة أكبر من مجرد حدث تاريخي) (Naim, 2023). The first article is originally in English, and as mentioned all English texts must be translated to Arabic. Since the other article is in Arabic, no work is needed to be done there at this point. The following example is a text excerpt from (Bronstein, 2009), followed by the translation Gemini provided.

"From early on, Zionism ignored the existence of the Arab inhabitants of Palestine. It is, therefore, not possible that some 800,000 persons were ethnically cleansed from the country and that more than 500 Palestinian villages were destroyed".

" تجاهلت الصهيونية منذ وقت مبكر وجود السكان العرب في فلسطين. ومن ثم، فإنه ليس من الممكن أن يتم تطهير ما يقرب من 800000 شخص عرقياَ من البلاد، وأن يتم تدمير أكثر من 500 قرية فلسطينية".

3.3 Summarization

The aim of using Summarization is to reduce data complexity and improve the efficiency of similarity and contradiction analysis. Summarization is used to extract the main points from the text and focus on relevant information. This process separates content into actionable, high-quality content, avoiding irrelevant details. We experimented with different summarization approaches on the same text about Nakba, and below is a discussion of the results of this experimentation.

Using TextRank:

As mentioned earlier, the TextRank algorithm is used to retrieve sentences from the original text, after it ranks the sentences with importance scores, providing an extractive summary of the text at hand. The example below shows a group of facts (sentences) that were extracted and retrieved by the TextRank algorithm when applied to (Naim, 2023).

- "أن كل الأهوال التي مر بها شعبنا الفلسطيني في تلك الفترة كانت جزءًا من مخطط متعمد من القيادة العليا للحركة الصهيونية،"
- "تم تدمير أكثر من 530 قرية فلسطينية والسيطرة على أكثر من 700 قرية ومدينة،"
- "وتهجير أكثر من 750 ألف فلسطيني (نحو 50% من الفلسطينيين الذين كانوا يقيمون في فلسطين التاريخية)،"
- "فقد سيطر اليهود بالقوة عام 1948 على نحو 78% من أراضي فلسطين التاريخية، وأنشؤوا دولتهم على هذه المساحة."

Using Gemini:

The second approach we used is Google's Gemini. Gemini, unlike traditional summarization techniques, can be prompted to summarize text in a list of the main points or ideas from the text, providing an abstractive summary that uses paraphrasing of the original text. For illustration purposes, Gemini was prompted to summarize (Naim, 2023), and the example below shows a sample of the extracted facts.

- "النكبة هي كلمة عربية تعني الكارثة، وهي حدث أليم استمر نحو سنتين من منتصف عام 1947 إلى منتصف عام 1949."
- "تضمنت النكبة تدمير أكثر من 530 قرية فلسطينية والسيطرة على أكثر من 700 قرية ومدينة وتهجير أكثر من 750 ألف فلسطيني."
- "روّج الصهاينة أن فلسطين كانت صحراء خالية من السكان، لكن هذه الرواية لا تصمد أمام حقائق التاريخ."
- "منذ النكبة، وضعت القيادة الصهيونية خطة للسيطرة على الشعب الفلسطيني وإحباط قدرته على الثورة والرفض."

Using both of these models comes with advantages and disadvantages. TextRank for example is unsupervised and can extract the exact "problem" sentences which can hold some contradiction to others. However, if the original text holds some ambiguity in its wording, the sentence will be passed as is. In contrast, Gemini reduces the complexity of some sentences by paraphrasing, which makes comparing and finding contradictions easier. This, however, can be problematic if paraphrasing changes the intended meaning.

3.4 Similarity and Contradictions

The core of our work is to determine if two texts of different sources have contradicting statements. Two sentences are said to be contradicting each other if they are generally about the same idea, with conflicting information found in both. An example on contradicting sentences can be seen in the following example:

Sentence 1 (Originally in English): "From early on, Zionism ignored the existence of the Arab inhabitants of Palestine. It is, therefore, not possible that some 800,000 persons were ethnically cleansed from the country and that more than 500 Palestinian villages were destroyed." (Bronstein, 2009)

(Translation:

تجاهلت الصهيونية منذ وقت مبكر وجود السكان العرب في فلسطين. ومن ثم، فإنه ليس من الممكن أن يتم تطهير ما يقرب من 800000 شخص عرقيًا من البلاد، وأن يتم تدمير أكثر من 500 قرية فلسطينية.

Sentence 2 (Originally in Arabic):

في تلك الفترة، تم تدمير أكثر من 530 قرية فلسطينية والسيطرة على أكثر من 700 قرية ومدينة، وتهجير أكثر من 750 ألف فلسطيني (نحو 50% من الفلسطينيين الذين كانوا يقيمون في فلسطين التاريخية). (2023 ,Naim)

(Translation: "During that time, more than 530 Palestinian villages were destroyed, over 700 villages and towns were seized, and more than 750,000 Palestinians (approximately 50% of those living in historic Palestine) were displaced.")

Both sentences are on the same topic, but present contradictory statements.

To detect such contradictions, the facts extracted from both subject texts are compared using two Natural Language Inference (NLI) models, XLM-RoBERTa (xlm-roberta-large-xnli) and BART (bart-large-mnli). This is done by pairing one fact (sentence) from each list of the extracted facts at a time and identifying their relationships as Contradiction, Neutral, or Entailment. Each pair created is assigned different probabilities representing each of these labels, with the highest probability determining the final label given to the pair. If the highest probability is given to the contradiction label, then the sentences are considered to be contradicting.

For comparison purposes, this process is performed twice: once for the facts extracted from both subject texts using Gemini, and again for the facts extracted using the Textrank algorithm. As there are differences in the type of sentences retrieved by each approach, not all facts found in one approach are necessarily found in the other. Tables 1 and 2 shows a sample of pairs with the labels assigned by each NLI model and their corresponding probabilities. In both tables, the premise comes from the facts extracted from (Naim, 2023), while the hypothesis comes from the facts extracted from (Bronstein, 2009).

From table 1, the reader can infer that the premise and the hypothesis are contradictory based on the overall meanings of the sentences of examples 1 and 2 (i.e. The Nakba led to contrasting outcomes for both Palestinians and Zionists). Both models correctly labeled the pair as a contradiction.

In the third example, the reader can also infer a contradiction (i.e. Describing the Nakba as a catastrophe in the premise, and denying the Nakba in the hypothesis), but because the wording can be complex as seen in the hypothesis, the models did not assign the same label to the pair.

Finally, the last example also shows a case of disagreement between the models. Even though the sentences are contradictory (i.e. the premise discusses the expulsion of 750,000 Palestinians, while the hypothesis doubts both the expulsion of said refugees and even their existence), XLM-RoBERTa (xlm-roberta-large-xnli) was not able to detect the contradiction, and BART-NLI (bart-large-mnli) assigned a lower contradiction score. This indicates that the models were not able to identify this contradiction correctly.

From table 2, the reader can clearly see that the premise and the hypothesis of example 1 are contradictory(i.e. Premise detailing the expulsion of 750,000 refugees, and the hypothesis denying the possibility of that happening). Both models resulted in labeling the pair as a contradiction.

Example 2 is more complicated in the sense that the contradiction is inferred from the meaning of the pair (i.e premise references torture and detainment of more than 1,000,000 Palestinians, while the hypothesis claims Zionists ignored Arabs in Palestine). This contradiction is more subtle than the first, therefore the models did not assign the same label, and the contradiction score given was low. In contrast, the last example shows an inferred contradiction (i.e premise states that the tragedies happening at the time (Nakba) was a deliberate plan by Zionist leaders, and the hypothesis clearly implies the Nakba did not happen in the past but continues to happen today (because of the discourse around the topic). The models successfully detected a contradiction between the pair.

The models however failed to detect that the pair in example 3 were actually not contradictory (i.e both the premise and the hypothesis state that refugees had been evicted, in the premise by force, and in the hypothesis as a means for the Zionist

Table 1: Samples of Comparison Results for facts Extracted Using Gemini

#	Premise	Hypothesis	XLM-RoBERTa Label	XLM-RoBERTa Probability	BART Label	BART Label Probability
1	تضمنت النكبة تدمير أكثر من 530 قرية فلسطينية والسيطرة على أكثر من 700 قرية ومدينة وتهجير أكثر من 750 ألف فلسطيني.	النكبة هي حدث ضروري، لأنها حققت ذاتية صهيونية نقية مغلقة ومستقلة من الناحية العرقية.	Contradiction	0.999	Contradiction	0.902
2	أدت النكبة إلى تقسيم الشعب الفلسطيني إلى معازل مفصولة وتعرض لأكثر من مليون فلسطيني للاعتقال والتعذيب والحرمان منذ عام 1967.	النكبة هي حدث ضروري، لأنها حققت ذاتية صهيونية نقية مغلقة ومستقلة من الناحية العرقية.	Contradiction	0.999	Contradiction	0.906
3	النكبة هي كلمة عربية تعني الكارثة، وهي حدث أليم استمر نحو سنتين من منتصف عام 1947 إلى منتصف عام 1949.	تستمر النكبة كحدث لم يحدث في الماضي في الحدوث أيضًا اليوم.	Neutral	0.931	Contradiction	0.885
4	تضمنت النكبة تدمير أكثر من 530 قرية فلسطينية والسيطرة على أكثر من 700 قرية ومدينة وتهجير أكثر من 750 ألف فلسطيني.	إذا لم يكن الفلسطينيون متواجدين 'حقًا'، فلا يمكن أن يحدث طردهم أيضًا.	Neutral	0.996	Contradiction	0.546

Table 2: Samples of Comparison Results for facts Extracted Using TextRank

#	Premise	Hypothesis	XLM-RoBERTa Label	XLM-RoBERTa Probability	BART Label	BART Label Probability
1	وتهجير أكثر من 750 ألف فلسطيني،	فإنه ليس من الممكن أن يتم تطهير ما يقرب من 800000 شخص عرقيًا من البلاد،	Contradiction	0.982	Contradiction	0.946
2	أكثر من مليون فلسطيني تعرض للاعتقال والتعذيب والحرمان منذ احتلال عام 1967،	تجاهلت الصهيونية منذ وقت مبكر وجود السكان العرب في فلسطين.	Neutral	0.779	Contradiction	0.506
3	فقد سيطر اليهود بالقوة عام 1948 على نحو 78% من أراضي فلسطين التاريخية، وأنشؤوا دولتهم على هذه المساحة .	كان على المشروع الصهيوني إخلاء سكان البلاد من أجل تحقيق ذاته.	Neutral	0.998	Contradiction	0.810
4	أن كل الأهوال التي مر بها شعبنا الفلسطيني في تلك الفترة كانت جزءًا من مخطط متعمد من القيادة العليا للحركة الصهيونية،	تستمر النكبة كحدث لم يحدث في الماضي في الحدوث أيضًا اليوم.	Contradiction	0.967	Contradiction	0.855

project to "realize itself"). This pair was mislabeled by both models.

Since comparing the different summarization approaches (using Gemini or TextRank) was not feasible due to the limitations of the NLI task, it is more effective to select the appropriate approach based on the specific use case. We recommend that if a researcher wants to quote the translation as it is and point to contradictions without external paraphrasing, then using the TextRank algorithm is preferred. However, if the text requires paraphrasing or further explanation, then benefiting from the abilities of Google's Gemini might be a better choice. In other words, if the researcher prefers an extractive summary, TextRank should be used, but if an abstractive summary is needed, then Gemini is the appropriate choice.

3.5 Finding Missing Facts

This section addresses the other important aspect of the paper: determining whether a specific fact can be found in one of the subject texts but not in the other. This approach allows the reader to detect biases in narratives, and find patterns of what facts tend to be omitted frequently.

Each sentence in the extracted facts lists is embedded using a sentence transformer model. This generates a vector embedding for each sentence, and therefore comparing a pair of sentences can be done using cosine similarity between their respective vectors. Every pair combination from the two lists are compared. If a specific sentence scores a low similarity when paired with every sentence of the other list, this sentence is considered to be a unique facts, meaning that the other text does not contain a similar sentence, indicating that such a fact is dropped or left out from the other narrative, or simply that the topic of the fact is not found in the other text.

Some facts mentioned in (Naim, 2023) but not in (Bronstein, 2009) discuss some crucial implications of the Nakba. This includes the statement "7,000,000 Palestinian (Refugees) in the diaspora suffer from deprivation of the most basic rights and are subjected to persecution and harassment" (original: "أن 7 ملايين فلسطيني في الشتات يعانون الحرمان من أبسط الحقوق الأساسية"). Such an important fact was not found in (Bronstein, 2009), which might be an indication of bias. Other facts from (Naim, 2023) that are not mentioned in (Bronstein, 2009) can be found in tables 4 and 6 of the appendix.

On the other hand, (Bronstein, 2009) speaks more on the views of the Zionists leaders regarding the Nakba, a stance which is not found in (Naim, 2023). An example is "Attitudes of the leaders and architects of Zionism towards the indigenous inhabitants of 'Zion' were situated between their perception as (temporary) guardians or holders of the land on one end". Other facts from (Bronstein, 2009) that are not mentioned in (Naim, 2023) can be found in tables 3 and 5 in the appendix.

4 Limitations and Future Work

4.1 Limitations

One of the main limitations of the summarization approach using Gemini is that it may not capture all the key points accurately, potentially omitting or misrepresenting some of them. This can lead to contradictions when comparing the summarized information with other texts. The accuracy of the model remains a concern, as it may struggle to extract or interpret some of the essential details correctly, affecting the reliability of the summaries.

A significant limitation to address is the translation model's inability to distinguish effectively between past and present contexts. For example, the sentence "it is, therefore, not possible that some 800,000 persons were ethnically cleansed from the country " was translated as "فإنه ليس من الممكن أن يتم تطهير ما يقرب من 800000 شخص عرقيًا من البلاد." which does not properly capture the past context of the event, and instead reflects a present action. Such subtle contradictions may be harder to detect.

Some sentences in Arabic have different syntax structures not found in English. For example, a sentence like "الشعب الفلسطيني تحت الاحتلال" (The Palestinian people (is) under occupation) lacks a verb but conveys a clear fact. Many tools rely on complete sentence structures, making it hard to handle nominal or verbless sentences while preserving their meaning.

4.2 Future Work

A key direction for future work includes a quantitative evaluation of the proposed approach to measure its performance and reliability in contradiction detection.

Future work could focus on improving the translated model to handle text translation from any language to Arabic. This enhancement would help ensure that the model can process a broader range of content. Additionally, by refining the model, it may be possible to detect contradictions more effectively across various texts. For instance, when discussing historical events like the Nakba, the model can be trained to prioritize Arabic sources, as they are more likely to contain the correct points about the event compared to other languages.

Furthermore, the approach we presented in this paper can be the foundation for other work focusing on other pieces of Nakba history, such as oral history related to the Nakba and the 1948 war, providing a more comprehensive understanding of this historical event.

5 Conclusion

In this paper we proposed a method of contradiction detection in historical texts about the Nakba, and the sensitivity of dealing with the different narratives surrounding the issue. We proposed the use of Google's Gemini to provide context-aware translations of texts in English, as the audience this work is directed towards is Arabic-speaking historians and experts. In addition, we also compared prompting Gemini to provide facts summarized from textual content, in addition to using the TextRank algorithm for the same purpose. The core of the paper then employs NLI models such as XLM-RoBERTa (xlm-roberta-large-xnli) and BART (bart-large-mnli) to detect contradictions in pairs of statements taken from different texts about the Nakba. The findings suggest that the performance of these models on this specific task is influenced by the complexity of the sentences and the Arabic linguistic features in general. Another important part of this paper is a suggested method of finding sentences or topics that are not mentioned in a specific text with a specific narrative. Our aim was that the methodologies suggested in this paper enable an expert in history to gain deeper analysis of biases, contradictions, and gaps in historical narratives from both sides of history.

References

Guangsheng Bao, Zebin Ou, and Yue Zhang. 2023. Gemini: controlling the sentence-level summary style in abstractive text summarization. In *Proceedings of the 2023 Conference on Empirical Methods in Natural Language Processing*, pages 831–842.

Rugved Bongale, Talha Chafekar, Mayank Chowdhary, and Tushar Bapecha. 2022. Automatic news summarizer using textrank. In *2022 IEEE 7th International conference for Convergence in Technology (I2CT)*, pages 1–5. IEEE.

Eitan Bronstein. 2009. The Nakba: Something that did not occur (although it had to occur). https://www.zochrot.org/publication_articles/view/50644/en?The_Nakba_Something_That_Did_Not_Occur__Although_It_Had_to_Occur__.

Khloud Al Jallad and Nada Ghneim. 2022. Arnli: Arabic natural language inference for entailment and contradiction detection. *arXiv preprint arXiv:2209.13953*.

Chirantana Mallick, Ajit Kumar Das, Madhurima Dutta, Asit Kumar Das, and Apurba Sarkar. 2019. Graph-based text summarization using modified textrank. In *Soft Computing in Data Analytics: Proceedings of International Conference on SCDA 2018*, pages 137–146. Springer.

Diana Muir. 2008. A land without a people for a people without a land. *Middle East Quarterly*, 15(2).

Aya Murra, Nada Hamarsheh, and Zahia Elabour. 2024. *Automated Generation and Improvement of Arabic Wikipedia Web Pages*. Graduation project report, Electrical and Computer Engineering Department, Birzeit University.

Balaji N., Deepa Kumari, Bhavatarini N., Megha N., Sunil Kumar, et al. 2022. Text summarization using nlp technique. In *2022 International Conference on Distributed Computing, VLSI, Electrical Circuits and Robotics (DISCOVER)*, pages 30–35. IEEE.

Basem Naim. 2023. النكبة...أكبر من مجرد حدث تاريخي [the Nakba ..more than just a historical event]. https://www.aljazeera.net/opinions/2023/6/4/%D8%A7%D9%84%D9%86%D9%83%D8%A8%D8%A9-%D8%A3%D9%83%D8%A8%D8%B1-%D9%85%D9%86-%D9%85%D8%AC%D8%B1%D8%AF-%D8%AD%D8%AF%D8%AB-%D8%AA%D8%A7%D8%B1%D9%8A%D8%AE%D9%8A.

Yixin Nie, Yicheng Wang, and Mohit Bansal. 2019. Analyzing compositionality-sensitivity of nli models. In *Proceedings of the AAAI conference on artificial intelligence*, volume 33, pages 6867–6874.

Palestinian Central Bureau of Statistics (PCBS). 2008. Special Report on the 60th Anniversary of the Nakba. https://www.pcbs.gov.ps/Portals/_pcbs/PressRelease/nakba%2060.pdf.

Palestinian Central Bureau of Statistics (PCBS). 2021. Statistical Review on the 73rd Annual Commemoration of the Palestinian Nakba. https://www.pcbs.gov.ps/portals/_pcbs/PressRelease/Press_En_10-5-2021-nakba-en.pdf.

Adnan Souri, Mohammed Al Achhab, Badr Eddine El Mohajir, Mohamed Naoum, Outman El Hichami, and Abdelali Zbakh. 2023. Arabic text summarization challenges using deep learning techniques: A review. *International Journal on Recent and Innovation Trends in Computing and Communication*, 11(11s):134–142.

United Nations. 2024. About the Nakba - Question of Palestine. https://www.un.org/unispal/about-the-nakba/. Retrieved November 10, 2024.

A Appendix

Unique TextRank with original excerpts from (Bronstein, 2009)		
نُظمت مراسم لإحياء الذكرى قرب 'سينما سيتي' (هيرتسليا) عن قرية إجليل الفلسطينية التي كانت قائمة في ذلك الموقع حتى عام 1948.	"In March 2004 a commemoration was held near the 'Cinema City' (Herzliya) for the Palestinian village of Ijlil which existed at the site until 1948"	(Bronstein, 2009)
كانت مواقف قادة ومعماريي الصهيونية تجاه السكان الأصليين لـ 'صهيون' في مكان ما بين اعتبارهم أوصياء (مؤقتين) أو حائزين للأرض في أحد طرفي نقيض.	"Attitudes of the leaders and architects of Zionism towards the indigenous inhabitants of 'Zion' were situated between their perception as (temporary) guardians or holders of the land on one end"	(Bronstein, 2009)
"تم الإشارة إلى ماضي عام 1948 فقط بما يتماشى مع السرد الصهيوني الذي يرى أنه 'كما لم يقبلونا هنا في الماضي (على سبيل المثال وفقًا لخطة تقسيم الأمم المتحدة)،"	"Reference to the past of 1948 is made only in line with the Zionist narrative which holds that, 'just like they did not accept us here in the past (e.g. according to the UN Partition Plan)"	(Bronstein, 2009)

Table 3: Unique TextRank facts from (Bronstein, 2009)

Unique TextRank facts with translations from (Naim, 2023)		
"تم تدمير أكثر من 530 قرية فلسطينية والسيطرة على أكثر من 700 قرية ومدينة"	"More than 530 Palestinian villages were destroyed, and control was established over more than 700 villages and towns."	(Naim, 2023)
"أُسست أول جمعية نسائية في فلسطين عام 1903،"	"The first women's association in Palestine was established in 1903."	(Naim, 2023)
"فقد سيطر اليهود بالقوة عام 1948 على نحو 78% من أراضي فلسطين التاريخية، وأنشؤوا دولتهم على هذه المساحة."	"In 1948, Jews seized nearly 78% of historical Palestine by force and established their state on this land."	(Naim, 2023)
"أكثر من 76% من مساحة الضفة الغربية تحت السيطرة الإسرائيلية الكاملة،"	"More than 76% of the West Bank is under full Israeli control."	(Naim, 2023)
"أن 7 ملايين فلسطيني في الشتات يعانون الحرمان من أبسط الحقوق الأساسية"	"Seven million Palestinians in the diaspora suffer from deprivation of basic human rights."	(Naim, 2023)
"ويتعرضون بشكل متكرر لموجات من الاضطهاد والملاحقة في الدول المختلفة،"	"They are repeatedly subjected to waves of persecution and harassment in various countries."	(Naim, 2023)

Table 4: Unique TextRank facts from (Naim, 2023)

Unique Gemini facts with translations from (Bronstein, 2009)		
بُنيت الهوية الصهيونية منذ البداية على نفي مزدوج: نفي زمن ومكان اليهود خارج صهيون، ونفي زمن ومكان السكان الأصليين لإقليم صهيون.	"Zionist identity was built from the beginning on a two-fold negation: it negates time and space of the Jews outside Zion, a 'negation of exile' which extends beyond the realm of religion, and it negates time and space of those indigenous to the territory of Zion"	(Bronstein, 2009)
وفقًا للصهيونية، فقد وقعت الأحداث العنيفة التي حدثت في حوالي عام 1948 بالفعل، ولكن فقط في شكل رد غير قابل للتجنب على الاضطرابات التي تسبب فيها 'السكان المحليون' الذين لم يقبلوا بإنشاء الكيان الجديد، الدولة اليهودية.	"According to Zionism, the violent events around 1948 did in fact occur, but only in form of an unavoidable response to the disturbance caused by the 'locals,' who did not accept the establishment of the new entity, the Jewish State."	(Bronstein, 2009)
النكبة هي حدث ضروري، لأنها حققت ذاتية صهيونية نقية مغلقة ومستقلة من الناحية العرقية.	"On the other hand, and paradoxically, the Nakba – the violent expulsion of the inhabitants of the country and the transformation of those remaining into refugees in their homeland, or into second-class citizens – is a necessary event, because it brought about the realization of the ethnically pure, closed and autonomous Zionist subject which builds itself in the framework of a state aimed exclusively for him/her."	(Bronstein, 2009)
يصف يوسف فايتس، أحد رؤساء الصندوق القومي اليهودي في ذلك الوقت، تدمير قرية زرنوقة بعد طرد سكانها، على الرغم من دعوات عديدة من اليهود بالامتناع عن طردهم.	"Yosef Weitz, one of the heads of the Jewish National Fund at the time, provides evidence which is surprising in its honesty. He tells of the destruction of the village of Zarnuqa after its inhabitants had been expelled, despite of numerous calls by Jews to abstain from their expulsion."	(Bronstein, 2009)

Table 5: Unique Gemini facts with original excerpts from (Bronstein, 2009)

Unique Gemini facts with translation from (Naim, 2023)		
تضمنت النكبة تدمير أكثر من 530 قرية فلسطينية والسيطرة على أكثر من 700 قرية ومدينة وتهجير أكثر من 750 ألف فلسطيني.	"The Nakba included the destruction of more than 530 Palestinian villages, the control of over 700 villages and towns, and the displacement of more than 750,000 Palestinians."	(Naim, 2023)
أكثر من 76% من مساحة الضفة الغربية تحت السيطرة الإسرائيلية الكاملة، وقطاع غزة تحت حصار إسرائيلي خانق منذ أكثر من 17 عامًا.	"More than 76% of the West Bank is under full Israeli control, while the Gaza Strip has been under a suffocating Israeli blockade for more than 17 years."	(Naim, 2023)
يعاني 7 ملايين فلسطيني في الشتات من الحرمان من أبسط الحقوق الأساسية ويتعرضون للاضطهاد والملاحقة.	"Seven million Palestinians in the diaspora suffer from deprivation of basic rights and are subjected to persecution and harassment."	(Naim, 2023)

Table 6: Unique Gemini facts with translation from (Naim, 2023)

Multilingual Propaganda Detection: Exploring Transformer-Based Models mBERT, XLM-RoBERTa, and mT5

Mohamed Ibrahim Ragab[1], Ensaf Hussein Mohamed[1], Walaa Medhat[2]
School of Information Technology and Computer Science, CIS,
Nile University, Giza, Egypt
Correspondence: moragab@nu.edu.eg, enmohamed@nu.edu.eg, wmedhat@nu.edu.eg

Abstract

This research focuses on the detection of multilingual propaganda using transformer-based embeddings from state-of-the-art models, including mBERT, XLM-RoBERTa, and mT5. A balanced dataset was employed to ensure equal representation across propaganda classes, enabling robust model evaluation. The mT5 model demonstrated the highest performance, achieving an accuracy of 99.61% and an F1-score of 0.9961, showcasing its effectiveness in multilingual contexts. Similarly, mBERT and XLM-RoBERTa achieved strong results, with accuracies of 92% and 91.41%, respectively, highlighting their capabilities in capturing linguistic and contextual nuances. Despite these high overall performances, the results revealed challenges in detecting subtle propaganda elements, suggesting the need for further improvements in handling nuanced classification tasks.

1 Introduction

Propaganda detection is a critical step in combating the spread of misinformation and biased content designed to manipulate public opinion. Propaganda content often relies on subtle linguistic cues, making its detection a complex task even in monolingual contexts. While recent advancements in natural language processing (NLP), particularly transformer-based models, have significantly improved propaganda detection in English, multilingual detection remains a challenging frontier. This challenge stems from linguistic diversity, contextual variability, and the scarcity of high-quality annotated datasets for non-English languages, which limits the generalizability of existing models.

Previous studies have focused on monolingual approaches, leveraging machine learning and deep learning models to identify and categorize propagandistic content. Transformer-based architectures, such as BERT and its multilingual variants, have demonstrated strong performance in capturing complex linguistic patterns. However, these approaches often face limitations in multilingual settings due to imbalanced datasets, inconsistent performance across languages, and challenges in distinguishing nuanced propaganda categories. Existing models also struggle to balance precision and recall across diverse classes, particularly in low-resource languages.

In this paper, we address these limitations by integrating transformer-based models—mBERT, XLM-RoBERTa, and mT5—into ensemble frameworks designed to enhance multilingual propaganda detection. We aim to improve classification robustness and performance across languages. Our approach leverages the strengths of individual models while mitigating their weaknesses through ensemble learning, offering a more balanced and effective solution for multilingual classification tasks.

The rest of the paper is organized as follows: Section 2 shows related work on the Propaganda classification problem. Section 3.1 describes the dataset and preprocessing techniques used in this study, Section 3.2 details the transformer models and ensemble frameworks implemented. Section 4 presents the experimental results, including individual model performance and ensemble outcomes. Finally, Section 5 discusses the findings, limitations, and potential directions for future research.

2 Related Work

In this section, we review recent advancements in related fields, focusing on propaganda detection, political bias detection, extremism detection, and multilingual misinformation detection. These studies provide a foundation for understanding the challenges and methodologies in multilingual classification tasks, highlighting limitations in existing approaches and motivating the contributions of this work.

The SAFARI (Azizov et al., 2024) study evaluates cross-lingual political bias and factuality

Proceedings of the Proceedings of the 1st International Workshop on Nakba Narratives as Language Resources, pages 75–82
January 20, 2025.

detection using media- and article-level datasets. Ensemble models with soft voting and Multilingual Pre-trained Language Models (MPLMs) like mBERT and XLM-R performed best on English datasets, achieving F1 scores of 84.96% for factuality and 84.95% for political bias. Multilingual datasets showed weaker results due to limited training data, with the best F1 score for political bias reaching 29.05%. Article-level models performed strongly on English-distant supervision datasets (F1: 82.62%) but less so on expert-annotated and multilingual data, highlighting challenges in cross-lingual transfer. Joint modeling, combining political bias and factuality detection, achieved its highest F1 score of 83.81% using soft voting. Large Language Models (LLMs), including Mistral7B and LLaMA27B, underperformed MPLMs in zero-shot settings, with F1 scores up to 46.84%. The study employed clustering techniques for data curation and evaluated models using F1 scores, accuracy, and recall. While ensemble methods and MPLMs proved effective, challenges remain in multilingual adaptation and fine-grained zero-shot learning.

Recent advancements (Modzelewski et al., 2024) in propaganda detection have utilized diverse methods, including fine-tuned transformers, few-shot GPT prompting, and classical machine learning. Studies focused on a dataset of tweets by diplomats from China, Russia, the U.S., and the EU in English and Spanish, tackling binary to fine-grained multilabel classification tasks. Among these, XLM-RoBERTa (XLM-BI) emerged as the top-performing model, excelling in multilingual and Spanish tasks, while RoBERTa (ROB-EN) demonstrated strong performance on English-specific tasks. Few-shot prompting with GPT-3.5 and GPT-4o showed potential for binary classification, with GPT-4o outperforming GPT-3.5 but not reaching the accuracy of fine-tuned BERT models. Classical machine learning approaches, including LightGBM and XGBoost with StyloMetrix linguistic features, offered competitive performance, particularly in English binary classification, where LightGBM's F1 score rivaled that of BERT-based models. These findings highlight the strength of fine-tuned transformers for complex multilingual tasks, while also recognizing the effectiveness of classical machine learning and GPT-based methods in specific contexts.

Advancements in extremism and radicalization detection (Zerrouki and Benblidia, 2024) have explored multilingual datasets and sophisticated classification techniques. Recent research introduced a multilingual corpus for binary and multiclass classification tasks, encompassing texts on extremism and radicalization from diverse sources such as ISIS-related content and hate speech in languages like English, Arabic, Indian, Korean, and Kazakh. The dataset includes 17,100 samples for binary extremism, 5,000 for binary radicalization, and 11,400 for multiclass extremism. The study utilized preprocessing methods such as language-specific cleaning, TF-IDF, and word embeddings, alongside machine learning models (e.g., L.SVC, Random Forest) and deep learning approaches (Bi-LSTM, DistilBERT-Multi). Bi-LSTM achieved high accuracy for binary classification (97.8% for radicalization, 96.81% for extremism), while transformer-based models excelled in multiclass classification with 91.07% accuracy. These results highlight the effectiveness of deep learning and transformer models for multilingual extremism detection tasks.

Recent efforts in political bias detection (Agrawal et al., 2022) have introduced an annotated dataset of 1,388 Hindi news articles and headlines from diverse sources, balanced across three categories: biased towards BJP, biased against BJP, and neutral. Articles were annotated for coverage and tonality bias with a kappa score of 0.65, highlighting the subjective challenges in labeling neutrality. The dataset features class-specific averages in word and sentence counts, providing insights into linguistic characteristics. The study evaluated transformer-based models, including mBERT, XLM-RoBERTa, and IndicBERT, alongside traditional machine learning approaches like SVM, Logistic Regression, and Random Forest. XLM-RoBERTa achieved the best results with 83% accuracy and an F1-macro score of 76.4%, significantly outperforming traditional models, which scored below 60% in F1-macro. The findings emphasize the effectiveness of multilingual transformers in bias detection tasks and highlight challenges in accurately identifying neutral articles due to their subjective nature.

Recent research (Panda and Levitan, 2021) on misinformation detection has focused on multilingual datasets and transformer-based models. A study using tweets related to COVID-19 from the NLP4IF 2021 shared task investigated misinformation detection in English, Bulgarian, and Arabic. The dataset included binary annotations for seven questions assessing misinformation characteristics, with 451–3,000 training samples and up to 1,000 test samples per language. The study evaluated logistic regression, a transformer encoder, and BERT-based models. English BERT (Capuozzo et al., 2020) achieved the best results for English (F1: 0.729), while multilingual BERT (m-BERT) demonstrated strong cross-lingual generalization, achieving F1 scores of 0.843 for Bulgarian and 0.741 for Arabic. Experimental setups, including zero-shot, few-shot, and target-only training, highlighted the potential of m-BERT to perform well in low-resource settings with minimal target-language data. These findings emphasize the effectiveness of contextualized embeddings and multilingual transformers in detecting misinformation across diverse languages.

Gap Analysis of Related Work: Despite the advancements in multilingual propaganda detection, several gaps remain that highlight the need for further exploration:

Limited Multilingual Representation: While studies like SAFARI and NLP4IF have explored multilingual contexts, their datasets are often limited in linguistic diversity, focusing on high-resource languages like English and Spanish. Low-resource languages, which are equally vulnerable to propaganda and misinformation, remain under-represented, impacting the generalizability of existing models.

Overreliance on Individual Models: Transformer models like mBERT, XLM-RoBERTa, and mT5 have shown strong standalone performance, but their reliance on pretraining data biases can limit robustness in real-world scenarios. Ensemble methods are underexplored in mitigating these weaknesses, particularly in balancing class-specific performance.

3 Materials and Methods

This section describes the methodology for detecting multilingual propaganda using transformer-based embeddings and ensemble learning. The process involves balancing the dataset to ensure equal class representation and preprocessing steps like tokenization. Transformer models—mBERT, XLM-RoBERTa, and mT5—were fine-tuned to extract multilingual embeddings, capturing linguistic and contextual nuances. These embeddings were then used in classification frameworks to evaluate the models' effectiveness in handling multilingual propaganda detection tasks.

3.1 The used Dataset

The dataset (Duaibes et al., 2024) utilized in this study, curated by SinaLab (2024), consists of a comprehensive collection of 13,500 rows and 13 columns, representing a rich and diverse array of Facebook posts. Developed as part of the FigNews 2024 Shared Task on News Media Narratives, the dataset focuses on the framing of the Israeli War on Gaza, providing valuable insights into bias and propaganda in media. The corpus spans five languages—Arabic, English, Hebrew, French, and Hindi—with an equal distribution of 2,400 posts per language, ensuring linguistic diversity and balance. Each post is meticulously annotated for attributes related to bias and propaganda, making this dataset a critical resource for advancing multilingual analysis of media narratives.

The dataset includes the following notable columns: Text is the original text of the Facebook post, as it appeared in its source language. English MT is a machine-translated version of the text in English, facilitating cross-lingual analysis and ensuring uniformity for annotators who are not fluent in the source language. Arabic MT is a machine-translated version of the text in Arabic, aiding linguistic diversity and analysis. Propaganda This column indicates whether the post contains propaganda types.

A particular focus of our analysis is the Propaganda column, which captures whether a post contains propaganda. As shown in Table 1 and Figure 1, this column consists of four distinct classes, with the distribution of instances as follows:

Class	Number of Instances
Not Propaganda	7098
Propaganda	3301
Unclear	269
Not Applicable	132

Table 1: Distribution of instances in the Propaganda column across the dataset.

These labels provide a foundation for investigating the prevalence and characteristics of propaganda within the dataset. The predominance of "Not Propaganda" suggests that most posts lack propagandistic content, yet the substantial presence of "Propaganda" emphasizes the significance of its impact in framing narratives. The smaller proportions of "Unclear" and "Not Applicable" highlight the challenges and ambiguities faced during anno-

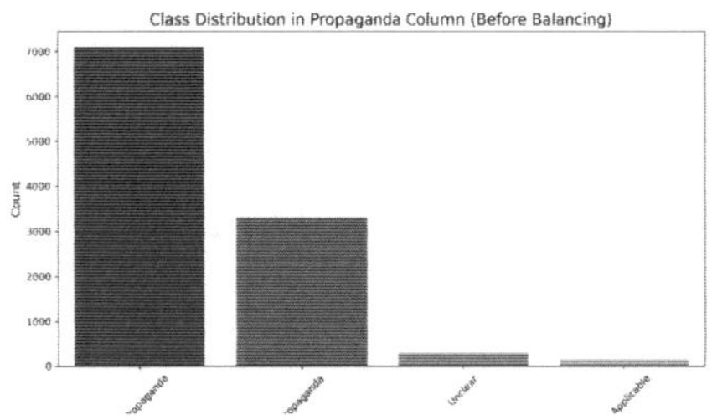

Figure 1: Distribution of instances in the Propaganda column across the dataset.

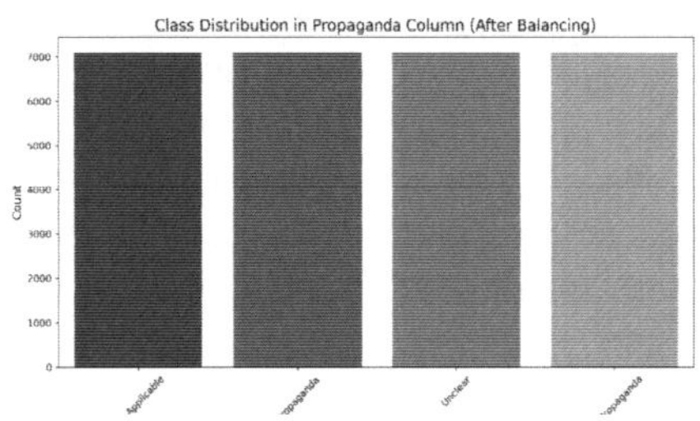

Figure 2: Class Distribution in the Propaganda Column After Applying the Balancing Step.

tation.

Class	Number of Instances
Not Propaganda	7098
Propaganda	7098
Unclear	7098
Not Applicable	7098

Table 2: Class Distribution in the Propaganda Column After Applying the Balancing Step.

As shown in Table 2 and Figure 2, After applying the balancing step to the dataset, each class in the Propaganda column was adjusted to have an equal number of instances, with 7,098 samples per class. This ensured that the dataset was balanced, eliminating any bias towards overrepresented classes and providing a more even distribution for training the model.

The dataset also includes metadata such as the language of the post, bias-related annotations, and machine-translated versions of the text for cross-lingual analysis. These features enable a comprehensive exploration of linguistic and cultural patterns in bias and propaganda.

Figure 3 provides a snapshot of the dataset used in this study. It showcases the key columns, including the Text column containing the multilingual propaganda content and the Propaganda column indicating class labels. The figure highlights the structure of the data, demonstrating how text samples are paired with corresponding annotations, which serve as the basis for training and evaluating the models.

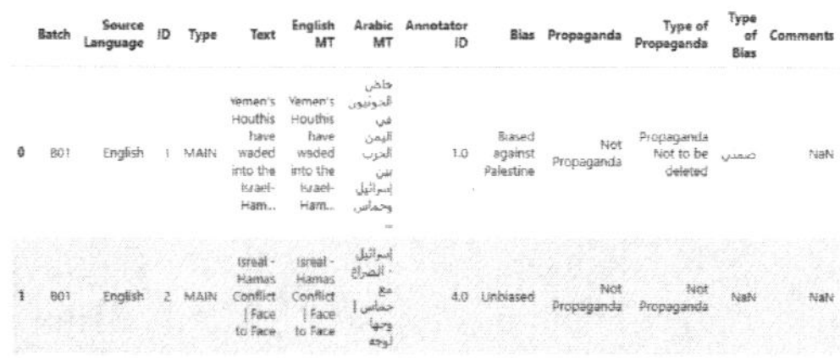

	Batch	Source Language	ID	Type	Text	English MT	Arabic MT	Annotator ID	Bias	Propaganda	Type of Propaganda	Type of Bias	Comments
0	B01	English	1	MAIN	Yemen's Houthis have waded into the Israel-Ham...	Yemen's Houthis have waded into the Israel-Ham...	خاض الحوثيون في اليمن الحرب بين إسرائيل وحماس ...	1.0	Biased against Palestine	Not Propaganda	Propaganda Not to be deleted	ضمني	NaN
1	B01	English	2	MAIN	Isreal - Hamas Conflict | Face to Face	Isreal - Hamas Conflict | Face to Face	إسرائيل - الصراع مع حماس | وجها لوجه	4.0	Unbiased	Not Propaganda	Not Propaganda	NaN	NaN

Figure 3: An Overview of the Dataset: Sample Columns and Rows

3.2 Methodology

In this study, we implemented state-of-the-art multilingual models to classify propaganda and bias in Facebook posts. The models include mBERT, mT5, and XLM-RoBERTa.

As shown in Figure 4, the proposed architecture for multilingual propaganda detection leverages XLM-Roberta, a powerful multilingual transformer model, combined with robust preprocessing and training strategies. The first step involves preparing the dataset by loading text data in multiple languages (e.g., English, and Arabic) and their corresponding propaganda labels. To address the class imbalance, oversampling is applied to minority classes to ensure balanced representation across all categories. Text data is preprocessed by removing punctuation and converting to lowercase to standardize inputs, followed by label encoding to convert categorical labels into numerical values.

The next stage utilizes the Model tokenizer to tokenize the preprocessed text while applying padding and truncation to ensure uniform input lengths. A HuggingFace dataset is created and split into training and testing subsets. The architecture uses the MBert, XLM-Roberta, and MT5) models for sequence classification, configured for four output classes corresponding to the encoded labels. Training configurations include a low learning rate, small batch size, weight decay for regularization, and an evaluation strategy that monitors performance after each epoch.

Training is conducted with a HuggingFace Trainer, integrating a manual early stopping mechanism to prevent overfitting. The model evaluates validation loss at the end of each epoch, saving

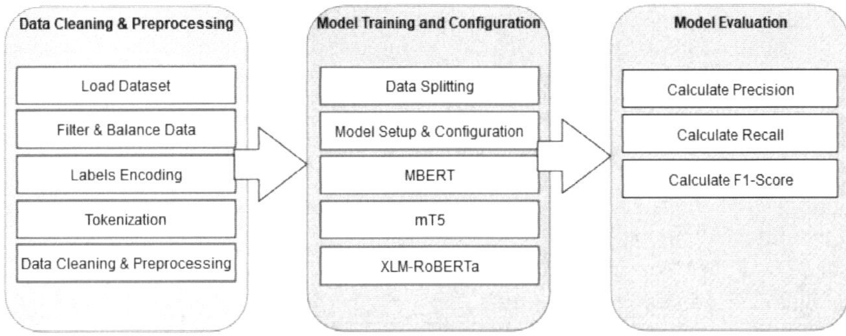

Figure 4: Multilingual Propaganda Detection Architecture Utilizing XLM-Roberta, MBert, and MT5 with Balanced Class Handling and Early Stopping for Optimized Performance.

the best-performing model when improvements are detected and halting training if no improvement occurs for a specified number of consecutive epochs. Finally, the best model is evaluated on the test set, with metrics such as accuracy, precision, recall, and F1-score reported to assess classification performance. This architecture effectively combines XLM-Roberta's multilingual capabilities with balanced data handling and efficient training strategies to achieve robust propaganda detection.

Multilingual BERT (MBERT) is a variant of BERT pre-trained on Wikipedia data across 104 languages, as described by Libovický et al. (2019). Designed to process input at the token level, it utilizes deep bidirectional attention mechanisms to capture intricate linguistic relationships and contextual nuances effectively. Its multilingual pretraining makes it particularly suited for tasks involving cross-lingual understanding and classification, rendering it an ideal choice for analyzing diverse datasets like the one used in this study. mBERT's versatility has been demonstrated across a wide range of multilingual and cross-lingual natural language processing applications.

mT5 (Multilingual T5) is an extension of the T5 model, pre-trained on over 100 languages, as described by Fuadi et al. (2023). It employs a text-to-text framework, where all tasks—ranging from classification to text generation—are reformulated as text generation problems. This unified approach allows mT5 to handle a wide variety of language processing tasks with remarkable flexibility and consistency. Its multilingual training on diverse linguistic data makes it particularly robust, even in low-resource language settings, enabling effective performance across a broad spectrum of multilingual and cross-lingual tasks.

XLM-RoBERTa It builds on RoBERTa, an optimized version of BERT (Wiciaputra et al., 2021), by pretraining on a massive multilingual corpus spanning 100 languages. It achieves state-of-the-art performance on various multilingual benchmarks and is particularly effective in handling languages with limited resources.

4 Results and Discussion

4.1 Experiment Setup

We employed three transformer-based models — **mBERT**, **mT5**, and **XLM-RoBERTa** — for multilingual propaganda detection. The experiment setup consisted of data preprocessing, model fine-tuning, and evaluation.

4.1.1 Computational Resources

The experiments were conducted on the Kaggle platform, leveraging a P100 GPU for accelerated computations. The P100 GPU provided the necessary computational power for handling large datasets and fine-tuning transformer-based models efficiently. The use of a high-performance GPU significantly reduced training time, especially for resource-intensive models like mT5. Kaggle's environment also facilitated seamless access to datasets and libraries required for the experiments.

4.1.2 Data Preprocessing

- **Cleansing**: Rows with missing values were removed to ensure data consistency.

- **Class Balancing**: Oversampling techniques were employed to balance the number of instances across all classes, mitigating potential bias during training.

- **Tokenization**: Each model utilized its respective tokenizer - mBERT: `BertTokenizer` - mT5: `T5Tokenizer` - XLM-RoBERTa: `XLM-RoBERTaTokenizer` The text data was tokenized into subword units, ensuring compatibility with the transformer architectures.

- **Label Encoding**: Categorical labels, such as "Propaganda" and "Not Propaganda," were numerically encoded to facilitate classification.

- **Dataset Splits**: The dataset was converted into PyTorch tensors and split into training, validation, and test sets. An 80-10-10 split ratio was maintained to balance the training and evaluation phases.

4.1.3 Model Fine-Tuning

- **mBERT**: `BertForSequenceClassification`, learning rate 2×10^{-5}, batch size: 16, epochs: 50 (early stopping applied), no. of labels: 4.

- **mT5**: `MT5ForConditionalGeneration`, learning rate 5×10^{-5}, batch size: 8, epochs: 50 (early stopping applied), no. of labels: 4.

- **XLM-RoBERTa**: HuggingFace `Trainer`, learning rate 1×10^{-5}, batch size: 8, epochs: 50 (early stopping applied), no. of labels: 4.

All models were optimized using the AdamW optimizer, with weight decay set to 0.05. Early stopping was implemented for all models to prevent overfitting, with training halting after three consecutive epochs without validation loss improvement. Learning rate schedulers were utilized to adjust learning rates dynamically during training.

4.2 Result

In the Results section, we analyze and compare the performance of three transformer-based models—mBERT, MT5, and XLM-RoBERTa—on the task of multilingual propaganda detection. The analysis includes a detailed evaluation of the models' performance with and without data balancing techniques to address class imbalances. Key evaluation metrics, including accuracy, precision, recall, F1-score, training loss, validation loss, and the number of training epochs, are used to assess and compare the effectiveness of each model under both scenarios.

Performance on Imbalanced Data (Without Balancing) As shown in Table 3, the performance of the models varied significantly when trained on imbalanced data, highlighting the challenges posed by class distribution. The MT5 model achieved a remarkable accuracy of 98.86%, precision of 0.9911, recall of 0.9886, and F1-score of 0.9882, showcasing its ability to handle imbalanced datasets effectively. This superiority can be attributed to MT5's text-to-text framework, which allows it to model nuanced relationships within the data.

In contrast, mBERT struggled with imbalanced data, achieving an accuracy of only 53.00%, with precision, recall, and F1-score all around 0.65. This indicates difficulty in generalizing across uneven class distributions. Similarly, XLM-RoBERTa achieved moderate performance, with an accuracy of 69.70% and an F1-score of 0.5595, suggesting it was able to identify positive instances (recall of 0.6870) but lacked precision (0.4720). These results underscore the necessity of addressing class imbalances to improve model performance.

Performance on Balanced Data (After Balancing) After addressing class imbalances through oversampling techniques, all models showed significant improvements in their performance metrics, as detailed in Table 4. The MT5 model continued to outperform the other models, achieving an accuracy of 99.61%, precision of 0.9961, recall of 0.9961, and F1-score of 0.9962. This further highlights MT5's robustness in handling balanced datasets and extracting nuanced features from multilingual text.

The mBERT model demonstrated substantial improvement, achieving an accuracy of 92.0%, with balanced precision, recall, and F1-scores of 0.92. Its ability to generalize effectively after balancing emphasizes the importance of preprocessing in enhancing performance. XLM-RoBERTa, while still lagging behind MT5 and mBERT, improved to an accuracy of 89.51%, with an F1-score of 0.8934, indicating better adaptation to the balanced dataset.

Training and Validation Loss Table 5 provides insights into the training and validation loss for each model. The MT5 model exhibited the most efficient learning, achieving the lowest training loss of 0.0080 and validation loss of 0.0102, highlighting its excellent generalization capabilities. The mBERT model followed with a training loss of 0.0755 and validation loss of 0.2719, reflecting steady learning and robust generalization. XLM-RoBERTa, however, recorded a training loss of 0.0467 but struggled with a validation loss of 0.7156, indicating potential overfitting or difficulty in adapting to the multilingual dataset's complex-

Model	Accuracy (%)	Precision	Recall	F1-Score	No. Epocs
mBERT	53.00	0.66	0.64	0.65	5
MT5	98.86	0.9911	0.9886	0.9882	24
XLM-RoBERTa	69.70	0.4720	0.6870	0.5595	15

Table 3: Performance Metrics of mBERT, MT5, and XLM-RoBERTa Models Without Balancing Techniques.

Model	Accuracy (%)	Precision	Recall	F1-Score	No. Epocs
mBERT	92.0	0.98	0.92	0.92	8
MT5	99.61	0.9961	0.996	0.9962	27
XLM-RoBERTa	89.51	0.9006	0.8951	0.8934	16

Table 4: Performance Metrics of mBERT, MT5, and XLM-RoBERTa Models Using Balancing Techniques.

ity.

Model	Training	Validation
mBERT	0.0755	0.2719
MT5	0.0080	0.0102
XLM-RoBERTa	0.0467	0.7156

Table 5: Training and Validation Loss of mBERT, MT5, and XLM-Roberta Models.

Analysis of Performance Differences: MT5's Dominance: MT5 consistently outperformed the other models across all metrics, both with and without data balancing. Its text-to-text framework enables it to capture subtle linguistic and contextual nuances, making it highly effective for multilingual propaganda detection, making it highly effective for multilingual propaganda detection with an accuracy of 99%.

mBERT's Consistency: Despite not achieving the same level of accuracy as MT5, mBERT demonstrated commendable performance with an accuracy of 92% and competitive scores across all metrics. Its ability to leverage multilingual pretraining makes it a robust choice for tasks where efficiency is prioritized over peak accuracy.

Challenges with XLM-Roberta: While XLM-RoBERTa showed promise with an accuracy of 89.51%, its higher validation loss suggests issues with overfitting or insufficient adaptation to the dataset's multilingual nature. This could stem from its reliance on pretraining that may not fully capture the nuanced biases present in propaganda detection tasks.

Generalization and Efficiency: The results highlight the importance of achieving a balance between learning efficiency and generalization. While all models employed early stopping to mitigate overfitting, MT5's consistently low validation loss underscores its superior ability to generalize, whereas XLM-RoBERTa's performance suggests room for improvement in adapting to diverse linguistic inputs.

The analysis reveals that data balancing significantly enhances model performance, especially for models like mBERT and XLM-RoBERTa, which struggled with imbalanced datasets. MT5's consistently high performance underscores its suitability for multilingual tasks, while the improvements seen in mBERT demonstrate its potential when coupled with effective preprocessing techniques. These findings emphasize the critical role of balancing and preprocessing in ensuring fair and robust evaluations.

Overall, these findings demonstrate that while MT5 is the most effective model for this task, further research could focus on improving the generalization capabilities of models like XLM-RoBERTa to better handle the complexities of multilingual propaganda detection.

5 Conclusion

This study implemented and evaluated three transformer-based models—mBERT, XLM-RoBERTa, and mT5—to address the challenge of multilingual propaganda detection. By leveraging these models' multilingual capabilities and employing advanced preprocessing techniques, including data balancing, we conducted a comprehensive assessment of their performance. Key evaluation metrics such as accuracy, precision, recall, F1-score, and loss values were used to determine the models' effectiveness across diverse propaganda categories.

The mT5 model consistently outperformed its counterparts, achieving an outstanding accuracy of 99.61% and an F1-score of 0.9961, demonstrating its exceptional ability to handle multilingual content and detect propaganda with high precision. Its text-to-text framework allowed it to effectively model linguistic nuances across multiple languages, making it the most reliable model for this task. The mBERT model also showcased strong performance, achieving an accuracy of 92.0% and an F1-score of 0.92, excelling in the "Not Propaganda" and "Not Applicable" categories. Despite these results, it showed room for improvement in more nuanced categories. The XLM-RoBERTa model achieved a respectable accuracy of 89.51%, with an F1-score of 0.8934, but faced challenges with generalization, as evidenced by its higher validation loss compared to the other models.

The results emphasize the transformative potential of transformer-based embeddings in multilingual propaganda detection. While mT5 emerged as the most effective model, mBERT demonstrated computational efficiency and solid performance, making it a viable choice for practical applications. On the other hand, XLM-RoBERTa highlighted areas for future improvement, particularly in adapting to complex multilingual tasks.

Limitations and Future Work: These future directions aim to refine and enhance the capabilities of multilingual propaganda detection, expanding the models' adaptability, accuracy, and generalization across various contexts and languages.

Hyperparameter Optimization and Fine-Tuning: Future work could explore the fine-tuning of hyperparameters such as learning rate, batch size, and number of epochs for each model, especially mBERT and XLM-RoBERTa. Optimizing these parameters could lead to improved performance, particularly in terms of accuracy, precision, and recall across different propaganda categories.

Exploring Advanced Ensemble Techniques: While individual models like mT5, mBERT, and XLM-RoBERTa demonstrated strong performance, future research could investigate the use of more advanced ensemble methods, such as stacking and boosting, to combine the strengths of multiple models. This could help in improving performance, especially in identifying subtle propaganda elements that individual models may miss.

Cross-Lingual Transfer Learning: One promising direction is to explore cross-lingual transfer learning by leveraging pre-trained multilingual models to better handle low-resource languages.

6 References

Samyak Agrawal, Kshitij Gupta, Devansh Gautam, and Radhika Mamidi. 2022. Towards detecting political bias in hindi news articles. In *Proceedings of the 60th annual meeting of the association for computational linguistics: student research workshop*, pages 239–244.

Dilshod Azizov, Zain Mujahid, Hilal AlQuabeh, Preslav Nakov, and Shangsong Liang. 2024. Safari: Cross-lingual bias and factuality detection in news media and news articles. In *Findings of the Association for Computational Linguistics: EMNLP 2024*, pages 12217–12231.

Pasquale Capuozzo, Ivano Lauriola, Carlo Strapparava, Fabio Aiolli, Giuseppe Sartori, et al. 2020. Automatic detection of cross-language verbal deception. In *42nd Annual Conference of the Cognitive Science Society (CogSci'20)*, pages 1756–1762.

Lina Duaibes, Areej Jaber, Mustafa Jarrar, Ahmad Qadi, and Mais Qandeel. 2024. Sina at FigNews 2024: Multilingual Datasets Annotated with Bias and Propaganda. In *Proceedings of the Second Arabic Natural Language Processing Conference (ArabicNLP 2024)*, Bangkok, Thailand. Association for Computational Linguistics.

Mukhlish Fuadi, Adhi Dharma Wibawa, and Surya Sumpeno. 2023. Adaptation of multilingual t5 transformer for indonesian language. In *2023 IEEE 9th Information Technology International Seminar (ITIS)*, pages 1–6. IEEE.

Jindřich Libovickỳ, Rudolf Rosa, and Alexander Fraser. 2019. How language-neutral is multilingual bert? *arXiv preprint arXiv:1911.03310*.

Arkadiusz Modzelewski, Paweł Golik, and Adam Wierzbicki. 2024. Bilingual propaganda detection in diplomats' tweets using language models and linguistic features. *IberLEF@ SEPLN*.

Subhadarshi Panda and Sarah Ita Levitan. 2021. Detecting multilingual covid-19 misinformation on social media via contextualized embeddings. In *Proceedings of the Fourth Workshop on NLP for Internet Freedom: Censorship, Disinformation, and Propaganda*, pages 125–129.

Yakobus Keenan Wiciaputra, Julio Christian Young, and Andre Rusli. 2021. Bilingual text classification in english and indonesian via transfer learning using xlm-roberta. *International Journal of Advances in Soft Computing & Its Applications*, 13(3).

Khadidja Zerrouki and Nadjia Benblidia. 2024. Multilingual text preprocessing and classification for the detection of extremism and radicalization in social networks.

Collective Memory and Narrative Cohesion: A Computational Study of Palestinian Refugee Oral Histories in Lebanon

Ghadeer Awwad and Tamara N. Rayan and Lavinia Dunagan and David Gamba
School of Information
University of Michigan
Ann Arbor, MI, USA

Abstract

This study uses the Palestinian Oral History Archive (POHA) to investigate how Palestinian refugee groups in Lebanon sustain a cohesive collective memory of the Nakba through shared narratives. Grounded in Halbwachs' theory of group memory, we employ statistical analysis of pairwise similarity of narratives, focusing on the influence of shared gender and location. We use textual representation and semantic embeddings of narratives to represent the interviews themselves. Our analysis demonstrates that shared origin is a powerful determinant of narrative similarity across thematic keywords, landmarks, and significant figures, as well as in semantic embeddings of the narratives. Meanwhile, shared residence fosters cohesion, with its impact significantly amplified when paired with shared origin. Additionally, women's narratives exhibit heightened thematic cohesion, particularly in recounting experiences of the British occupation, underscoring the gendered dimensions of memory formation. This research deepens the understanding of collective memory in diasporic settings, emphasizing the critical role of oral histories in safeguarding Palestinian identity and resisting erasure.

1 Introduction

The Nakba, a pivotal moment in Palestinian history marked by the mass displacement of approximately 770,000 Palestinians during the forcible establishment of Israel (Bisharat, 1994; Khalidi, 1992; Abū-Sitta, 2016; Khoury, 2012; Khalidi, 1997; Masalha, 2012), embodies a broader colonial project to establish an ethnocratic state (Khoury, 2012; Pappé, 2007; Benvenisti et al., 2007; Masalha, 2012). The memory of the Nakba and the immense suffering caused by forced displacement, loss of land, and erasure of the Palestinian presence remains central to the national consciousness of Palestinians (Allan, 2013; Sa'di and Abu-Lughod, 2007; Jayyusi, 2007; Khalidi, 1997). Among Palestinians, refugees in Lebanon are exemplary in their resilience and their maintainance of a collective identity despite being intensely marginalized and disadvantaged. Denied basic rights under Lebanese law, they experience profound spatial, institutional, and economic exclusion (Siklawi, 2019; Rmeileh, 2021). Against these hardships, camps have historically served as spaces of resistance, particularly during the 1970s and 1980s when they became bases for the Palestinian Liberation Organization (Siklawi, 2019; Rmeileh, 2021). Beyond armed resistance, cultural efforts such as storytelling and poetry are crucial for preserving their national identity and asserting the right to return (Siklawi, 2019; Rmeileh, 2021; Sayigh, 2015, 1998).

In consideration of the unique social and political context in which Palestinian refugees in Lebanon are situated, this study is centered on the following research questions: Do Palestinian refugee groups in Lebanon, physically isolated from their homeland, maintain cohesive collective memory formation in their remembrance of the Nakba? And if so, what are the indicators of similarity in their narratives?

To answer these questions, we employ natural language processing (NLP) techniques in one of the most comprehensive digital repositories of oral histories told by refugees of the Nakba, the Palestinian Oral History Archive (POHA) (Sleiman and Chebaro, 2018). POHA has been used extensively to study collective memories and narratives of refugees. We contrast and complement prolific interpretive approaches (Davis, 2011; Barakat, 2019; Swedenburg, 1995; Moon, 2023) that study the sociohistoric impacts of the Nakba and extend other quantitative studies, such as Banat et al. (2018), which demonstrate the persistence of collective memory in Palestinian youth. Our methodology uses various textual representations of archive interviews that encode themes, specific entities, and semantic content. We then statistically compare

Proceedings of the Proceedings of the 1st International Workshop on Nakba Narratives as Language Resources, pages 83–102
January 20, 2025.

pairwise similarities of textual representations of the refugees' narratives. Through this, we measure the degree of similarity within different refugee communities in Lebanon in terms of how members remember the Nakba. As a theoretical framework, we use Halbwachs' (1992) concept of group memory to understand how Palestinian remembrance of the Nakba in the diaspora is shaped by boundary-making identity markers, in this case, location and gender. Our main findings show that sharing origin is a strong indicator of higher similarity in refugee narratives, sharing residence in Lebanon is also an indicator of similarity, and sharing both is in many cases an even stronger indicator of cohesion. We also find that the same gender is an indicator of cohesion, although to a smaller degree, as women's narratives are weakly similar to other women. By analyzing the narratives documented within POHA, which represents more than 50 cities and refugee camps in Lebanon, this study contributes understanding of how collective memory formation functions on a larger scale within the Palestinian context.

2 Background

Memory work, through oral histories, counters Zionist narratives and challenges the erasure of Palestinian experiences (Khoury, 2012; Bisharat, 1994; Hanafi and Knudsen, 2011; Sayigh, 2015; Masalha, 2012; Massad, 2006). By documenting the lived experiences of women, refugees, and everyday Palestinians that are underrepresented in national archival records and historiography (Sleiman and Chebaro, 2018; Allan, 2021; Farah Aboubakr, 2017; Hanafi and Knudsen, 2011), oral histories provide a more complex account of the Nakba.

This complexity is seen in how refugees diverge in how they remember the Nakba. Collective memory formation and positionality often dictate which events, people, and places are remembered based on the concerns that were and continue to be relevant for refugees (Ben-Ze'ev, 2002, p.14). As Silmi found in her analysis of oral histories within the Nakba Archive, different "economic, social, and political locations entail different positions, frames of reference and value systems... [such] different positionalities are reflected in the way they remember and tell their stories of life in Palestine and Arab-Jewish relations before the Nakba" (2021, p.61). Gender produces further multiplicity, seen in Rosemary Sayigh's (1979; 1998; 2007) extensive analysis of recorded testimonies in Lebanon's refugee camps. Sayigh was one of the first to assert that "women are often 'subversive' tellers of national history" (1998, p.47) because they include internal conflicts within the resistance movement and detailed accounts of atrocities suppressed within official historiographies. Similarly, Humphries and Khalili (2007) and Khoury (2018) found that Palestinian women choose to transmit information based on what is meaningful within their lived experiences, causing their stories to diverge from "official" histories significantly.

Oral history archives, especially in audiovisual formats, present unique challenges for computational methods due to their non-textual medium (Pessanha and Salah, 2021). Greenberg (1998) observes that NLP is particularly well-suited for archival collections, as numerous studies have demonstrated its ability to induce new metadata fields and values from archival records or existing metadata. More broadly, NLP can enrich archival practices—it can identify recurring themes, topics, and significant entities such as people, places, or events (Colavizza et al., 2021; Jaillant and Rees, 2023). Notably, there is also substantial work in NLP interested in capturing narrative structure (Piper, 2023; Zhu et al., 2023; Shuttleworth and Padilla, 2022; Santana et al., 2023; Szojka et al., 2020; Bendevski et al., 2021; Akter and Santu, 2024). This line of research at times even pertains to biographical narratives (Bamman and Smith, 2014; Brookshire and Reiter, 2024), similar to those in POHA. We largely do not take advantage of these techniques for two reasons—POHA's interviews have been explicitly given structure by archivists and there are few pre-existing resources available for Arabic—but our study speaks to a more collective direction for computational narrative analysis.

Using computational methods, we uncover cohesion in narratives of dispossession and resilience, highlighting how these stories redefine Palestinian identity through collective experiences of loss and resistance (Bisharat, 1994; Qumsiyeh, 2011). In this paper, we leverage both the metadata included in POHA and transcriptions of interview speech to construct a holistic representation of Nakba narratives. The Nakba-POHA collection thus stands as a testament to the enduring fight for Palestinian rights and dignity and an example of how computational tools can uncover deeper insights from underrepresented histories.

3 Theoretical Framework and Hypothesis

To understand how Palestinians remember the Nakba, we build upon Halbwachs' (1992) theoretical framework of group memory. This theory is appropriate for our analysis of narrative cohesion within refugee communities because it outlines how individual memories are co-constructed through external social relations. Halbwachs observes that individuals will retrieve their memories in alignment with the logic of the group to which they belong. This can involve the reconstruction or rearranging of individual memories so that they have greater coherence with other group members' memories. In this process, the individual memories of group members will resemble each other and reflect the overall interests and thoughts of the group. However, this phenomenon only holds when the group is strongly established, long-lasting, and able to resist external modes of thinking. If group membership is interrupted through contact with externalities, such as outside beliefs or exposure to a different social context (Halbwachs, 1992, p.188), the cohesion of recollection can also be interrupted.

Halbwachs delineates groups as families, religious groups, and social classes that have developed a distinctive unity of outlooks over time (1992, p.52). Additionally, other potential group formations particular to the Palestinian context, such as the nature of trauma, age group, class, and tribe, could have an impact on narrative cohesion. However we limit our analysis to gender and geography because prior work has proven these aspects to be central identity markers that shape refugees' experiences of community (2018). As discussed in the background section, Palestinian women exhibit their own gendered memory of the Nakba. Therefore, we situate gender as a boundary-making identity marker. Additionally, geographical displacement from an original location to a foreign location is the key aspect that shapes Palestinian refugee groups and their experience (Sayigh, 1979; Safran, 1991). Therefore we situate place of origin and place of residence as another boundary-making identity marker.

Using this theoretical framework, we test the cohesiveness of the memories of Palestinians that have formed groups within Lebanon. While Palestinian refugees remember the Nakba in a multiplicity of ways, we expect that refugees' boundary-making identity markers will reflect higher cohesion in their narratives.

H1. *We hypothesize that same interviewee gender would be associated with increased cohesion in narratives (more so than across genders).*

H2. *We hypothesize that two interviewees belonging to the same spatial group will be associated with increased cohesion in their narratives.*

For our analysis, we define groups as interviewees who have the same gender, place of residence at the time of the interview and/or share the same place of origin from which they were displaced during the Nakba. Cohesion of group memories will be measured in the broader narratives around themes pertaining to the Nakba experience, such as the narration of Zionist invasions and their expulsion, as well as mentions of specific landmarks, significant figures, keywords and places. We expect that when refugees belong to the same group, there will be a higher similarity in how group members remember these entities.

4 Data & Methods

4.1 The Palestinian Oral History Archive

POHA is an archive of over a thousand video and audio interviews with Palestinian refugees in Lebanon displaced during the Nakba (Sleiman and Chebaro, 2018).[1] Although POHA is designed as an audiovisual archive (Sleiman and Chebaro, 2018), our approach focuses on the transcripts of the interviews. We opted for textual processing techniques to facilitate medium to large-scale analysis, acknowledging the potential for future multimodal analyses incorporating audiovisual features. Each POHA interview entry also includes metadata about the interviewee(s), interviewer(s), and content. We extracted this information from the POHA website. The content metadata includes keywords, headers summarizing main topics, significant figures, landmarks mentioned, and Table of Contents headers (TOCs) outlining each interview's structure. Details about the origin and residence of interviewees provide valuable context for understanding the narratives (see appendix A.1 for extraction details). To convert the audio content into text, we used the API of a transcription service, Transkriptor (Transkriptor, n.d.). We discuss this process in appendix A.5.

[1]POHA houses distinct archival collections to preserve Palestinian oral history. While its focus is largely on the Nakba, it also includes interviews documenting folklore and traditional tales; we filtered these out for our analysis.

Table 1: Aspects that we represent in different vectors and the sources for representation, specifying which ones use a BoW representation and which one use a semantic embedding using a LLM.

Aspect	Source	Representation
Keywords/themes	Metadata	BoW
Significant Figures	Metadata	BoW
Families	Metadata	BoW
Landmarks	Metadata	BoW
NER	Transcripts	BoW
Semantic by theme	Transcripts	Semantic Emb

4.2 Measuring Interviewees' Narrative Cohesion

We measure cohesion among interviews by comparing their similarities on different representations. We use various aspects of the interviewee narratives data to construct these representations. Table 1 outlines the different aspects we encode into representations and the methods used. We employ two main forms of representation:

Bag-of-Words (BoW): Applied primarily to metadata to represent specific entities and themes (denoted by curated keywords).

Semantic Embeddings: Dense vector representations obtained from the transcripts using a large language model, interpreted as capturing broader semantic similarity.

In the following sections, we provide more specifics on these representations.

4.2.1 Bag-of-Words Representations of Key Entities

We use bag-of-words (BoW) representations to capture specific entities related to various aspects of the interviews. These are listed in the metadata curated by archivists, focusing on landmarks, families, significant figures, and keywords. The keywords are curated to form a thematic representation of the interview (Sleiman and Chebaro, 2018). Additionally, we extract general named entities from the transcripts using an Arabic NER model from the CAMeL Tools library (Obeid et al., 2020) (details in appendix B.1). These entities capture mentions of places or landmarks without proper names, contributing to a nuanced understanding of similarity. Comparisons using BoW representations emphasize narrative similarity based on shared entities like families or significant figures. In contrast, keyword-based similarity reflects shared broad themes between interviews.

4.2.2 Semantic Embeddings from Transcripts

We complement our analysis by measuring narrative similarity through semantic embeddings of the transcripts. Utilizing instruction-conditioned embeddings (Su et al., 2023) and OpenAI's `text-embedding-3-large` model, we generated vector representations for interview sections (see appendix B.3). Notably, we did not filter out interviewers' speech; since we wanted to retain the full narrative structure of each interview as a text, and since Sleiman and Chebaro (2018) describe a high degree of consistency in their approach. This indicates that the interviewers follow the same structure and that the embeddings reflect the interviewees' narratives.[2]

To avoid oversimplifying the diverse interview content, we partitioned transcripts thematically using metadata-derived characteristics. Each interview's archivist-curated Table of Contents (TOC) provides descriptive headers for sections. We perform thematic narrative comparisons, by extracting embeddings from excerpts corresponding to TOC subheaders. We categorized the TOC headers into themes to compare excerpts across interviews (details in appendix B.2). The resulting embeddings are visualized using UMAP (McInnes et al., 2018) in fig. 1. Additional details on obtaining the embeddings are provided in appendix B.3.

For analysis, we focused on the four more prevalent themes closely related to the Nakba—Zionist Attacks During and After the Nakba; Exile, Expulsion, and Displacement; British Mandate Colonialism and Occupation; and Resistance and Popular Struggles—we created embeddings for transcript excerpts within these themes.

4.2.3 Similarity as cohesion

Given representations $\mathbf{e}_i^A, \mathbf{e}_j^A$ of interviews i, j, where the e_i^A could be BoW representations of metadata entities or semantic embeddings of the transcripts, we measure the cohesion of the interviews via the cosine similarity $\sigma(\mathbf{e}_j^A, \mathbf{e}_j^A)$ between the representations

$$\sigma(\mathbf{e}_j^A, \mathbf{e}_j^A) = \frac{\mathbf{e}_j^A \cdot \mathbf{e}_j^A}{\|\mathbf{e}_j^A\| \|\mathbf{e}_j^A\|}. \quad (1)$$

[2]Any filtering method barring that based on speaker identity could also potentially eliminate valuable testimony from interviewees.

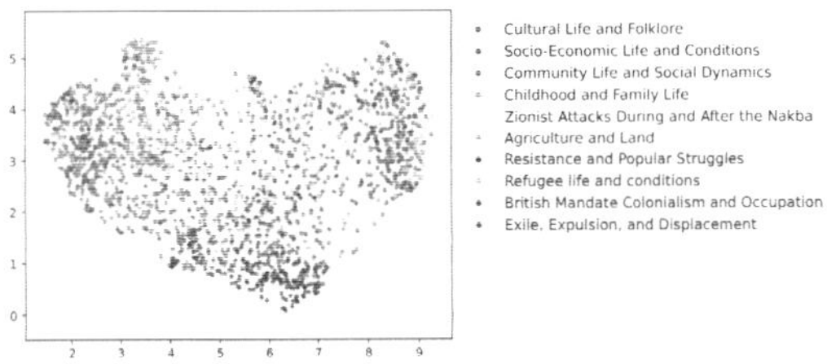

Figure 1: UMAP of instruction-based embeddings of interview transcript sections for all themes. Related themes are visually indistinguishable in this decomposition, while different themes are distant from each other.

Despite using the same measure for similarity, We heavily lean into the meanings of each of the aspects to interpret the meaning of similarity and cohesion contingent on what is being represented.

4.3 Statistical Analysis of Narrative Cohesion

We aim to compare pairs of interviews given interviewee identity markers. For example, we test whether pairs where both interviewees are female are more or less similar than pairs where both are male. To achieve this, we estimate models where the dependent variable is the similarity score, and the independent variables encode identity or community comparisons of interest.

4.3.1 Analysis by Gender Pairings

To analyze differences by gender, we use the following model with the standarized similarity $\sigma_{ij}^A = \sigma(\mathbf{e}_i^A, \mathbf{e}_j^A)$ as the dependent variable:

$$\sigma_{ij}^A = \sum_{X \in \{FF, FM, MM\}} \beta_X \, g_{ij}^X + \mu_i + \eta_j + \epsilon_{ij}. \quad (2)$$

Here, $g_{ij}^X = \mathbb{1}(g_{ij} = X)$ are dummy variables indicating gender pairing ($X \in \{FF, FM, MM\}$). Then, β_X captures the effects of the gender pairings. Random effects $\mu_i \sim \mathcal{N}(0, \sigma_\mu^2)$ and $\eta_j \sim \mathcal{N}(0, \sigma_\eta^2)$ account for interviews i and j, respectively, and the residual error is $\epsilon_{ij} \sim \mathcal{N}(0, \sigma_\epsilon^2)$.

4.3.2 Analysis by Community(Location) Pairings

To compare similarities σ^T (per theme) based on location, we use:

$$\sigma_{ij}^T = \beta_0 + \beta_1 s_{ij}^o + \beta_2 s_{ij}^r + \beta_3 (s_{ij}^o \times s_{ij}^r) + \mu_i + \eta_j + \epsilon_{ij}. \quad (3)$$

In this model, s_{ij}^o and s_{ij}^r are binary indicators of whether interviews i and j share the same origin or residence, respectively. The interaction term captures the combined effect of shared origin and residence. Random effects and residuals are defined as before.

Due to imbalance—with few pairs sharing both origin and residence—we apply an inverse weighting scheme based on the prevalence of each pairing type (details in appendix B.4.1). To better capture uncertainty, we also ran the models within a Bayesian framework using the `brms` package (Bürkner, 2017), allowing us to compare credible intervals with the frequentist results, we detail more in appendix B.5.

5 Findings

Using the models outlined, we test cohesion for both gender and location along a set of different aspects. As discussed in Section 3, we hypothesize that narrative cohesion will be higher 1) within same-gender pairs and 2) within same-community pairs (place of origin and place of residence). We refer to analyses of BOW representations of metadata and extracted named entities as relating to "factual" aspects of the interviews and the analyses using embeddings of different interview sections as "thematic."

5.1 Women's narratives are slightly more cohesive

We begin by testing cohesion within same-gender pairs. Palestinian women testify to different experiences of all three temporalities represented in POHA's biographies (pre-1948 village life, the Nakba, and refugee life); we also assume that group memory is operative on some level. While we do not expect that woman-woman or man-man pairs will necessarily display more or less cohesion according to our measure, we do expect that their levels of cohesion will be separable compared to the standard of man-woman pairs.

We use the model specified above in 4.3.1 to iteratively test the relationship between gender and different bag-of-words descriptors of the narrative. This yields the coefficients displayed in Figure 2. Our results suggest that there is evidence for women displaying thematic narrative cohesion but not necessarily factual cohesion.

Our original hypothesis about the particularity of women's experiences is only partially supported.

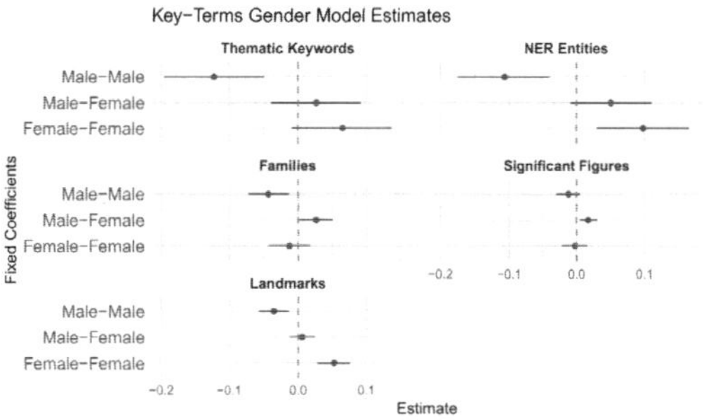

Figure 2: Model coefficients reflecting the relationship between factual mention-based cohesion and gender. Pairs of interviews where both interviewees are men tend to be less similar than those where both interviewees are women or those where one is a man and one is a woman; interviews where both interviewees are women are usually more similar, especially for the less specific measures.

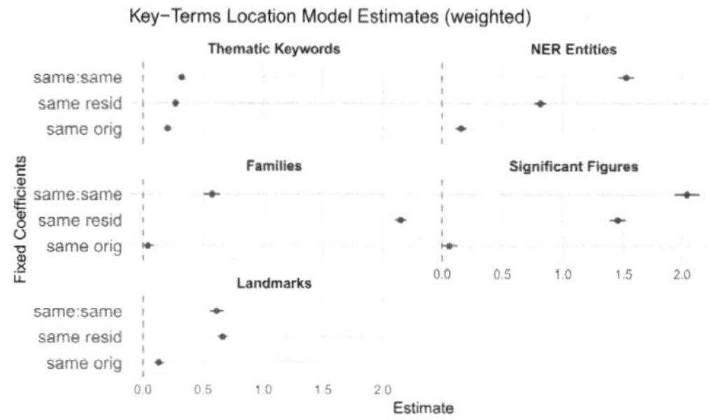

Figure 4: Model coefficients reflecting the relationship between factual mention-based cohesion and shared location. Same origin and resid. consistently predicts the mention of similar entities and (for the keywords) broader concepts. Being from the same place and living in the same place often has a large positive correlation with similarity.

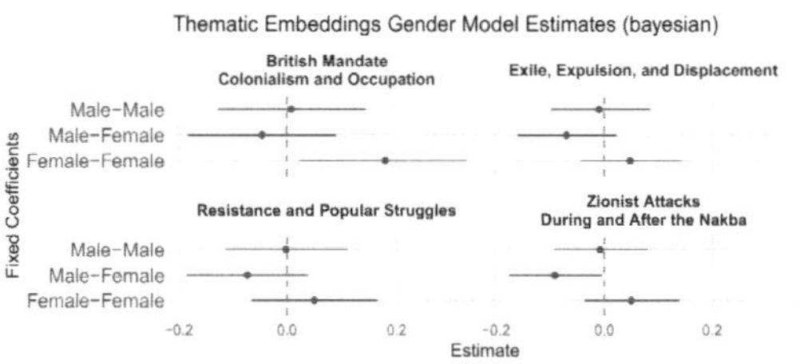

Figure 3: Model coefficients reflecting the relationship between thematic cohesion within topics and gender. Pairs of interviews where both interviewees are men may be slightly more similar than the reference class of man-woman pairs, and pairs of interviewees where both interviewees are women are the most similar of all.

In the context of factual mentions, women display only more cohesion than men in the context of landmarks and named entities actually found in the transcript. Otherwise, men seem to diverge in their mentions of landmarks and families as well as keywords and named entities. Thematically, women are observably cohesive only in discussions of the British Mandate. This speaks to how gender is not necessarily primary to the parties and places mentioned in life narratives in POHA.

The specific contexts in which there is observable similarity within gender pairs confirm arguments made in the qualitative literature we inventory in Section 2. The segments of interviews in which women talk about subjects related to village life in the pre-Nakba period are particulary cohesive; however, women also display significant similarity in discussions of Zionist attacks. In contrast, men appear to have descriptions of both the pre-Nakba period and the post-Nakba period (corresponding to the British Mandate and refugee life categories) that are not notably similar.

5.2 Shared communities lead to shared narratives

We also test group memory cohesion in the context of locations. Qualitative work on the experience of Palestinians in Lebanon has observed the development of shared narratives about both refugee life and the Nakba itself. We expect that both interviewees' origins and their current community impact their personal narration of Palestinian history.

We use a mixed effects model, including an interaction term representing the sharing of both original and current residences. This corresponds to an unusual commonality in experiences, given the importance of both interviewees' places of origin and their condition in exile. As shown in Figures 4 and 5, we find that shared origin *and* shared residence in Lebanon predict shared themes while narrating certain salient aspects of the Nakba.

We find strong support for our original hypothesis. Nevertheless, our results speak to a more nuanced relationship between shared current residence and narrative similarity than one might previously expect. Shared current residence alone predicts similarity along every axis we examine aside from discussions of community life (implicitly in the pre-Nakba context); shared origin alone predicts cohesiveness in both factual mentions and thematic narration, albeit moreso for factual mentions. However, sharing *both* residence *and* place of origin is more predictive than place of origin

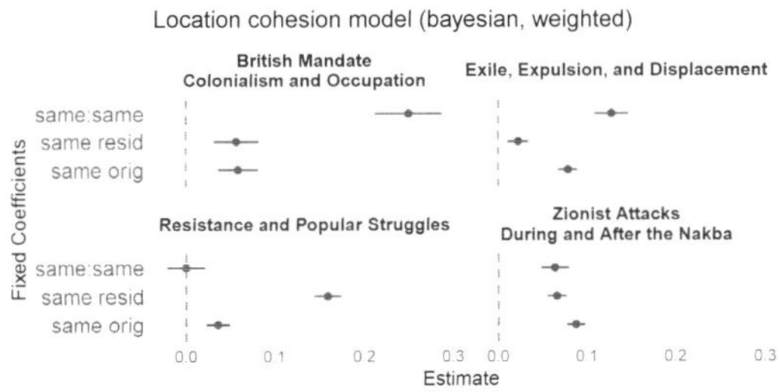

Figure 5: Model coefficients reflecting the relationship between thematic cohesion within topics and shared location. Similar to Figure 4, being from the same homeplace or residence consistently predicts higher similarities in every major theme. Living in the same place *and* being from the same location is quite predictive of narrating major historical events similarly

alone for categories related to both the pre and post-expulsion periods. This suggests processes of collective narration in the refugee context mediate the inclusion of shared themes in individuals' life narratives, depending on whether or not those individuals are from the same place originally.

6 Discussion

We observe evidence of group memory in several different scenarios concerning boundary-making identity markers. When interviewees share a community space (same origin or same residence), there is higher similarity within their narratives. Critically, sharing both same origin and residence often results in an even stronger similarity in interviewees' narratives. This indicates that the cohesiveness of narratives depends on the continuity of the group, which, in turn, depends on the continuity of shared space. As well, we observe weaker evidence that gender is an indicator of similarity, though women's narratives tend to be more similar.

The cohesion of narratives based on location can be reasonably explained through the theoretical framework of group memory. Refugees sharing same origin but not the same residence still have cohesive narratives, demonstrating that group members' bond to other members of their original village are not severed in exile. As Toivanen and Baser (2019) state, diasporic memory is not constrained by spatial boundaries, therefore refugees can participate in group recollection with others from the same origins even when they are physically separate. When traumatic experiences threaten group bonds, members will "erase from its memory all that might separate individuals" (Halbwachs, 1992, p.183), allowing for a collective narrative to emerge from individual memories. Therefore, the cohesion of narratives when refugees share the same origin but not the same residence is evidence of the strength and continuity of their bond despite the violent expulsion of the Nakba.

Refugees who share the same residence but not the same origin also have cohesive narratives, which shows that the Nakba itself was a catalyst for the formation of new group boundaries. It is anticipated that place of residence impacts group formation because studies (Brubaker, 2005; Safran, 1991; Butler, 2001) show that different segments of a diaspora will engage in boundary-maintenance and preserve a distinct identity due to self-segregation or social exclusion from the host society. Considering Palestinian refugees in Lebanon continue to be denied citizenship, legal identity, or work visas, their isolation from the rest of Lebanese society has caused refugees to turn inwards and develop strong group bonds with each other. Sharing the same place of residence, even without a continous bond stretching back to the homeland, therefore contributes to preserving a shared identity and cohesive memory as a group.

Finally, sharing the same origin and place of residence is often a strong indicator of similarity. This is consistent with the framework of group memory, which states that groups maintain cohesive memories so long as they are resistant to outside influences (Halbwachs, 1992). When Palestinians from the same village were forcibly displaced to the same place in Lebanon, their group continuity was maintained. This is not the case for all memories, however, as refugees in the same residence narrativize refugee life and conditions dissimilarly. These memories are newer compared to those from the Nakba period, so it is possible this specific theme has not yet been subjected to the processes of group memory. Overall, however, existing research states that diasporic group memory is shaped by both the homeland and the host country (Toivanen and Baser, 2019; Voytiv, 2024), therefore it is not unexpected that Palestinian refugees who share the same past and present location have an even stronger similarity in their narratives than refugees who ohare only one location.

Our findings regarding gender merit further discussion. Gender narrative similarity is more variable and there is no single identifier of a stronger similarity or dissimilarity. This speaks to an overall shared understanding of the Nakba transcending gender boundaries. However, we highlight significant differences. Namely, increased cohesion concerning themes in general (keywords) and pre-Nakba village context. This connects to two factors that influence group memory. First, the constructed social and cultural roles of gender among Palestinians in refugee camps, and second, the nature of refugee camps as spaces of displacement and vulnerability, which operate under unique socio-economic constraints that profoundly shape gender dynamics. Second, pre-Nakba, villages were closely knit communities where women's roles and responsibilities were shaped by communal practices and survival strategies, including supporting resistance (Sayigh, 2007; Tamari, 2008; Nimr, 2008; Yahya, 2017). In these settings, women often internalized dominant national narratives shaped by the era, which laid the foundation for their role in the broader narrative of resistance (Tamari, 2008; Sayigh, 1998; Yahya, 2017).

Women's factual cohesion appears strongest when referencing specific landmarks or entities in transcripts. This can be associated with their emotional connection to physical places. In contrast, men's narratives exhibit notable divergence in their descriptions of landmarks, families, and other entities. This suggests that men's experiences are either more individualized or less influenced by communal memory practices. Sayigh's ethnography corroborates this, highlighting men's fragmented recollections shaped by personal trajectories and interactions with political and economic systems (Sayigh, 1998, 2015).

Overall, our findings challenge the notion that same-gender pairs inherently produce cohesive narratives (Tamari, 2008; Nimr, 2008; Sayigh, 2015, 1998). Instead, cohesion reflects the collective memory fostered by women's roles in village life and under colonial rule, even as factual details vary.

7 Conclusion

This paper constitutes a large-scale computational analysis of an oral history archive of the Nakba using natural language processing. Drawing from qualitative literature on Palestinian refugees' experiences, we explore how boundary-making identity markers shape their life narratives. Comparing the narratives of Palestinians beyond Lebanon or the narratives of those from rural vs. urban contexts are opportunities for further research into how locality shapes narrative cohesion. This study, however, is bound by the scope of POHA which focuses solely on Lebanon and offers a preliminary foray into one means of capturing multidimensional narrative cohesion in an archive. With these findings, we hope to both reaffirm and extend prior scholarship on Palestinian collective memory, by providing empirical evidence of how oral narratives allow refugees to build continuity and counteract the violent fragmentation of Palestinian society after the Nakba.

Limitations

From a substantive standpoint, the analysis and interviews (which represent just a fraction of the Palestinian refugee population in Lebanon) provide only a partial perspective on the Nakba. Capturing the depth of this historical tragedy in a single analysis is inherently difficult, especially when the Nakba remains an ongoing condition of exile.

Our analysis uses mixed effects models to explore the relationship between cohesion and community membership; here, we identify assumptions that may not be robust. Although we tried a triangulation approach with different aspects, the textual representations are limited in capturing narrative structure. Generally, our focused approach only begins to characterize POHA. Future research could explore other methods for understanding oral history archives, complementing interpretive approaches that engage directly with individual interviews. In addition, the metadata results in this paper partly reflect curation decisions by the POHA team. Archivists' positionality often influences descriptive practices (King, 2024; Carbajal and Caswell, 2021), introducing potential bias in metadata terminology. Discrete metadata fields also risk reducing the rich lived experiences in interviews to simplified categories, although we use semantic embeddings to counteract these limitations.

Acknowledgments

We deeply honor the courage and resilience of Palestinians who have shared their powerful and often overwhelming experiences. Their stories are a testament to the unyielding spirit of resistance, serving not only as a bridge to future generations but as a vital contribution to the ongoing journey toward justice and liberation. We are also grateful to the American University of Beirut librarians for their support in addressing our inquiries.

References

Salmān Abū-Sitta. 2016. *Mapping My Return: A Palestinian Memoir.* American University in Cairo Press, Cairo New York.

Mousumi Akter and Shubhra Kanti Karmaker Santu. 2024. FaNS: A Facet-based Narrative Similarity Metric. *Preprint*, arXiv:2309.04823.

Amirah Allan. 2021. Introduction: Past Continuous. In Diana Allan, editor, *Voices of the Nakba: A Living History of Palestine*, pages 61–81. Pluto Press.

Diana Allan. 2013. *Refugees of the Revolution: Experiences of Palestinian Exile.* Stanford University Press.

David Bamman and Noah A. Smith. 2014. Unsupervised Discovery of Biographical Structure from Text. *Transactions of the Association for Computational Linguistics*, 2:363–376.

Bassam Yousef Ibrahim Banat, Francisco Entrena-Durán, and Jawad Dayyeh. 2018. Palestinian Refugee Youth: Reproduction of Collective Memory of the Nakba. *ASS*, 14(12):147.

Rana Barakat. 2019. Reading Palestinian agency in mandate history: The narrative of the Buraq Revolt as anti-relational. *Contemporary Levant*, 4(1):28–38.

Efrat Ben-Ze'ev. 2002. The Palestinian village of Ijzim during the 1948 war: Forming an anthropological history through villagers accounts and army documents. *History and Anthropology*, 13(1):13–30.

Vinamra Benara, Chandan Singh, John X. Morris, Richard Antonello, Ion Stoica, Alexander G. Huth, and Jianfeng Gao. 2024. Crafting Interpretable Embeddings by Asking LLMs Questions.

Filip Bendevski, Jumana Ibrahim, Tina Krulec, Theodore Waters, Nizar Habash, Hanan Salam, Himadri Mukherjee, and Christin Camia. 2021. Towards Automatic Narrative Coherence Prediction. In *Proceedings of the 2021 International Conference on Multimodal Interaction*, ICMI '21, pages 539–547, New York, NY, USA. Association for Computing Machinery.

Eyal Benvenisti, Chaim Gans, and Sari Hanafi, editors. 2007. *Israel and the Palestinian Refugees.* Number 189 in Beiträge zum ausländischen öffentlichen Recht und Völkerrecht. Springer Berlin Heidelberg, Berlin, Heidelberg.

George E. Bisharat. 1994. Displacement and Social Identity: Palestinian Refugees in the West Bank. *Cent Migr Stud Spec Iss*, 11(4):163–188.

Patrick Brookshire and Nils Reiter. 2024. Modeling Moravian Memoirs: Ternary Sentiment Analysis in a Low Resource Setting. In *Proceedings of the 8th Joint SIGHUM Workshop on Computational Linguistics for Cultural Heritage, Social Sciences, Humanities and Literature (LaTeCH-CLfL 2024)*, pages 91–100, St. Julians, Malta. Association for Computational Linguistics.

Rogers Brubaker. 2005. The 'diaspora' diaspora. *Ethnic and Racial Studies*, 28(1):1–19.

Paul-Christian Bürkner. 2017. Brms: An R Package for Bayesian Multilevel Models Using Stan. *Journal of Statistical Software*, 80:1–28.

Kim D. Butler. 2001. Defining Diaspora, Refining a Discourse. *dsp*, 10(2):189–219.

Itza A. Carbajal and Michelle Caswell. 2021. Critical Digital Archives: A Review from Archival Studies. *The American Historical Review*, 126(3):1102–1120.

Giovanni Colavizza, Tobias Blanke, Charles Jeurgens, and Julia Noordegraaf. 2021. Archives and AI: An Overview of Current Debates and Future Perspectives. *Journal on Computing and Cultural Heritage*, 15(1):4:1–4:15.

Rochelle A. Davis. 2011. *Palestinian Village Histories: Geographies of the Displaced.* Stanford Studies in Middle Eastern and Islamic Societies and Cultures. Stanford University Press, Stanford, Calif.

Farah Aboubakr. 2017. Peasantry in Palestinian Folktales: Sites of Memory, Homeland, and Collectivity. *Marvels & Tales*, 31(2):217.

Edwin Farley and R. Gutman. 2020. A Bayesian Approach to Linking Data Without Unique Identifiers. *arXiv: Computation.*

Jane Greenberg. 1998. The Applicability of Natural Language Processing (NLP) to Archival Properties and Objectives. *The American Archivist*, 61(2):400–425.

Maurice Halbwachs. 1992. *On Collective Memory.* University of Chicago Press.

Sari Hanafi and Are J. Knudsen, editors. 2011. *Palestinian Refugees: Identity, Space and Place in the Levant.* Routeldge, Milton Park, Abingdon, Oxon New York.

Isabelle Humphries and Laleh Khalili. 2007. Gender of Nakba Memory. In Ahmad H. Sa'di and Lila Abu-Lughod, editors, *Nakba: Palestine, 1948, and the Claims of Memory*, Cultures of History, pages 207–228. Columbia University Press, New York.

Go Inoue, Bashar Alhafni, Nurpeiis Baimukan, Houda Bouamor, and Nizar Habash. 2021. The Interplay of Variant, Size, and Task Type in Arabic Pre-trained Language Models. In *Proceedings of the Sixth Arabic Natural Language Processing Workshop*, Kyiv, Ukraine (Online). Association for Computational Linguistics.

Lise Jaillant and Arran Rees. 2023. Applying AI to digital archives: trust, collaboration and shared professional ethics. *Digital Scholarship in the Humanities*, 38(2):571–585.

Lena Jayyusi. 2007. Iterability, Cumulativity, and Presence: The Relational Figures of Palestinian Memory. In Ahmed H. Sa'di and Lila Abu-Lughod, editors, *Nakba: Palestine, 1948, and the Claims of Memory*, Cultures of History, pages 107–134. Columbia University Press, New York.

Rashid Khalidi. 1997. *Palestinian Identity*. Columbia University Press.

Walid Khalidi. 1992. *All That Remains: The Palestinian Villages Occupied and Depopulated by Israel in 1948*. Institute for Palestine Studies.

Elias Khoury. 2012. Rethinking the *Nakba*. *Critical Inquiry*, 38(2):250–266.

Laura Khoury. 2018. Shu'fat refugee camp women authenticate an old "Nakba" and frame something "new" while narrating it. In Nahla Abdo-Zubi and Nur Masalha, editors, *An Oral History of the Palestinian Nakba*, pages 136–158. ZED, London, UK.

Owen C. King. 2024. Archival meta-metadata: Revision history and positionality of finding aids. *Arch Sci*, 24(3):509–529.

Nur Masalha. 2012. *The Palestine Nakba: Decolonising History, Narrating the Subaltern, Reclaiming Memory*. Zed Books, London.

Nur Masalha. 2018. Decolonizing methodology, reclaiming memory: Palestinian oral histories and memories of the Nakba. In Nahla Abdo-Zubi and Nur Masalha, editors, *An Oral History of the Palestinian Nakba*, pages 6–39. ZED, London, UK.

Joseph Andoni Massad. 2006. *The Persistence of the Palestinian Question: Essays on Zionism and the Palestinians*. Routledge Kegan Paul, London New York, NY.

Leland McInnes, John Healy, Nathaniel Saul, and Lukas Großberger. 2018. UMAP: Uniform Manifold Approximation and Projection. *Journal of Open Source Software*, 3(29):861.

Roxy Moon. 2023. Outside the Locus of Control: Palestinian Digital Archives Resist Israeli Settler-Colonial Erasure. *Journal of Palestine Studies*, 52(4):37–52.

Sonia Nimr. 2008. Fast Forward to the Past: A Look into Palestinian Collective Memory. *clo*, 63–64:338–349.

Ossama Obeid, Nasser Zalmout, Salam Khalifa, Dima Taji, Mai Oudah, Bashar Alhafni, Go Inoue, Fadhl Eryani, Alexander Erdmann, and Nizar Habash. 2020. CAMeL Tools: An Open Source Python Toolkit for Arabic Natural Language Processing. In *Proceedings of the 12th Language Resources and Evaluation Conference*, pages 7022–7032, Marseille, France. European Language Resources Association.

OpenAI. Hello GPT-4o.

OpenAI, Josh Achiam, Steven Adler, Sandhini Agarwal, Lama Ahmad, Ilge Akkaya, Florencia Leoni Aleman, Diogo Almeida, Janko Altenschmidt, Sam Altman, Shyamal Anadkat, Red Avila, Igor Babuschkin, Suchir Balaji, Valerie Balcom, Paul Baltescu, Haiming Bao, Mohammad Bavarian, Jeff Belgum, Irwan Bello, Jake Berdine, Gabriel Bernadett-Shapiro, Christopher Berner, Lenny Bogdonoff, Oleg Boiko, Madelaine Boyd, Anna-Luisa Brakman, Greg Brockman, Tim Brooks, Miles Brundage, Kevin Button, Trevor Cai, Rosie Campbell, Andrew Cann, Brittany Carey, Chelsea Carlson, Rory Carmichael, Brooke Chan, Che Chang, Fotis Chantzis, Derek Chen, Sully Chen, Ruby Chen, Jason Chen, Mark Chen, Ben Chess, Chester Cho, Casey Chu, Hyung Won Chung, Dave Cummings, Jeremiah Currier, Yunxing Dai, Cory Decareaux, Thomas Degry, Noah Deutsch, Damien Deville, Arka Dhar, David Dohan, Steve Dowling, Sheila Dunning, Adrien Ecoffet, Atty Eleti, Tyna Eloundou, David Farhi, Liam Fedus, Niko Felix, Simón Posada Fishman, Juston Forte, Isabella Fulford, Leo Gao, Elie Georges, Christian Gibson, Vik Goel, Tarun Gogineni, Gabriel Goh, Rapha Gontijo-Lopes, Jonathan Gordon, Morgan Grafstein, Scott Gray, Ryan Greene, Joshua Gross, Shixiang Shane Gu, Yufei Guo, Chris Hallacy, Jesse Han, Jeff Harris, Yuchen He, Mike Heaton, Johannes Heidecke, Chris Hesse, Alan Hickey, Wade Hickey, Peter Hoeschele, Brandon Houghton, Kenny Hsu, Shengli Hu, Xin Hu, Joost Huizinga, Shantanu Jain, Shawn Jain, Joanne Jang, Angela Jiang, Roger Jiang, Haozhun Jin, Denny Jin, Shino Jomoto, Billie Jonn, Heewoo Jun, Tomer Kaftan, Łukasz Kaiser, Ali Kamali, Ingmar Kanitscheider, Nitish Shirish Keskar, Tabarak Khan, Logan Kilpatrick, Jong Wook Kim, Christina Kim, Yongjik Kim, Jan Hendrik Kirchner, Jamie Kiros, Matt Knight, Daniel Kokotajlo, Łukasz Kondraciuk, Andrew Kondrich, Aris Konstantinidis, Kyle Kosic, Gretchen Krueger, Vishal Kuo, Michael Lampe, Ikai Lan, Teddy Lee, Jan Leike, Jade Leung, Daniel Levy, Chak Ming Li, Rachel Lim, Molly Lin, Stephanie Lin, Mateusz Litwin, Theresa Lopez, Ryan Lowe, Patricia Lue, Anna Makanju, Kim Malfacini, Sam Manning, Todor Markov, Yaniv Markovski, Bianca Martin, Katie Mayer, Andrew Mayne, Bob McGrew, Scott Mayer McKinney, Christine McLeavey, Paul McMillan, Jake McNeil, David Medina, Aalok Mehta, Jacob Menick, Luke Metz, Andrey Mishchenko, Pamela Mishkin, Vinnie Monaco, Evan Morikawa, Daniel Mossing, Tong Mu, Mira Murati, Oleg Murk, David Mély, Ashvin Nair, Reiichiro Nakano, Rajeev Nayak, Arvind Neelakantan, Richard Ngo, Hyeonwoo Noh, Long Ouyang, Cullen O'Keefe, Jakub Pachocki, Alex Paino, Joe Palermo, Ashley Pantuliano, Giambattista Parascandolo, Joel Parish, Emy Parparita, Alex Passos, Mikhail Pavlov, Andrew Peng, Adam Perelman, Filipe de Avila Belbute Peres, Michael Petrov, Henrique Ponde de Oliveira Pinto, Michael, Pokorny, Michelle Pokrass, Vitchyr H. Pong, Tolly Powell, Alethea Power, Boris Power, Elizabeth Proehl, Raul Puri, Alec Radford, Jack Rae, Aditya Ramesh,

Cameron Raymond, Francis Real, Kendra Rimbach, Carl Ross, Bob Rotsted, Henri Roussez, Nick Ryder, Mario Saltarelli, Ted Sanders, Shibani Santurkar, Girish Sastry, Heather Schmidt, David Schnurr, John Schulman, Daniel Selsam, Kyla Sheppard, Toki Sherbakov, Jessica Shieh, Sarah Shoker, Pranav Shyam, Szymon Sidor, Eric Sigler, Maddie Simens, Jordan Sitkin, Katarina Slama, Ian Sohl, Benjamin Sokolowsky, Yang Song, Natalie Staudacher, Felipe Petroski Such, Natalie Summers, Ilya Sutskever, Jie Tang, Nikolas Tezak, Madeleine B. Thompson, Phil Tillet, Amin Tootoonchian, Elizabeth Tseng, Preston Tuggle, Nick Turley, Jerry Tworek, Juan Felipe Cerón Uribe, Andrea Vallone, Arun Vijayvergiya, Chelsea Voss, Carroll Wainwright, Justin Jay Wang, Alvin Wang, Ben Wang, Jonathan Ward, Jason Wei, CJ Weinmann, Akila Welihinda, Peter Welinder, Jiayi Weng, Lilian Weng, Matt Wiethoff, Dave Willner, Clemens Winter, Samuel Wolrich, Hannah Wong, Lauren Workman, Sherwin Wu, Jeff Wu, Michael Wu, Kai Xiao, Tao Xu, Sarah Yoo, Kevin Yu, Qiming Yuan, Wojciech Zaremba, Rowan Zellers, Chong Zhang, Marvin Zhang, Shengjia Zhao, Tianhao Zheng, Juntang Zhuang, William Zhuk, and Barret Zoph. 2024. GPT-4 Technical Report. *Preprint*, arXiv:2303.08774.

Ilan Pappé. 2007. *The Ethnic Cleansing of Palestine*. Oneworld Publications, New York.

Francisca Pessanha and Almila Akdag Salah. 2021. A Computational Look at Oral History Archives. *Journal on Computing and Cultural Heritage*, 15(1):6:1–6:16.

Andrew Piper. 2023. Computational Narrative Understanding: A Big Picture Analysis. In *Proceedings of the Big Picture Workshop*, pages 28–39, Singapore. Association for Computational Linguistics.

Mazin B Qumsiyeh. 2011. *Popular Resistance in Palestine: A History of Hope and Empowerment*. Pluto Press, New York, NY.

Alec Radford, Jong Wook Kim, Tao Xu, Greg Brockman, Christine McLeavey, and Ilya Sutskever. 2022. Robust Speech Recognition via Large-Scale Weak Supervision. *Preprint*, arXiv:2212.04356.

Leonard Richardson. Beautiful soup.

Rami Rmeileh. 2021. "sumud is to always be one hand": Culturally informed resilience among palestinian refugee men in lebanon. Master's thesis.

Ahmad H. Sa'di and Lila Abu-Lughod. 2007. Introduction: The Claims of Memory. In Ahmed H. Sa'di and Lila Abu-Lughod, editors, *Nakba: Palestine, 1948, and the Claims of Memory*, Cultures of History, pages 1–24. Columbia University Press, New York.

William Safran. 1991. Diasporas in Modern Societies: Myths of Homeland and Return. *dsp*, 1(1):83–99.

Brenda Santana, Ricardo Campos, Evelin Amorim, Alípio Jorge, Purificação Silvano, and Sérgio Nunes. 2023. A survey on narrative extraction from textual data. *Artif Intell Rev*, 56(8):8393–8435.

Rosemary Sayigh. 1979. *The Palestinians: From Peasants to Revolutionaries*. Zed Books Ltd.

Rosemary Sayigh. 1998. Palestinian Camp Women as Tellers of History. *Journal of Palestine Studies*, 27(2):42–58.

Rosemary Sayigh. 2007. Product and Producer of Palestinian History: Stereotypes of "Self" in Camp Women's Life Stories. *Journal of Middle East Women's Studies*, 3(1):86–105.

Rosemary Sayigh. 2015. Oral history, colonialist dispossession, and the state: The Palestinian case. *Settler Colonial Studies*, 5(3):193–204.

David Shuttleworth and Jose Padilla. 2022. From Narratives to Conceptual Models via Natural Language Processing. In *2022 Winter Simulation Conference (WSC)*, pages 2222–2233.

Rami Siklawi. 2019. The Palestinian Refugee Camps in Lebanon Post 1990: Dilemmas of Survival and Return to Palestine. *Arab Studies Quarterly*, 41(1).

Amirah Silmi. 2021. The Margin and the Centre in Narrating Pre-1948 Palestine. In Diana Allan, editor, *Voices of the Nakba: A Living History of Palestine*, pages 61–81. Pluto Press.

Hana Sleiman and Kaoukab Chebaro. 2018. Narrating Palestine: The Palestinian Oral History Archive Project. *Journal of Palestine Studies*, 47(2):63–76.

Stan Development Team. 2024. RStan: The R interface to Stan.

Hongjin Su, Weijia Shi, Jungo Kasai, Yizhong Wang, Yushi Hu, Mari Ostendorf, Wen-tau Yih, Noah A. Smith, Luke Zettlemoyer, and Tao Yu. 2023. One Embedder, Any Task: Instruction-Finetuned Text Embeddings. In *Findings of the Association for Computational Linguistics: ACL 2023*, pages 1102–1121, Toronto, Canada. Association for Computational Linguistics.

Ted Swedenburg. 1995. *Memories of Revolt: The 1936 - 1939 Rebellion and the Palestinian National Past*. University of Minnesota Press, Minneapolis, Minn.

Zsofia A. Szojka, Annabelle Nicol, and David La Rooy. 2020. Narrative coherence in multiple forensic interviews with child witnesses alleging physical and sexual abuse. *Applied Cognitive Psychology*, 34(5):943–960.

Salim Tamari. 2008. *Mountain against the Sea: Essays on Palestinian Society and Culture*. University of California Press.

Mari Toivanen and Bahar Baser. 2019. Remembering the Past in Diasporic Spaces: Kurdish Reflections on Genocide Memorialization for Anfal. *Genocide Studies International*, 13(1):10–33.

Transkriptor. n.d. Transkriptor API.

Sofiya Voytiv. 2024. Diasporic group boundaries and solidarity in the making: Collective memory in the anti-war protests in Sweden. *Ethnic and Racial Studies*, 47(2):391–410.

Abbad Yahya. 2017. Oral History and Dual Marginalization:. *Jerusalem Quarterly*.

Lixing Zhu, Runcong Zhao, Lin Gui, and Yulan He. 2023. Are NLP Models Good at Tracing Thoughts: An Overview of Narrative Understanding. *Preprint*, arXiv:2310.18783.

A Data Appendix

A.1 Extraction of POHA data

We extracted both audio files and corresponding metadata from the Palestinian Oral History Archive by scraping their website, located on the American University of Beirut's website at libraries.aub.edu.lb/poha/. Every record in POHA has its own dedicated ID, running from 4158 to 4887; each record's page has the URL `https://libraries.aub.edu.lb/poha/Record/{]`

For each interview page, we use the `BeautifulSoup` library (Richardson) to extract data from the HTML. Some of the fields (e.g., significant figures who appear in an interview) are variously present and absent; we flexibly add these to JSON representations of the metadata. Interview audio was downloaded from the "Interview Audio/Video" field present for most interviews. A minority of the interviews did not have available recordings; after this scraping process, during which we excluded those, we were left with 720 interviews.

A.2 Extracting Information from Bios

Our initial extracted metadata directly from POHA did not include specific fields for gender or place of residence. However, this information was sometimes present also within the metadata, just not in a structured format. When available, such information was often embedded within the *bio* field.

To extract gender and place of residence from the bios—which was essential for our study—we utilized a large language model. We compiled the bios in both Arabic and English and supplied them to `gpt-4o` (OpenAI et al., 2024) using the following prompt:

```
From the following *interview
    description* + *metadata on names
    and places of origin* extract the
    following information in JSON format
    .

The input data has the following
    structure.

{{
  "en": {{"bio": "<bio in english>",
          interviewee: ["<name person
               1>", "<name person 2>",
               ...],
          place_of_origin: ["<origin
               person 1>", "<origin
               person 2>", ...]}}
  "ar": {{"bio": "<bio in arabic>",
          interviewee: ["<name person
               1>", "<name person 2>",
               ...],
          place_of_origin: ["<origin
               person 1>", "<origin
               person 2>", ...]}},
}}


The output data must have the following
    structure. Not all fields might be
    present, in that case, omit those

```json
{{
  "en": {{  # for english data
      extraction
    "interview_date": ""
    "interview_location": ""
    "interviewees": [
      {{
        "name": "",
        "place_of_origin": "",
        "gender": "",
        "birth_date": "",
        "place_of_residence": "",
        "occupation": "",
        "occupation_entity": ""
      }},
    ]
  }},
  "ar": {{  # for arabic data extraction
    "interview_date": ""
    "interview_location": ""
    "interviewees": [
      {{
        "name": "",
        "place_of_origin": "",
        "gender": "",
        "birth_date": "",
        "place_of_residence": "",
        "occupation": "",
        "occupation_entity": ""
      }},
    ]
  }}
}}
```

Notes:
- The interview might have more than one
     interviewee.
- The description is given in english
    and in arabic, extract the data for
    both versions, make sure the order
    of interviewees is the same for both
     versions
```

```
- Output the `name` as it appears in `
    interviewee` list. If the name does
    not appear in the interview list use
     the name as it appears on the bio
- Output the `place_of_origin` as it
    appears in `place_or_origin` list.
    If the place does not appear in the
    place_of_origin list use the place
    as it appears on the bio
- Use date format %Y-%m-%d (eg.
    2024-08-25) if possible, if not, use
     %Y (eg. 2024)
- Be careful with keeping the correct
    transliteration of arabic names and
    places

----------------------
Interview description:

{{
  "en": {{"bio": "{data["en_bio"]}",
          interviewee: {data["
              en_interviewee"]},
          place_of_origin: {data["
              en_place_of_origin"]}}}
  "ar": {{"bio": "{data["ar_bio"]}",
          interviewee: {data["
              ar_interviewee"]},
          place_of_origin: {data["
              ar_place_of_origin"]}}}
}}
```

Listing 1: Prompt to extract structured information from the bios

Note that in addition to the bios, we provided the interviewees' names and places of origin as recorded in the metadata. This ensured that the model used consistent names, simplifying the process of linking all data together.

A.3 Curating Places of Residence

Initially, our metadata extraction did not include direct information about the place of residence for each interviewee. While the bios sometimes contained additional details beyond the specified metadata—including place of residence—this was not always the case. As explained in the previous section, we used `gpt-4o` to extract structured data from the bios.

After this process, many interviews still lacked specified places of residence in the bios, necessitating an alternative extraction method.

In our second approach, we focused on interviews for which no metadata was available. Arabic-speaking team members manually read the interview transcripts to identify the interviewees' places of residence. This task was inherently time-consuming, requiring approximately 30 minutes per interview for a native speaker due to the length of the interviews and the challenge of obtaining full context.

To expedite this process, we utilized `gpt-4o` with the following prompt:

```
From the following excerpt of an
    interview, extract the place of
    residence of the interviewee if such
     place is mentioned.

Notes:
- Do not confuse the place of residence
    with the place of origin of the
    interviewee.
- Attempt to identify the place where
    the interviewee is living at the
    time of the interview.
- It is very unlikely that the place of
    residence is within Palestine, as
    these are stories of exiled refugees
    .

Respond with the place of residence of
    the interviewee, the timestamp, and
    the line of text where you found it.
Also, add a short explanation of why the
     place is likely to be the place of
    residence.
If no place of residence can be
    reasonably identified, add a short
    explanation of why.

Text:
--------
speaker_id; timestamp; text
{text here}
```

Listing 2: Prompt to Extract Place of Residence from Interview Excerpt

Here, the text is formatted as specified in the prompt: `speaker_id; timestamp; text`.

Given that the interviews often exceeded the model's context window, we partitioned them by their table of contents and submitted each section individually. After processing a few interviews, our team members gained insights into which sections were more likely to mention the place of residence. Combining these insights with the model's suggestions, we efficiently processed approximately 250 interviews to obtain places of residence.

Out of the interviews that initially lacked residence information, we successfully identified the place of residence for 207 interviews. This left us with 52 interviews where the place of residence remained unidentified or unclear.

A.4 Deduplication of Places

We frequently encountered variations in how places of origin and places of residence were referenced within the metadata and bios. For example, a single refugee camp might be referred to in up to eight different ways due to the addition or omission of words, or the inclusion of the area or country name. This inconsistency posed challenges for grouping and matching interviews based on places of origin and residence.

To resolve this issue, we performed a deduplication process using the `RecordLinker` library (Farley and Gutman, 2020). This tool allowed us to match locations by comparing both the Arabic and English versions of the names, utilizing edit distance metrics for each language. The process clustered records that likely referred to the same entity. We chose the most prevalent name in the data as the representative name for each cluster, effectively minimizing the impact of misspellings and variations by standardizing the names across the dataset.

After this process, we reduced the number of unique places to approximately 150 different places of origin and 100 different places of residence. We then manually curated these lists to finalize the mappings, ensuring accurate and consistent duplication of the interview information.

A.5 Transcriptions and validation

Filtering out interviews about folktales, we are left with 724 interviews. This still comprises about a thousand hours of audio and video. We use Transkriptor, a commercial transcription tool, to transcribe the interviews (Transkriptor, n.d.). Transcriptor supports transcription optimized for specific dialects of Arabic; this is important for the fidelity of our transcriptions of POHA, given that many of the interviews are in Levantine Arabic rather than MSA. While we explored using smaller Whisper (Radford et al., 2022) models, the large volume of interviews and specificity of the data led to low-quality and slowly obtained results.

Two Arabic-speaking members of our team conducted a qualitative assessment of the interviews to validate transcriptions. This process involved manually reviewing a subset of the transcriptions to ensure accuracy and consistency, particularly for dialect-specific nuances.

The translator effectively captured the local Palestinian dialect without censoring words or omitting context, achieving 90 percent accuracy. However, challenges arose from factors such as the quality of the interviews and their structural design. In some cases, the transcription tool struggled to recognize sentence boundaries and properly connect the text, requiring careful contextual interpretation without re-listening to the audio. Additionally, there were minor issues with reading the local dialect, as the transcription tool spelled words differently than how native speakers would naturally express them.

B Methods Appendix

B.1 Extracting named entities

In order to extract named entities, we use the CAMeL Tools library (Obeid et al., 2020). In particular, we used the `CAMeL-Lab/bert-base-arabic-camelbert-msa-ner` model available on HuggingFace to conduct flat token classification. Inoue et al. (2021) describes this model as having a F1 score of 74.1 on dialectal Arabic (under which Levantine Arabic falls), which is sufficient for our purposes given the complementary nature of our analyses.

B.2 Defining the Themes

Overall, the Table of Contents (TOC) headers contain over 3,000 entries. Unlike keywords and other entities in the metadata—which required selection from a specific list of entities (Sleiman and Chebaro, 2018)—the TOC headers were largely left to the discretion of the archivists. Each interview is unique; the flexibility of the headers allows for a broad characterization of an interview's content without imposing a strict classification system. This means that although many headers are very similar, there is no unique categorization of TOCs.

To generate the themes, we first took a random sample of the headers in English and then prompted `gpt-4o` (OpenAI) to generate a list of potential themes to cluster the exemplars. This followed an approach similar to QAEmb, where a large language model is prompted to generate a rubric (Benara et al., 2024). We used this as a starting point for manual curation, adding and modifying themes and relocating exemplars as needed.

In the end, we arrived at the following themes:

Childhood and Family Life Experiences and memories of childhood and family life, including upbringing, education, community interactions, and daily life before displacement.

Education and Intellectual Life Educational experiences, curricula, teaching methods, and intellectual pursuits both within Palestine before 1948 and among the Palestinian diaspora.

Community Life and Social Dynamics Community structures, social customs, celebrations, and dynamics within Palestinian towns. Mostly represents community pre-Nakba.

Zionist Attacks During and After the Nakba Zionist attacks, occupation, and conflicts; during and after the Nakba, including invasions, occupations, massacres, battles, and their effects on Palestinians.

Exile, Expulsion, and Displacement Accounts of expulsion, exile, and displacement during the Nakba, detailing the journeys, hardships, and experiences of leaving Palestine.

Socio-Economic Life and Conditions Examinations of socio-economic conditions before the Nakba, including employment, agriculture, economic activities, social relations, and health care in Palestinian communities.

Cultural Life and Folklore Explorations of Palestinian cultural life and folklore, including traditional songs, customs, and stories.

British Mandate Colonialism and Occupation Discussions of the British Mandate period (1920–1948), focusing on British administration, policies, the role in Zionist colonization, and Palestinian resistance prior to the Nakba.

Resistance and Popular Struggles Accounts of Palestinian resistance movements and popular struggles against colonialism and occupation.

Women's Roles Exploration of women's roles in society, including contributions to community rebuilding, activism, rights, and political involvement during displacement.

Agriculture and Land Descriptions of agricultural practices, land use, and the importance of agriculture to community life in Palestine before the Nakba.

Reflections and Final Thoughts Personal reflections on the refugee experience, aspirations for the future, attempts to return, and thoughts on migration and displacement.

Refugee Life and Conditions Examinations of life as refugees, focusing on living conditions, education, aid, social conditions in exile, and discussions on the right of return.

We then classified all TOCs using a multilabel approach by manually annotating a sample of 340 headers. For classification features, we embedded the headers using instructed embeddings with the instruction: "Represent the Interview Section Header for classifying its main theme." We used a test split and compared the performance of different multi-label models, with a one-vs-rest Support Vector Machine Classifier (SVC) offering the best performance with an AUC of 0.98. We also conducted a qualitative spot-check of the results to verify that the assigned themes were appropriate.

table 2 contains the list of curated themes and the associated number of interview TOCs that were classified as belonging to the theme.

B.3 Thematic Embeddings

To capture additional semantic similarities beyond what could be established from the POHA metadata, we utilized embeddings generated by Large Language Models (LLMs). Specifically, we employed OpenAI's `text-embedding-ada-002` model.

Given that individual sections specified in the Table of Contents (TOC) headers could fall into multiple themes, we designed our approach to focus the embeddings on specific themes. This was crucial because themes in personal narratives often intersect; for instance, discussions of expulsions are frequently preceded by accounts of Zionist attacks.

To ensure the embeddings were theme-specific, we constructed prompts by prepending a thematic instruction to the text. The instructions were provided in both English and Arabic to avoid potential biases arising from language differences. Experiments showed no significant differences between the two languages; however, we proceeded with the Arabic prompt for consistency. The instructions used were:

```
Represent the following interview
    transcript for analyzing the theme
```

Listing 3: Instruction prepended to generate embeddings (in English)

A key challenge was generating a single representation per theme in an interview. Often, multiple headers pertained to the same theme, and individual sections could exceed the model's maximum context window of 8,091 tokens. To address this, we divided the interview texts into manageable chunks, each prepended with the instruction. We

Table 2: Themes and count of interviews headers with such theme, roughly corresponds to the number of interviews that contain the theme. In bold we note the themes that we focus on for analysis because they are both more related to the Nakba topically and are prevalent as well

Theme	TOCs count
Zionist Attacks During and After the Nakba	714
Community Life and Social Dynamics	697
Cultural Life and Folklore	580
Exile, Expulsion, and Displacement	548
Resistance and Popular Struggles	505
Socio-Economic Life and Conditions	327
British Mandate Colonialism and Occupation	259
Refugee life and conditions	255
Childhood and Family Life	233
Agriculture and Land	140
Reflections and Final Thoughts	51
Women's Roles	40
Education and Intellectual Life	27

obtained embeddings for each chunk and then combined them using max-pooling to create a single representation for the theme within the interview.

We performed validation procedures to ensure the quality of the embeddings. For instance, we verified that embeddings for the same theme were, on average, more similar to each other than to embeddings from different themes—a consistency that was consistently observed. The cosine similarities ranged from approximately 0.30 to 0.80, with the average often exceeding 0.60.

These thematic embeddings allowed us to capture nuanced semantic relationships within the interviews, facilitating more sophisticated analyses of the narratives.

B.4 Additional model details

B.4.1 Weighted Location Models

In our analysis of pairwise comparisons of interview similarity based on the same place of origin and the same place of residence, we identified a significant imbalance in the data. Most interview pairs did not share either place of origin or residence, and less than 1% of the data involved pairs sharing both place of residence and place of origin. table 3 details the counts for each condition comparing same origin and same residence. Addressing this imbalance was crucial, especially since we aimed to use this data for the analysis of themes, where the data would be further subdivided.

To mitigate the effects of this imbalance, we incorporated weights into the regression estimations of the mixed models. Specifically, we used an *inverse frequency weighting scheme*, where each observation is weighted inversely proportional to its frequency in the data. This means that rarer combinations (e.g., interview pairs sharing both place of origin and residence) receive higher weights, ensuring they have a proportionate influence on the model despite their low occurrence.

Table 3: Prevalence of conditions comparing same origin and residence among pairs of interviews in the data.

Location Pair Condition	Pairs
Same Origin +Same Residence	251036
Same Origin +Diff. Residence	18990
Diff. Origin +Same Residence	3338
Diff Origin +Diff Residence	634

We applied the same weights, defined by the general prevalence in our sample, to compute models for both Bag-of-Words (BoW) based representations—which use all interviews—and for themes, which involve pairings of interviews matching on the same theme. This approach ensured consistency in the weights applied to the observations across different analyses.

B.5 Bayesian Models

To complement the frequentist mixed models and to better understand the potential behavior of the parameters, we also implemented the models using a Bayesian framework. We estimated the parameters using Markov Chain Monte Carlo methods provided by the `brms` library (Bürkner, 2017), which utilizes the `Stan` (Stan Development Team, 2024) language and sampler to implement Bayesian multilevel models similar to the `lmer` models.

We chose Bayesian models because they allow for the estimation of credible intervals for the parameters, providing a probabilistic interpretation of the parameter estimates. This enabled us to confirm our results on the weak association of the parameters and to understand the variability in our estimates more clearly.

The models followed almost identical specifications to those described in section 4.3, both mathematically and in the code implementation. We delineate them here following.

To compare similarities σ_{ij}^T (per theme) based on location within a Bayesian framework, we use the model

$$\sigma_{ij}^T \sim \mathcal{N}(\mu_{ij}, \sigma^2), \quad (4)$$

$$\mu_{ij} = \beta_0 + \beta_1 s_{ij}^o + \beta_2 s_{ij}^r + \beta_3 (s_{ij}^o \times s_{ij}^r) + u_i + v_j, \quad (5)$$

where u_i and v_j are random effects associated with interviews i and j, respectively, accounting for unobserved heterogeneity. σ^2 is the residual variance (not similarity).

We specify the following prior distributions for the parameters:

$$\begin{aligned}
\beta_0 &\sim \text{Normal}(0, 0.1), \\
\beta_k &\sim \text{Normal}(0, 1), \quad \text{for } k = 1, 2, 3, \\
u_i &\sim \text{Normal}(0, \sigma_u^2), \quad \sigma_u \sim \text{Exponential}(1), \\
v_j &\sim \text{Normal}(0, \sigma_v^2), \quad \sigma_v \sim \text{Exponential}(1), \\
\sigma &\sim \text{Exponential}(1).
\end{aligned}$$

In this Bayesian model:

- β_0 is the intercept with a prior centered at 0 and a small variance, reflecting our initial belief about the central tendency of similarities.
- β_1, β_2, and β_3 are the coefficients for the fixed effects with priors reflecting moderate uncertainty.
- σ_u and σ_v are the standard deviations of the random effects, modeled with Exponential priors to ensure positivity and to express a preference for smaller values.
- The residual standard deviation σ also follows an Exponential prior, promoting regularization.

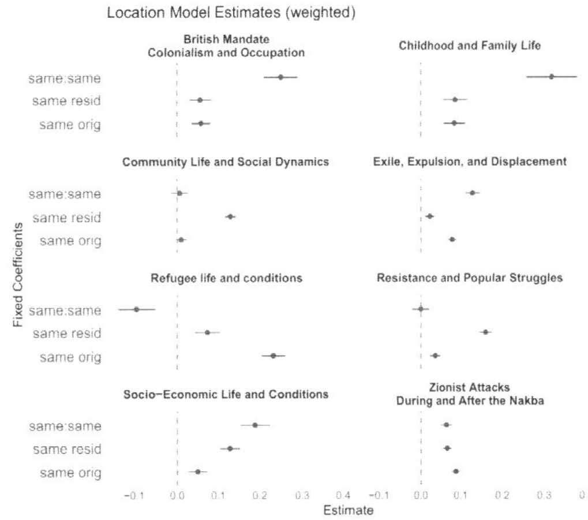

Figure 6: Mixed model for location estimates for all themes, following the same description as section 5.1.

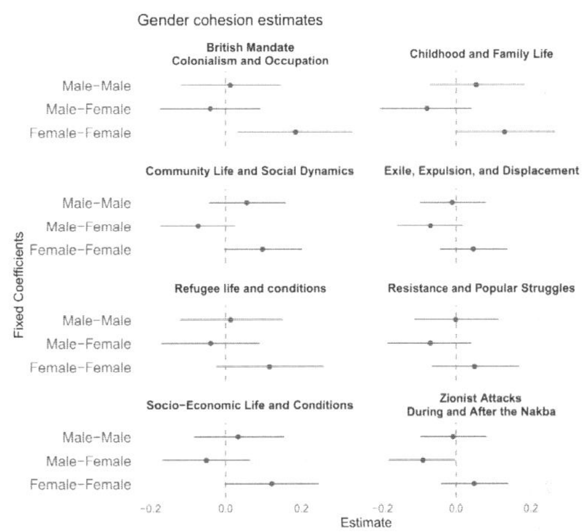

Figure 7: Mixed model for gender estimates for all themes, following the same description as section 5.1.

The gender model follows a very similar definition but uses the parameters as described in section 4.3

We show the results of the Bayesian models in section appendix C.2

C Results Appendix

C.1 Model results for all themes

In the main body, we selected the results for the key 4 themes as being more significant for our analysis perspective on the Nakba. Here we add the thematic plots of all themes, both for location (fig. 6) and gender (fig. 7).

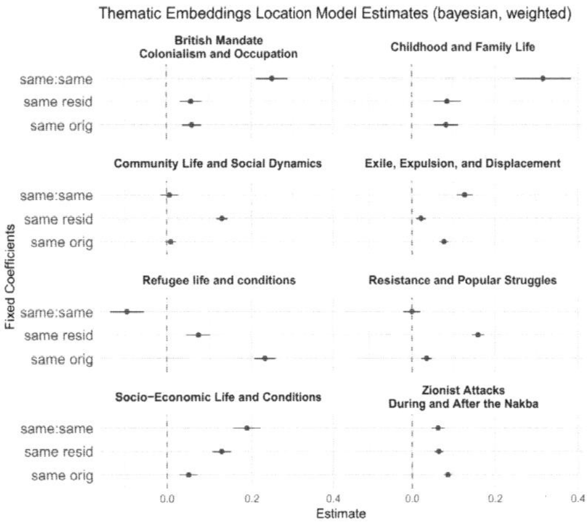

Figure 8: Bayesian model estimates with credible intervals for the models predicting similarity in themes according to location matches of the pairings of interviews.

C.2 Bayesian model results

Here we add the results of the Bayesian models on themes. Note here that although the representation we chose is the same, the intervals here mean credible intervals instead of confidence intervals. Results are for bayesian model for location cohesion analysis on fig. 8 and for gender cohesion analysis in fig. 9

C.3 Embedding similarity insights

POHA contains rich information about experiences in different parts of pre-1948 Palestine. Here, we present an additional table of contents-based plots.

We also explore the coocurrence of different themes. The theme scheme that we use engenders significant overlap among a couple of categories—namely, Zionist attacks, expulsion, and resistance.

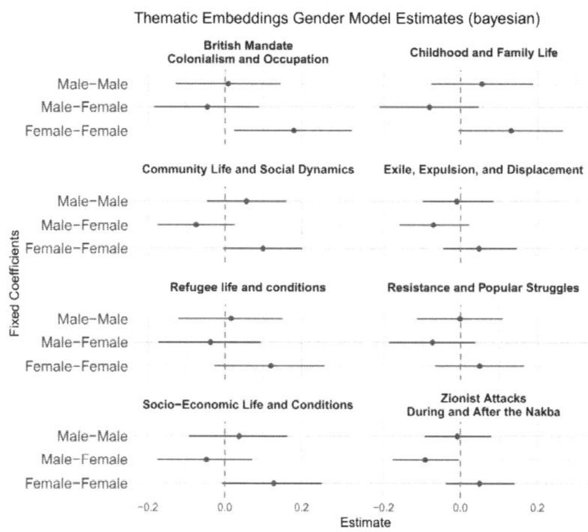

Figure 9: Bayesian model estimates with credible intervals for the models predicting similarity in themes according to gender matches of the pairings of interviews.

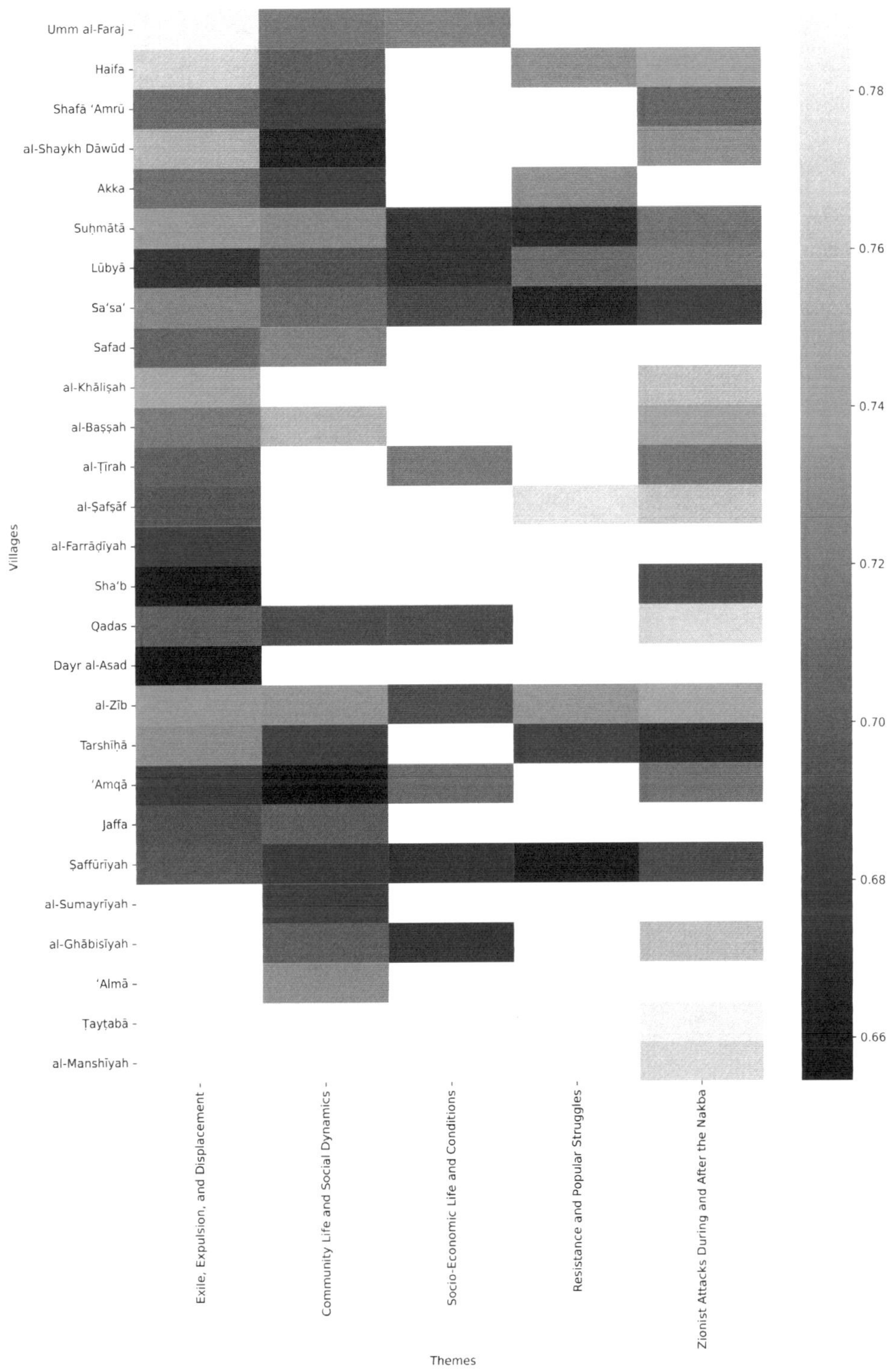

Figure 10: Average cosine similarity between the embeddings of two interview segments on the labeled theme for every place of origin in POHA. A blank rectangle represents a lack of data.

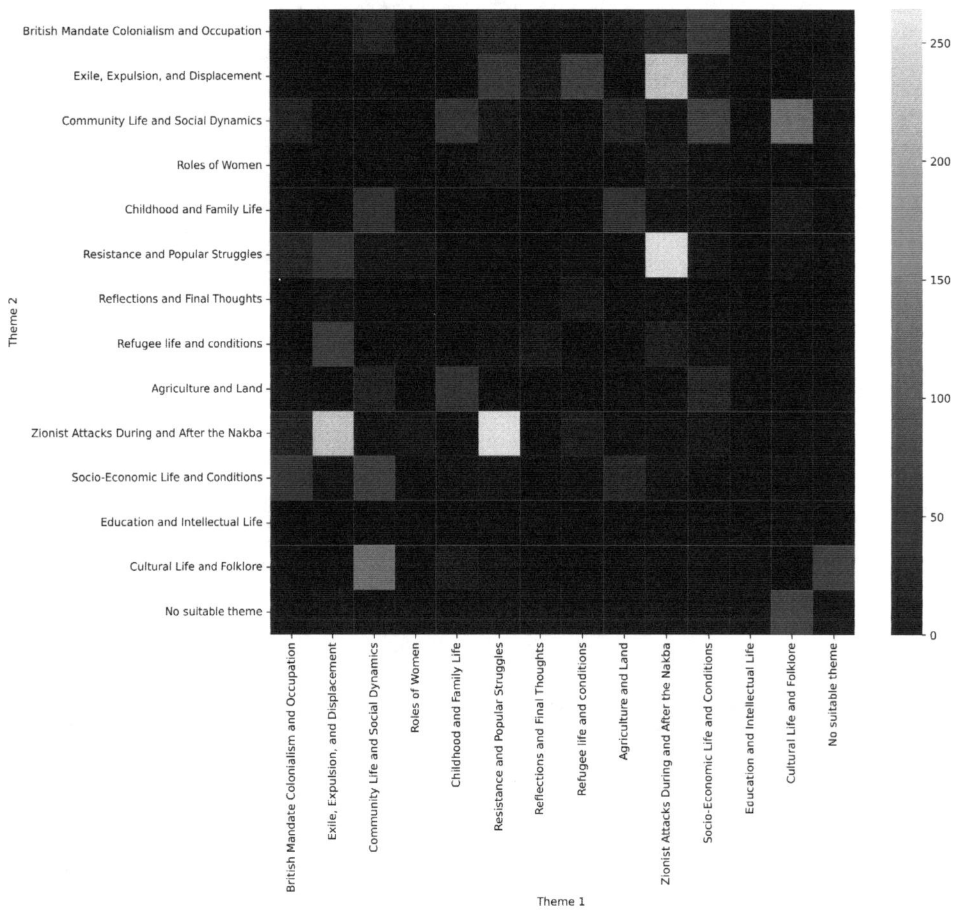

Figure 11: Cooccurrence between themes in POHA interview segments (i.e., the number of headers for which one theme and another both apply).

The Missing Cause: An Analysis of Causal Attributions in Reporting on Palestine

Paulina Garcia-Corral
Hertie School
corral@hertie-school.org

Hannah Béchara
Hertie School
bechara@hertie-school.org

Krishnamoorthy Manohara
Hertie School
manohara@hertie-school.org

Slava Jankin
University of Birmingham
v.jankin@bham.ac.uk

Abstract

Missing cause bias is a specific type of bias in media reporting that relies on consistently omitting causal attribution to specific events, for example when omitting specific actors as causes of incidents. Identifying these patterns in news outlets can be helpful in assessing the level of bias present in media content. In this paper, we examine the prevalence of this bias in reporting on Palestine by identifying causal constructions in headlines. We compare headlines from three main news media outlets: CNN, the BBC, and AJ (AlJazeera), that cover the Israel-Palestine conflict. We also collect and compare these findings to data related to the Ukraine-Russia war to analyze editorial style within press organizations. We annotate a subset of this data and evaluate two causal language models (UniCausal and GPT-4o) for the identification and extraction of causal language in news headlines. Using the top performing model, GPT-4o, we machine annotate the full corpus and analyze missing bias prevalence within and across news organizations. Our findings reveal that BBC headlines tend to avoid directly attributing causality to Israel for the violence in Gaza, both when compared to other news outlets, and to its own reporting on other conflicts.

1 Introduction

Media reporting of conflict is often perceived by various stakeholders as biased. Headlines, in particular, are frequently criticized for being misleading, incomplete, or lacking context, which can skew the information presented. Just last year, the BBC reported more than 1,500 complaints over Israel-Palestine coverage, being accused of bias from both sides of the conflict[1]. A significant source of contention is the lack of causal attribution in events. Reports may state that citizens "die" rather than are "killed", or that hospitals are "destroyed" rather than "bombed" by specific actors.

Missing cause bias (Gentzkow and Shapiro, 2006), is a special type of information omission that consistently omits attributing responsibility, placing blame or giving praise to specific acts or actors that caused an event, such as passively describing a violent attack by using sentences that do not contain a subject, or using the passive voice to avoid naming an actor. In the past year, the subject of missing cause bias has become controversial in the media's coverage of the Israel-Palestine conflict. In July 2024, activists decried the BBC's coverage of the death of Mohammad Bhar by using the passive voice and failing to mention the cause of his death[2]. In August 2024, the BBC changed headlines after criticism from the Israeli Foreign Ministry for failing to mention the fact that a bombing was triggered after rockets where allegedly fired from Gaza[3].

In this paper, we propose using a causal relation extraction model to machine annotate online newspaper headlines, to measure missing cause in news media. By using causal relation extraction models to perform span detection of cause and effect (Drury et al., 2022), we can quantify and compare assigned causes and omitted causes after matching articles that cover the same events. The main contributions of this paper include:

- Measure causal headline prevalence
- Measure the prevalence of omitted cause bias
- Control for editorial style by doing a cross

[1] https://www.theguardian.com/media/2023/oct/16/bbc-gets-1500-complaints-over-israel\-hamas-coverage-split-50-50-on-each-side

[2] https://www.newarab.com/news/shameful-bbc-story-israels-killing-disabled-man-revised

[3] https://x.com/EmmanuelNahshon/status/1027440634968326149

Proceedings of the Proceedings of the 1st International Workshop on Nakba Narratives as Language Resources, pages 103–113
January 20, 2025.

comparison of headlines from the Russia-Ukraine war

2 Related Work

2.1 Automatic Bias Detection

While media bias has a long tradition in the realms of social sciences, it remains a relatively young research topic in Natural Language Processing. Common NLP techniques such as sentiment analysis (Lin et al., 2011), topic modeling (Best et al., 2005) and lexical feature analysis (Hube and Fetahu, 2018) have been used to detect media bias. More recently, supervised machine learning classifiers trained on transformer-based models have achieved better results although some underlying issues persist (Rodrigo-Ginés et al., 2024). Altogether, media bias is a a multi-faceted problem with several competing definitions, and bias detection remains a complex task.

Several researchers have addressed the detection of media bias as a classification problem. This classification can be binary (either bias exists or it does not exist), or it can be treated as a multi-classification problem. One such paper, which rates articles by degree of polarization, identifies a set of 130 content-based features that span 7 categories: structure, complexity, sentiment, bias, morality, topic and engagement, and show that they all contribute towards media bias detection (Horne et al., 2018). In contrast, media bias has also been classified by its stance towards an event (Cremisini et al., 2019) or by its place on the political compass (Baly et al., 2020).

Given that supervised classification usually uses case-specific annotations, there are some relevant attempts for our case study. To detect media bias using NLP, Al-Sarraj and Lubbad (2018) compared three supervised machine learning algorithms trained on an Israel-Palestine conflict news dataset, a SVM with bio-grams achieved the highest performance of 91.76% accuracy and F1-score of 91.46%. Wei and Santos (2020) collected data from history book excerpts and newspaper articles of the same conflict, and trained a sequence classifiers to predict authorship provenance. Their best model to detect narrative origin achieved an F1-score of 85.10% for history book excerpts and 91.90% for newspaper articles. Additionally, Cremisini et al. (2019) manually classified pro-Russia and pro-Western bias of news articles. Using a baseline SVM classifier with doc2vec embeddings, they achieved an F1-score of 86%. However, their results suggest that models may be learning journalistic styles rather than actually modeling bias. Similarly, Potash et al. (2017) applied a novel methodology to a gold-labeled set of articles annotated for Pro-Russian bias, where a Naive Bayes classifier achieved 82.60% accuracy and a feed-forward neural networks achieved 85.60% accuracy.

2.2 Causal Language Modeling

Causality mining is the task of identifying causal language that connects events in a text. It is a subtask of information extraction, where causal relations are identified and mined from a collection of documents (Drury et al., 2022). Causal language can be expressed explicitly or implicitly. The former tends to use connectors such as "because" or "therefore" to signal a causal relationship between events. Causal verbs can also be used to express causality. Causality can be found inter or intra-sententially. Because causal language is a linguistically, syntactically and semantically complex construction used to express causal reasoning (Solstad and Bott, 2017; Neeleman and Van de Koot, 2012), it tends to rely on contextual information, and yields low inter-annotator agreement when annotated by humans (Dunietz et al., 2017).

Causal language is usually modelled in three steps: 1) causal sequence classification, 2) causal extraction and 3) pair classification (Tan et al., 2023). Causal mining used to be based on pattern matching by identifying causal connectors (Drury et al., 2022). Advances in machine learning allowed for statistical pattern recognition models, such as SVMs and Bayesian models (Hidey and Mckeown, 2016; Zhao et al., 2017). With the introduction of deep learning, a combination of architectures such as CNNs (Kruengkrai et al., 2017; de Silva et al., 2017), CRFs (Fu et al., 2011), or LSTMs (Li et al., 2019; Dasgupta et al., 2018) improved previous results. Moreover, fine-tuning transformer-based models such as BERT significantly improved both classification and extraction capabilities across domains (Yang et al., 2023; Tan et al., 2023; Khetan et al., 2022).

More recently, LLMs have been investigated for their causal extraction capabilities. Takayanagi et al. (2024) assessed the performance of ChatGPT across both domain-specific and non-English datasets. They found that while ChatGPT demonstrates a baseline proficiency in causal text mining, it can be outperformed by earlier models when sufficient training data is available. Similarly, Hobbhahn et al. (2022) explored GPT-3's capacity to identify causes and effects. Their results emphasize the significance of prompting, which suggests that GPT-3's predictions may be influenced more by the form of the input than by its content, raising questions about the model's true comprehension of causality. Luo et al. (2024) designed an LLM implementation that modifies causal datasets to optimize Event Causality Extraction. Experiments on both Chinese and English event causality extraction datasets achieved a 92% and 93% accuracy after using their proposed framework.

Furthermore, Causal language modeling has been tested on diverse news corpora. For example, Gusev and Tikhonov (2022) introduced HeadlineCause, a dataset annotated for implicit causal relations between paired news headlines in English (5,000 pairs) and Russian (9,000 pairs), annotated via crowdsourcing. Their XLM-RoBERTa-based model achieved 83.5% accuracy in English and 87.9% in Russian. Similarly, Tan et al. (2022) annotated protest-related news articles to create the Causal News Corpus, containing 3,559 sentences. They achieved an 81.20% F1-score on the test set and 83.46% in five-fold cross-validation. Additionally, Mariko et al. (2022) introduced FinCausal, a dataset designed to detect causal relationships in financial news. Lastly, Garcia Corral et al. (2024) developed a dataset to benchmark causal language detection that included data fro political press conferences.

Recent advancements in language modeling have enabled significant progress in causal event relation extraction. These advancements have, in turn, translated into significant improvements in downstream tasks that rely on causality mining to derive meaning from textual data. For example, Sun et al. (2024) achieved state-of-the-art results on the *Choice of Plausible Event in Sequence* (COPES) dataset. Their approach led to a 3.6%–16.6% improvement in correlation with human ratings in downstream narrative quality evaluation tasks, highlighting the importance of causality in computational narrative understanding. Similarly, Hosseini et al. (2019) demonstrated that causally and semantically coherent documents are more likely to be shared on social media, finding that coherence strongly influences online sharing behavior. These findings highlight how causal event detection can be leveraged for understanding textual organization and extracting key insights, such as underlying bias or positionality.

3 Methodology

To measure and analyze missing cause bias, we prepared a data selection and model evaluation pipeline to machine-annotate newspaper headlines at scale. We focused on headlines, as opposed to full articles, as they are optimized for contextual effect and processing effort, while directing readers to construct the optimal context for interpretation (Dor, 2003). This aligns with recent research that has shown that people can make inference from causal explanations (Kirfel et al., 2022). In other words, headlines give just enough information for readers to reconstruct the news story via inference, and omitting or including causal attributions in the headlines directly allows for implicit biases to be communicated without further information. Our data analysis and evaluation strategy can be divided into the following steps:

- Step 1: Data collection – We collected 4,993 headlines from AJ, the BBC and CNN, between May 2023 to February 2024. We scraped the Middle East and Europe sections of their online webpages, and filtered for relevant articles by searching for keywords around the Israel-Palestine and the Russia-Ukraine war.

- Step 2: Human Annotation – we labeled a subset of 541 random sentence to obtain a human "gold standard" for evaluation.

- Step 3: Model Comparison – We compared two models, one Bert-based and one LLM model, evaluated against the gold standard built in step 3.

- Step 4: Machine-Annotate Corpus – Using the best-performing model, we annotated the selected headlines for causal labels and causal spans.

- Step 5: Compare Explicit Cause Presence – Finally, after matching events across press organizations, we compared explicit cause presence across the different conflicts holding the event constant.

3.1 Data Collection

Our data collection process consisted of selecting three global news media outlets from different regions of the world, looking to maximize coverage diversity. We chose Al-Jazeera (AJ), British Broadcasting News (BBC) and Cable Network News (CNN). AlJazeera English is an English-language news channel headquartered in the Middle East and funded in part by the Qatari government. The BBC (British Broadcasting Corporation) is a British public service broadcaster, the oldest and largest in the United Kingdom, and is funded principally by a license fee charged by the British Government. Finally, CNN is a multinational news channel and website operating out of the USA. Both BBC and AJ can be considered "state media" and mainstream of their respective governments, for the purposes of this study. To include a third English language organization from a different region, we included CNN, a private American news broadcasting agency.

In order to establish that the differences in the prevalence of causal headlines and the causal attributions are not merely stylistic choices, we selected two on-going conflicts in two regions of the world. We collected data from the Ukraine-Russia war, and the Israel-Palestine war. We scraped the online web sections of AJ Ukraine- Russia war, and AJ Israel-Palestine Conflict, BBC Middle East, BBC Ukraine, and CNN-Europe and CNN-Middle East between 17/05/2023 and 17/02/2024. We filtered out any articles that made no mention of "Israel", "Palestine", "Russia" and "Ukraine" to create the final dataset of headlines. Table 1 describes the composition of our dataset, listing the number of articles and their proportion to the total dataset (N). Table 2 shows a cross-section headlines from each region and source. All the data will be available in our repository.

Region	Source	N
Pal	AJ	1,251 (0.48)
Pal	BBC	792 (0.30)
Pal	CNN	567 (0.22)
Ukr	AJ	1,018 (0.43)
Ukr	BBC	784 (0.33)
Ukr	CNN	581 (0.24)

Table 1: Statistics for the corpus of all collected news articles. "Region" is where the conflict is occurring, "Source" refers to the news organization (AJ, BBC or CNN), and N refers to the total number of articles with the relative proportion between parenthesis.

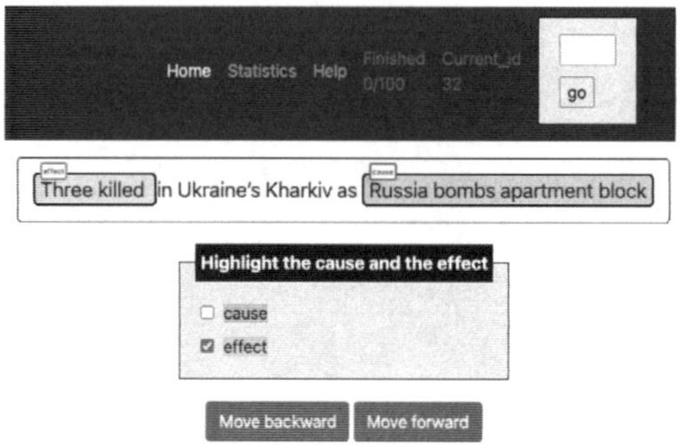

Figure 1: Potato annotation software example screen. We can see one headline from the Ukraine-Russia conflict with two spans selected for "cause" and "effect".

3.2 Corpus Annotation

In order to evaluate the selected model's accuracy in both the binary cause identification and span detection tasks, we created a gold standard of human-annotated data. We randomly selected 541 random headlines weighted across region and media outlets. We used a combination of Prolific[4] and Potato (Pei et al., 2022), a freely available web-based annotation tool which integrates with Prolific (See Figure 1 as reference). We hired and trained 8 students to annotate using the *Bring your own participants* (BYOP) option in Prolific. They annotated each headline's cause and effect from the subset we described in Section 3.1. The full statistics are detailed in Table 3. The human-annotated data has a distribution of 61% to 39% not causal to causal proportion, which is higher than what is expected from natural occurring (Dunietz et al., 2017). This might be due to a headline effect, where newspapers use causality more often than in natural occurring text, or a stylistic choice according to media organization, where click bait has heavily influence headlines style, such as phrasing headlines as questions. Alternatively, it could be an annotator drop-out rate effect where all the data was not consistently annotated across the weighted preselection.

We aggregated the causal label (0,1) by majority voting, and the causal spans using Overlap-Based Consensus, as we expect spans may vary slightly. To quantify the agreement between spans from different annotators, we used Intersection over Union (IoU) and a threshold of $\tau = 0.5$. Table 3 shows the descriptive statistics of human annotations.

[4]https://www.prolific.com/data-annotation

Date	Text	Region	Source
2024/02/12	Israel kills dozens in Rafah strikes, frees two captives	Palestine	AJ
2023/06/13	'Massive' Russian missile attack on Ukraine's Kryvyi Rih city	Ukraine	AJ
2024/01/26	Gaza war: ICJ to rule on call for Israel to stop military action - BBC News	Palestine	BBC
2024/01/28	Ukraine says it has uncovered major arms corruption - BBC News	Ukraine	BBC
2024/02/15	Israeli special forces raid largest functioning hospital in Gaza	Palestine	CNN
2023/08/24	Ukraine says it landed troops on the shores of Russian-occupied Crimea	Ukraine	CNN

Table 2: Example of headlines collected for the headline corpus from AJ, the BBC and CNN, for Middle East and Europe conflicts.

Region	Source	Causal	N	Perc
Palestine	Al Jazeera	0	73	0.549
		1	60	0.451
	BBC	0	53	0.602
		1	35	0.398
	CNN	0	43	0.597
		1	29	0.403
Ukraine	Al Jazeera	0	77	0.687
		1	35	0.313
	BBC	0	48	0.686
		1	22	0.314
	CNN	0	38	0.576
		1	28	0.424

Table 3: Human annotated subset and label statistics according to Region, Source and Causal headline label. "Perc" refers to the percentage of causal v. not causal headline in relation to the Region, Source and Causal label.

3.3 Model evaluation

To generate the machine annotations, we performed classification and causal span detection on all the collected headlines using two models. For both models, we ran inference with the out-of-the-box versions and did not perform fine-tuning with our human labeled data.

1 **UniCausal** (Tan et al., 2023), a BERT (Devlin et al., 2018) based causal language model fine-tuned on six, high-quality human-annotated corpora for causality. UniCausal is especially well-suited for our task as five of these six causal corpora include newspaper text. UniCausal achieved a 70.10% Binary F1-score for sequence classification, and a 52.42% F1-score on span detection on the overall corpus.

2 **GPT-4o** (OpenAI), a multilingual, multi-modal generative pre-trained transformer developed by OpenAI. Model hyper-parameters and prompt are included in the Appendix (c.f. Section A.2).

Model	Accuracy	Prec	Recall	F1
GPT-4o	0.746	0.649	0.751	0.696
Unicausal	0.712	0.685	0.478	0.563

Table 4: GPT-4o and Unicausal model results for causal sequence classification against human labeled data

Table 4 and 5 report the results of GPT-4o and UniCausal on both sequence and spans detection. In both tasks, we see better performance from GPT-4o, which achieved an overall F1-score of 70% on binary sequence classification, with a high accuracy of 75%. Meanwhile, Unicausal achieved an F1-score of 56%, with a with a high accuracy of 71% but a low recall value of 48%, highlighting the model's difficulty in distinguishing between classes. For causal span extraction, evaluation is based on the exact match between predicted and human labeled entities. We used Seqeval (Nakayama, 2018) library for evaluation metric computing. The difference between model performance is underscored even more in causal extraction. While GPT-4o achieves an overall F1-score of 42% in causal labeling (43% for Cause and 40% for Effect), Unicausal dramatically underperforms with a score of 9% overall F1-score (9.5% for Cause and 8% for Effect). In line with previous related work, our results demonstrate that for smaller, domain specific datasets, LLMs can outperform causal sequence identification and span extraction when tested against out-of-the-box, not fine-tuned smaller models. We include confusion matrices to analyze classification error type in Figures 2 and 3.

Model	Span	Accuracy	Precision	Recall	F1
GPT-4o	Cause		0.375	0.521	0.436
	Effect		0.372	0.448	0.406
	Overall	0.755	0.374	0.481	0.420
Unicausal	Cause		0.107	0.084	0.095
	Effect		0.100	0.070	0.083
	Overall	0.714	0.106	0.076	0.089

Table 5: Using Seqeval, reported metrics for GPT-4o and Unicausal causal span detection against human labeled data

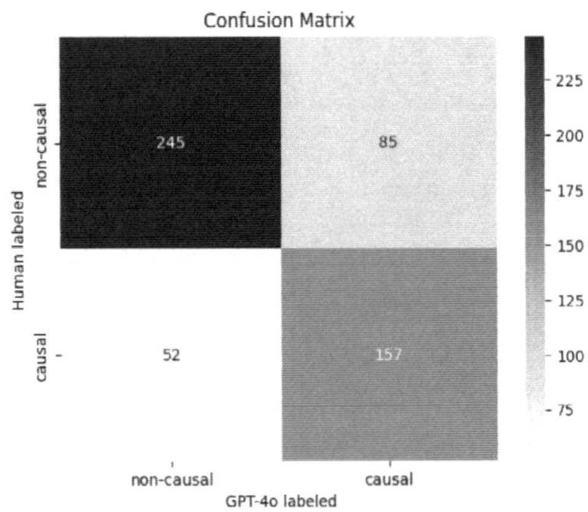

Figure 2: GPT-4o confusion matrix for sequence evaluation. The model achieves a reasonably high recall (75%), capturing most of the true causal instances. However, the model produces a fair number of false positives (85).

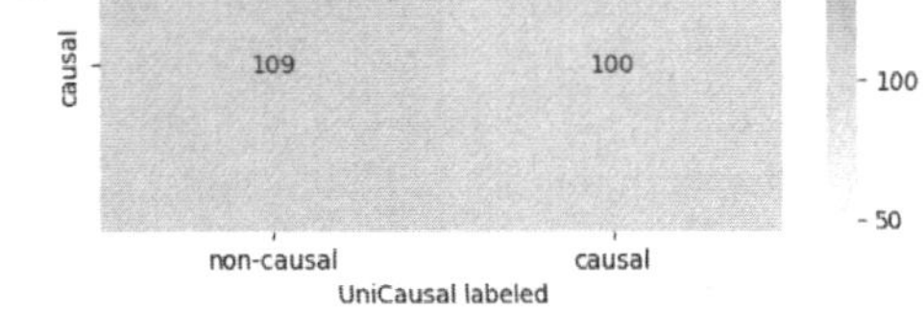

Figure 3: UniCausal confusion matrix for sequence evaluation. The model has a low recall (47%), failing to capture true causal instances. However, the model has a better precision compared to GPT-4o, better discerning true causal instances (100).

3.4 Matching Events with Cosine Similarity

To identify related articles across the three news organizations, and qualitatively analyze cause and effect spans, we matched headlines that refer to the same event across the news media outlets. To this end, we employed a temporal matching algorithm that linked articles from one source to another based on publication dates that fell within ±1 day of each other. Then, to evaluate the semantic alignment between matched pairs, we utilized a sentence-transformer model to compute cosine similarity scores between article headlines. Finally, all semantic similarity scores above 0.70 where qualitatively analyzed to confirm that the headlines were referring to the same event, and considered a complete match. Table 6 shows a sample of these aligned headlines.

4 Results

4.1 Sequence Classification

Based on our results, we compared the spans annotated by GPT-4o on all the collected headlines. We found that while 50% of AJ's headlines pertaining to Israel and Palestine are marked as causal, the same is true for only 35% of the BBC's headlines. CNN's headlines, on the other hand, were closer to AJ's in that 48% of headlines were marked as having a causal construction. The discrepancy between AJ and BBC diminishes when we look at headlines pertaining to the Ukraine-Russia conflict, where 38% of AJ's headlines are causal and 40% of BBC's headlines are causal. CNN's headlines, on the hand, do not vary greatly between regions. These results are summarized in Table 8. While these results give us a superficial look at how causality varies between regions and outlets, some of these differences can be attributed to editorial styles of each outlet. We therefore take a closer look at what is being left out.

4.2 Cause Identification

For a more fine-grained analysis, we take a closer look at the "cause" and "effect" spans annotated in the data. We selected for sentences in which the "effect" span includes references to violent acts as they tend to be contested in the context of conflict reporting. This search was based on relevant keywords. These keywords include the words: kill, murder, destroy, burn, dead/die, shot/shoot, strike, bomb, and attack.

AJ	BBC	CNN
Senior Hamas official Saleh al-Arouri killed in Beirut suburb	Hamas deputy leader Saleh al-Arouri killed in Beirut blast - BBC News	Senior Hamas leader killed in Beirut blast, heightening fears of wider regional conflict
Israel and Hamas agree to extend truce by two days, Qatar says	Israel-Hamas truce in Gaza extended for two days, Qatar says - BBC News	Deal reached to extend Israel-Hamas truce by two days, Qatar says
Gaza authorities say hundreds killed in Israeli air raid on hospital	Hospital blast in Gaza City kills hundreds - health officials - BBC News	Between 100 and 300 believed killed in Gaza hospital blast, according to preliminary US intelligence assessment
Family of Al Jazeera Gaza bureau chief killed in Israeli air raid	Wael Al-Dahdouh: Al Jazeera reporter's family killed in Gaza strike - BBC News	Journalist's family was killed in Gaza strike, says Al Jazeera

Table 6: A Sample of Aligned Headlines Using Temporal algorithm and Cosine Similarity scores to match.

Region	Source	Causal	N	Perc
Palestine	Al Jazeera	0	618	0.494
		1	633	0.506
	BBC	0	508	0.641
		1	284	0.359
	CNN	0	292	0.515
		1	275	0.485
Ukraine	Al Jazeera	0	630	0.619
		1	388	0.381
	BBC	0	465	0.593
		1	319	0.407
	CNN	0	284	0.489
		1	297	0.511

Table 7: GPT-4o machine labeled data contingency table by location, source and causal distribution of headlines.

Source	Isr-Pal	Rus-Ukr
AJ	50.6%	38%
BBC	35.8%	40%
CNN	48.5%	51%

Table 8: Percentage of positive sequences (causal sentences) in headlines by region and source as annotated by GPT-4o

Cause	AJ	BBC	CNN
Israel	40%	13%	25%
Russia	39%	34%	33%

Table 9: BBC vs AJ Headline Breakdown of Causal Sentences that Reference the Cause in Headlines Covering Violent Deaths

We then queried the cause span of the positive class for actors involved in the conflicts. Our aim was to determine whether or not there is a discrepancy between conflicts and outlets when it comes to directly identifying the actors. The results show a large gap between the number of headlines that explicitly name the cause in the headlines that refer Palestinian deaths. BBC's causal spans include Israel only 13% of the time, as opposed to AJ's 40% of the time and CNN's 25%. The results are summarized in Table 9. This discrepancy, while observable in the Russia-Ukraine headlines, is much less pronounced, suggesting a selective missing cause bias by conflict.

4.3 Direct Headline Comparison

In order to get a more conclusive look at the discrepancy between BBC, CNN and AJ's reporting on the Israel Palestine conflict, we further investigate a subset of sentences aligned using cosine similarity. We matched the headlines across all 3 outlets, leading to a final dataset of 50 headlines matched in this way. This allowed us to ensure that we are looking at headlines that cover the same event, and rule out the possibility that the missing cause bias that we observe is simply a result of these outlets focusing on different stories. We then filter out these headlines further to isolate only headlines that refer to violent acts, and find that the difference only diminishes very slightly. As seen in Table 10, only 10% of BBC and 17% of CNN's headlines explicitly name Israel as the cause of this violence, a opposed to 32% of AJ's headlines. To extend the generalizability of the findings, we also extended the same methods to the Russia-Ukraine reporting. We aligned the headlines between all three outlets using cosine similarity and once again directly compare direct references to the cause in the headlines. The results are also reported in Table 10, and compared directly to the Israel-Palestine results.

Cause	AJ	BBC	CNN
Israel	32%	10%	17%
Russia	50%	41%	41%

Table 10: AJ vs BBC vs CNN Headline Breakdown of Causal Sentences that Reference the Cause in Headlines Covering Violent Deaths in Aligned Headlines

Overall, our analysis shows that BBC headlines on the Israel-Palestine conflict often avoiding direct attribution of causality to the responsible actors for the deaths and destruction in Gaza. For example, phrases like "reported killed in latest strikes" or "scores were killed in the camp" are used without explicitly identifying Israel as the cause. This is evident in that only 10% of causal sentences that describe violence will attribute the cause directly the responsible party. This tendency reflects an implicit bias through omission or missing cause bias. This difference is highlighted in the example below, which describes the headlines for February 2, 2024. In all three headlines, the cause is emphasized in bold text.

AJ *__Israel__ kills dozens in Rafah strikes, frees two captives.*

BBC *Israel rescues two hostages in Rafah amid deadly strikes - BBC News.*

CNN *Israeli forces rescue 2 hostages as __airstrikes__ kill around 100 Palestinians in Rafah.*

5 Discussion and Conclusions

In this paper, we explored the use of causal language in media reporting on Israel and Palestine and how its detection can act as an indicator of bias, offering a window into the subtle ways in which narratives are shaped. We compared headlines from three different media outlets, AJ, BBC and CNN, pertaining to their reporting on the escalation of the Israel-Palestine conflict. We directly compared their reporting the Israel-Palestine conflict to their reporting the Russia-Ukraine conflict. Using a state-of-the-art causal extraction method, we automatically classified the headlines as causal and non-causal. We further extracted the cause and effect spans of each of the headlines. A comparison shows a clear bias by omission on the part of the BBC Israel-Palestine reporting, and to a lesser extend to CNN's Israel-Palestine reporting, especially when compared to opposed to AJ's reporting. Furthermore, it showed a clear omission bias when comparing the BBC's reporting to its own reporting on the Russia-Ukraine conflict.

6 Limitations

Our research is not without its limitations. The scope of the study was confined to just three media outlets, which do not represent the entire spectrum of journalistic practices. Further research could expand upon this work and incorporate headlines from different sources, including different languages and from various political leanings. Furthermore, this study focuses on headlines only, as they are crafted to capture the most attention. However, a future avenue of research could also focus on the articles themselves and the causal language and slant present therein.

7 Acknowledgements

The authors thank the DFG (EXC number 2055 – Project number 390715649, SCRIPTS) for providing funding for the annotation efforts. This project has also received funding from the European Union's Horizon Europe research and innovation program under Grant Agreement No 101057131, Climate Action To Advance HeaLthY Societies in Europe (CATALYSE).

References

Wael F. Al-Sarraj and Heba M. Lubbad. 2018. Bias detection of palestinian/israeli conflict in western media: A sentiment analysis experimental study. In *2018 International Conference on Promising Electronic Technologies (ICPET)*, pages 98–103.

Ramy Baly, Georgi Karadzhov, Jisun An, Haewoon Kwak, Yoan Dinkov, Ahmed Ali, James Glass, and Preslav Nakov. 2020. What was written vs. who read it: News media profiling using text analysis and social media context. In *Proceedings of the 58th Annual Meeting of the Association for Computational Linguistics*, pages 3364–3374, Online. Association for Computational Linguistics.

Clive Best, Erik van der Goot, Ken Blackler, Teófilo Garcia, and David Horby. 2005. Europe media monitor. *Technical Report EUR221 73 EN, European Commission.*

Andres Cremisini, Daniela Aguilar, and Mark A. Finlayson. 2019. A challenging dataset for bias detection: The case of the crisis in the ukraine. In *Social, Cultural, and Behavioral Modeling. SBP-BRiMS 2019*, volume 11549 of *Lecture Notes in Computer Science*. Springer, Cham.

Tirthankar Dasgupta, Rupsa Saha, Lipika Dey, and Abir Naskar. 2018. Automatic Extraction of Causal Relations from Text using Linguistically Informed Deep Neural Networks. In *Proceedings of the SIGDIAL 2018 Conference*, pages 12–14, Melbourne, Australia. Association for Computational Linguistics.

Tharini N. de Silva, Xiao Zhibo, Zhao Rui, and Mao Kezhi. 2017. Causal Relation Identification Using Convolutional Neural Networks and Knowledge Based Features. *International Journal of Computer and Systems Engineering*, 11(6).

Jacob Devlin, Ming-Wei Chang, Kenton Lee, and Kristina Toutanova. 2018. BERT: pre-training of deep bidirectional transformers for language understanding. *CoRR*, abs/1810.04805.

Daniel Dor. 2003. On newspaper headlines as relevance optimizers. *Journal of Pragmatics*, 35(5):695–721.

Brett Drury, Hugo Gonçalo Oliveira, and Alneu de Andrade Lopes. 2022. A survey of the extraction and applications of causal relations. *Natural Langauge Engineering*.

Jesse Dunietz, Lori Levin, and Jaime Carbonell. 2017. The BECauSE corpus 2.0: Annotating causality and overlapping relations. In *Proceedings of the 11th Linguistic Annotation Workshop*, pages 95–104, Valencia, Spain. Association for Computational Linguistics.

Jian-Feng Fu, Zong-Tian Liu, Wei Liu, and Wen Zhou. 2011. Event causal relation extraction based on cascaded conditional random fields. *Pattern Recognition and Artificial Intelligence*, 24(4):567.

Paulina Garcia Corral, Hanna Bechara, Ran Zhang, and Slava Jankin. 2024. PolitiCause: An annotation scheme and corpus for causality in political texts. In *Proceedings of the 2024 Joint International Conference on Computational Linguistics, Language Resources and Evaluation (LREC-COLING 2024)*, pages 12836–12845, Torino, Italia. ELRA and ICCL.

Matthew Gentzkow and Jesse M. Shapiro. 2006. Media bias and reputation. *Journal of Political Economy*, 114(2):280–316.

Ilya Gusev and Alexey Tikhonov. 2022. HeadlineCause: A dataset of news headlines for detecting causalities. In *Proceedings of the Thirteenth Language Resources and Evaluation Conference*, pages 6153–6161, Marseille, France. European Language Resources Association.

Christopher Hidey and Kathleen Mckeown. 2016. Identifying Causal Relations Using Parallel Wikipedia Articles. *54th Annual Meeting of the Association for Computational Linguistics, ACL 2016 - Long Papers*, 3:1424–1433. Publisher: Association for Computational Linguistics (ACL).

Marius Hobbhahn, Tom Lieberum, and David Seiler. 2022. Investigating causal understanding in LLMs. In *NeurIPS 2022 Workshop on Causality for Real-world Impact*.

Benjamin Horne, Sara Khedr, and Sibel Adali. 2018. Sampling the news producers: A large news and feature data set for the study of the complex media landscape. In *Proceedings of the International AAAI Conference on Web and Social Media*, volume 12.

P. Hosseini, M. Diab, and D. A. Broniatowski. 2019. Does causal coherence predict online spread of social media? In *Social, Cultural, and Behavioral Modeling. SBP-BRiMS 2019*, volume 11549 of *Lecture Notes in Computer Science*. Springer, Cham.

Christoph Hube and Besnik Fetahu. 2018. Detecting biased statements in wikipedia. In *Companion proceedings of the the web conference 2018*, pages 1779–1786.

Vivek Khetan, Roshni R. Ramnani, Mayuresh Anand, Shubhashis Sengupta, and Andrew E. Fano. 2022. Causal bert: Language models for causality detection between events expressed in text. In *Intelligent Computing. Lecture Notes in Networks and Systems*, volume vol 283.

Lara Kirfel, Thomas Icard, and Tobias Gerstenberg. 2022. Inference from explanation. *Journal of Experimental Psychology: General*, 151(7):1481–1501.

C. Kruengkrai, K. Torisawa, C. Hashimoto, J. Kloetzer, J.-H. Oh, and M. Tanaka. 2017. Improving event causality recognition with multiple background knowledge sources using multi-column convolutional neural networks. In *Proceedings of the AAAI Conference on Artificial Intelligence*, volume 31.

Zhaoning Li, Qi Li, Xiaotian Zou, and Jiangtao Ren. 2019. Causality extraction based on self-attentive bilstm-crf with transferred embeddings. *ArXiv*, abs/1904.07629.

Yu-Ru Lin, James Bagrow, and David Lazer. 2011. More voices than ever? quantifying media bias in networks. In *Proceedings of the international AAAI conference on web and social media*, volume 5, pages 193–200.

Kun Luo, Tong Zhou, Yubo Chen, Jun Zhao, and Kang Liu. 2024. Open event causality extraction by the assistance of LLM in task annotation, dataset, and method. In *Proceedings of the Workshop: Bridging Neurons and Symbols for Natural Language Processing and Knowledge Graphs Reasoning (NeusymBridge) @ LREC-COLING-2024*, pages 33–44, Torino, Italia. ELRA and ICCL.

Dominique Mariko, Hanna Abi-Akl, Kim Trottier, and Mahmoud El-Haj. 2022. The financial causality extraction shared task (FinCausal 2022). In *Proceedings of the 4th Financial Narrative Processing Workshop @LREC2022*, pages 105–107, Marseille, France. European Language Resources Association.

Hiroki Nakayama. 2018. seqeval: A python framework for sequence labeling evaluation. Software available from https://github.com/chakki-works/seqeval.

Ad Neeleman and Hans Van de Koot. 2012. The Linguistic Expression of Causation. In *The Theta System: Argument Structure at the Interface*. Oxford University Press, Oxford.

OpenAI. Gpt-4o system card. `https://openai.com/index/gpt-4o-system-card/`. Accessed: 2024-11-01.

Jiaxin Pei, Aparna Ananthasubramaniam, Xingyao Wang, Naitian Zhou, Apostolos Dedeloudis, Jackson Sargent, and David Jurgens. 2022. Potato: The portable text annotation tool. In *Proceedings of the 2022 Conference on Empirical Methods in Natural Language Processing: System Demonstrations*.

Peter Potash, Alexey Romanov, Mikhail Gronas, Anna Rumshisky, and Mikhail Gronas. 2017. Tracking bias in news sources using social media: the Russia-Ukraine maidan crisis of 2013–2014. In *Proceedings of the 2017 EMNLP Workshop: Natural Language Processing meets Journalism*, pages 13–18, Copenhagen, Denmark. Association for Computational Linguistics.

Francisco-Javier Rodrigo-Ginés, Jorge Carrillo de Albornoz, and Laura Plaza. 2024. A systematic review on media bias detection: What is media bias, how it is expressed, and how to detect it. *Expert Systems with Applications*, 237:121641.

Torgrim Solstad and Oliver Bott. 2017. 619Causality and Causal Reasoning in Natural Language. In *The Oxford Handbook of Causal Reasoning*. Oxford University Press.

Yidan Sun, Qin Chao, and Boyang Li. 2024. Event causality is key to computational story understanding. In *Proceedings of the 2024 Conference of the North American Chapter of the Association for Computational Linguistics: Human Language Technologies (Volume 1: Long Papers)*, pages 3493–3511, Mexico City, Mexico. Association for Computational Linguistics.

Takehiro Takayanagi, Masahiro Suzuki, Ryotaro Kobayashi, Hiroki Sakaji, and Kiyoshi Izumi. 2024. Is chatgpt the future of causal text mining? a comprehensive evaluation and analysis. *Preprint*, arXiv:2402.14484.

Fiona Anting Tan, Ali Hürriyetoğlu, Tommaso Caselli, Nelleke Oostdijk, Tadashi Nomoto, Hansi Hettiarachchi, Iqra Ameer, Onur Uca, Farhana Ferdousi Liza, and Tiancheng Hu. 2022. The causal news corpus: Annotating causal relations in event sentences from news. In *Proceedings of the Thirteenth Language Resources and Evaluation Conference*, pages 2298–2310, Marseille, France. European Language Resources Association.

Fiona Anting Tan, Xinyu Zuo, and See-Kiong Ng. 2023. Unicausal: Unified benchmark and repository for causal text mining. In *Big Data Analytics and Knowledge Discovery - 25th International Conference, DaWaK 2023, Penang, Malaysia, August 28-30, 2023, Proceedings*, volume 14148 of *Lecture Notes in Computer Science*, pages 248–262. Springer.

Jason Wei and Eugene Santos. 2020. Narrative origin classification of israeli-palestinian conflict texts. In *The Thirty-Third International FLAIRS Conference (FLAIRS-33)*.

Jiaoyun Yang, Hao Xiong, Hongjin Zhang, Min Hu, and Ning An. 2023. Causal pattern representation learning for extracting causality from literature. In *Proceedings of the 2022 5th International Conference on Machine Learning and Natural Language Processing*, MLNLP '22, page 229–233, New York, NY, USA. Association for Computing Machinery.

Sendong Zhao, Quan Wang, Sean Massung, Bing Qin, Ting Liu, Bin Wang, and Chengxiang Zhai. 2017. Constructing and Embedding Abstract Event Causality Networks from Text Snippets. In *Proceedings of the Tenth ACM International Conference on Web Search and Data Mining*, pages 335–344. ACM.

A Appendix

In Tables 11, 12, 13 we present the collected and filtered headlines that compose out dataset. The first table shows an almost 50-50 distribution of headlines according to conflict type. Second, we see that the majority of the headlines collected are from AJ, then from the BBC and finally from CNN. This is probably due to regional focus each press organization. Finally, we see a cross table comparison were headline count is distributed according to region and press.

A.1 Full corpus statistics

Region	N
Palestine	2,610 (0.52)
Ukraine	2,383 (0.48)

Table 11: Distribution by region of the whole corpus

Media	N
AJ	2,269 (0.45)
BBC	1,576 (0.32)
CNN	1,148 (0.23)

Table 12: Distribution by media outlet of whole corpus

Region	Source	N
Palestine	AJ	1,251 (0.25)
	BBC	792 (0.16)
	CNN	567 (0.11)
Ukraine	AJ	1,018 (0.20)
	BBC	784 (0.16)
	CNN	581 (0.12)
		4,993 (1.00)

Table 13: Corpus distribution per press organization

A.2 GPT-4o parameter and prompt specifications

To machine annotate all the headlines we used batched inference through the OpenAI API. Prompt was based on task standard prompts reported on LLM causal research papers. We selected it to follow convention and allow for cross comparison. Hyper parameter specifications were selected to reduce randomness and optimize for reproducibility.

Prompt:

"You are a causal language model that performs causal sequence classification and causal span detection. You will classify a headline as causal or not causal, and if it's causal you will extract the causes and effects. The output should be a json with label 1 or 0, cause, and effect value such as `{\n \"label\": ,\n \"cause\": ,\n \"effect\": \n}`

Hyperparameter specification

url = /v1/chat/completions

max tokens = 115

model = gpt-4o

temperature = 0.0

top p = 1

frequency penalty = 0

presence penalty = 0

Bias Detection in Media: Traditional Models vs. Transformers in Analyzing Social Media Coverage of the Israeli-Gaza Conflict

Marryam Yahya[1], Esraa Ismail[2], Mariam Nabil[3], Yomna Ashraf[4], Nada Radwan[5], Ziad Elshaer[6], Ensaf Mohamed[7]

School of Information Technology and Computer Science
Nile University, Giza, Egypt
Emails: {M.Yahya2163, E.Ismail2165, M.Nabil2184, Y.Ashraf2278, N.Ahmed2128, ZElshaer, EnMohamed}@nu.edu.eg

Abstract

Bias in news reporting significantly influences public perception, particularly in sensitive and polarized contexts like the Israel-Gaza conflict. Detecting bias in such cases presents unique challenges due to political, cultural, and ideological complexities, often amplifying disparities in reporting. While prior research has addressed media bias and dataset fairness, these approaches inadequately capture the nuanced dynamics of the Israel-Gaza conflict. To address this gap, we propose an NLP-based framework that leverages Nakba narratives as linguistic resources for bias detection in news coverage. Using a multilingual corpus focusing on Arabic texts, we apply rigorous data cleaning, pre-processing, and methods to mitigate imbalanced class distributions that could skew classification outcomes. Our study explores various approaches, including Machine Learning (ML), Deep Learning (DL), Transformer-based architectures, and generative models. The findings demonstrate promising advancements in automating bias detection, and enhancing fairness and accuracy in politically sensitive reporting.

Keywords: NLP, Text Classification, Bias-Detection, Nakba Narratives

1 Introduction

Bias detection in news reporting has become a crucial area of research, especially given its significant impact on public opinion and political polarization. In today's digital age, where information spreads rapidly through online platforms, news outlets are essential in shaping how people perceive events. However, media coverage often reflects underlying ideological or geopolitical biases, which can influence how audiences interpret the news. Detecting and understanding these biases is key to promoting ethical journalism and ensuring news reporting remains balanced and impartial. Recent advancements in Natural Language Processing (NLP) have introduced powerful new tools for identifying subtle biases in news articles. Machine learning models, in particular, have made significant strides in uncovering these hidden biases. Yet, these methods face unique challenges regarding sensitive and complex topics like the Israel-Gaza conflict. The language used in such coverage is heavily influenced by historical, cultural, and political factors, making it difficult for existing models to detect biases effectively. A more nuanced approach is needed to tackle this—one that goes beyond general bias detection methods and considers the conflict's specificities. While much of the existing research on bias detection in news has focused on more general forms of bias, such as political slant or ideological bias, the Israel-Gaza conflict presents a different set of challenges. Many studies have looked at these issues in languages like English, but often neglect the complexities of covering sensitive geopolitical topics. Additionally, the lack of annotated datasets focused on this conflict makes it even harder to develop effective bias detection tools. This paper addresses these gaps by creating a specialized NLP framework to detect and annotate biased coverage related to the Israel-Gaza conflict. Our work is based on the foundational project "BiasFignews" (SinaLab, 2024), which collected data on the Israeli-Gaza conflict. "BiasFignews" is a comprehensive multilingual corpus of 12,000 Facebook posts annotated for bias and propaganda. The corpus includes posts in Arabic, Hebrew, English, French, and Hindi, covering various events during the Israeli War on Gaza from October 7, 2023, to January 31, 2024.

Our main contributions include:

- Handling the imbalanced classes of the datasets to get the best performance for the models.
- Applying advanced linguistic and machine learning techniques to detect biases in news

Proceedings of the Proceedings of the 1st International Workshop on Nakba Narratives as Language Resources, pages 114–121
January 20, 2025. ©2025 Association for Computational Linguistics

content.

- Thoroughly evaluating the performance of these models.

By tackling the unique challenges of bias detection in conflict reporting, we hope to contribute to the development of more ethical journalism and improve the quality of media coverage in sensitive areas.

To achieve our goals, we use a comprehensive approach that includes data collection, cleaning, and pre-processing, followed by model development using various machine learning algorithms. Our first step is to create a multilingual annotated dataset scraped from social media platforms, focusing on news posts about the Israel-Gaza conflict. After addressing issues such as data imbalance, we apply advanced NLP techniques -such as transformer and sequential models like T5 and Bi-LSTM - and explore a variety of Machine Learning algorithms, including SVM, Random Forest, and XGBoost. Through experiments, we will benchmark these models and assess their performance in detecting bias, with a particular focus on how well they generalize across different languages and types of bias.

The rest of the paper is organized as follows: Section 2 will cover the Related Work, Section 3 will present our proposed Materials & Methods, Section 4 will present the Results & Discussion, Section 5 will Conclude the proposed work and discuss the recommendations of our future work and finally, Section 6 will represent the faced limitations in our work.

2 Related Work

This section reviews prominent studies on bias detection in NLP, focusing on their methodologies, challenges, and limitations. While existing work has explored media and language bias, few studies address the specific complexities of geopolitical conflicts like the Israel-Gaza conflict, especially in multilingual and culturally nuanced contexts.

Nadeem et al. (Nadeem and Raza, 2021) examine political bias in U.S. news articles, particularly content about former President Donald Trump. They apply a TensorFlow deep neural network (DNN) with Bag-of-Words (BoW) representation, TF-IDF weighting, and K-means clustering for pattern detection. The SimCSE framework outperforms these methods by effectively capturing subtle sentence-level biases.

Evans et al. (Evans et al., 2024) investigate how human biases influence NLP models, particularly in hate speech detection. Their work utilizes datasets to train the Emotion-Transformer model based on DistilBERT. While combining datasets improves bias detection for specific categories, they highlight persistent challenges in addressing imbalances in multi-target bias tasks.

Rodrigo-Gines et al. (Rodrigo-Ginés et al., 2024) conduct a systematic review categorizing types of media bias and distinguishing it from misinformation and disinformation. They emphasize the limitations of existing datasets and methods, calling for improved detection techniques to ensure accuracy and reliability in bias detection.

Khattak et al. (Donald et al., 2023) explore bias in customer interaction datasets, focusing on ethical data handling and fairness. They underscore the importance of mitigating bias during data preparation and advocate for enhanced methods to reduce biases in training datasets while ensuring compliance with GDPR.

Despite these advancements, existing studies lack a focus on media bias in the unique context of geopolitical conflicts, such as the Israel-Gaza conflict. The limited exploration of multilingual corpora, particularly in Arabic, and challenges with imbalanced data emphasize the need for specialized frameworks tailored to such sensitive and polarized scenarios.

3 Materials and Methods

This section provides a detailed overview of the dataset description and the proposed model pipeline, including data cleaning and preprocessing, handling imbalanced classes, the embedding models, and the classification models used.

3.1 Dataset Description

We employed a multilingual corpus annotated for bias and propaganda scraped from the Facebook platform (Duaibes et al., 2024) to implement our models. This corpus was constructed as a contribution to the FigNews 2024 Shared Task on News Media Narratives for framing the Israeli War on

Gaza. The dataset covers events during the war from October 7, 2023, to January 31, 2024. The corpus comprises 12,000 posts in five languages: Arabic, Hebrew, English, French, and Hindi, with 2,400 posts per language.

3.2 Methodology

The proposed model pipeline in Figure 1 consists of three phases: data cleaning and preprocessing, addressing class imbalance and ensuring class balance, and applying different models from various paradigms, including traditional machine learning models, transformer-based models, and generative models. These phases will be discussed in detail in the following subsections.

3.2.1 Data Cleaning & Pre-Processing

The initial phase of the pipeline involved cleaning and preparing the dataset to classify whether Arabic text is biased or not. Unnecessary columns such as Batch, Source Language, ID, Type, and others were removed, retaining only the "Arabic MT" and "Bias" columns. Null and duplicate fields were dropped, reducing the dataset to 10,800 rows.

Subsequently, text pre-processing was applied, including the removal of hashtags, URLs, emails, emojis, Arabic diacritics, and Tatweel. Arabic text normalization was performed by unifying Alif variants, replacing Taa Marbuta with Haa, and Alef Maqsura with Ya, as well as removing repeated characters. The dataset was then checked for class balance, as imbalanced data can lead to biased models favoring majority classes.

3.2.2 Handling Imbalanced Classes

To address the class imbalance, we employed Borderline-SMOTE (Han et al., 2005), which focuses on generating synthetic samples for minority class instances near the decision boundary. Unlike traditional SMOTE, this method emphasizes borderline samples likely to be misclassified due to proximity to majority class instances, enhancing model performance for minority classes.

We applied Borderline-SMOTE1, which generates synthetic samples exclusively from borderline minority samples. This approach improved decision boundary learning and classification performance. A comparison of label distributions before and after applying Borderline-SMOTE is shown in Figure 2.

3.2.3 Embeddings Model

To generate numerical representations of text data, we utilized the Multilingual E5 model (Wang et al., 2024), a large language model pre-trained on diverse languages and tasks. This model encodes text into high-dimensional vectors that capture semantic meaning. Using Hugging Face Transformers, the model tokenizes input text, encodes it via its encoder, and applies mean pooling to produce fixed-size embeddings. These embeddings map semantically similar words or phrases to vectors close to each other, enabling effective clustering, classification, and bias analysis.

In our research, we combined advanced large language models (LLMs), sequential, and transformer-based models to ensure robust and nuanced text representations for further bias detection.

3.2.4 Generative and Transformer-Based Models

- **Silma LLM:** A 9-billion-parameter generative model optimized for Arabic text tasks. It was used to detect bias in news articles by employing prompt engineering, which guides the model to classify text accurately and suggest neutralizing strategies for biased language.

- **T5 Encoder-Decoder Model:** The T5 model (Raffel et al., 2019) treats all tasks as text-to-text transformations, leveraging its pre-trained architecture to generate embeddings. This model captures complex semantic relationships in the dataset, enabling detailed and meaningful analysis for bias detection.

- **AraBERT Model:** AraBERT (Antoun et al., 2020), a BERT-based model tailored for Arabic, was fine-tuned using weighted sampling and Focal Loss to handle class imbalance. Despite its strong performance in general tasks, it struggled with minority class predictions in bias detection.

3.2.5 Deep Learning Models

Deep learning models are powerful tools for extracting complex patterns and representations from data. These models excel in analyzing text by capturing nuanced relationships and dependencies, making them essential for tasks like text classification, bias detection, and sentiment analysis.

- **LSTM:** Long Short-Term Memory (LSTM) networks (Hochreiter and Schmidhuber, 1997)

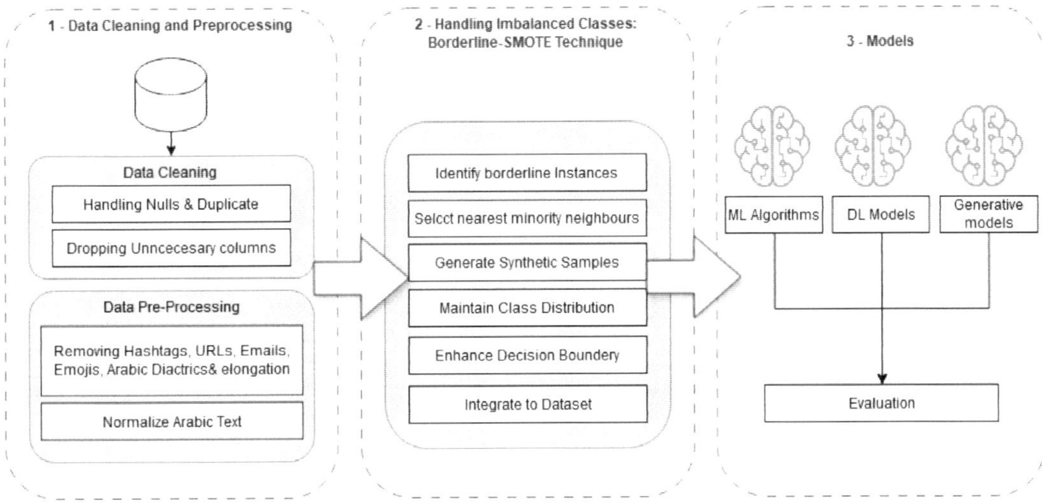

Figure 1: Model Pipeline

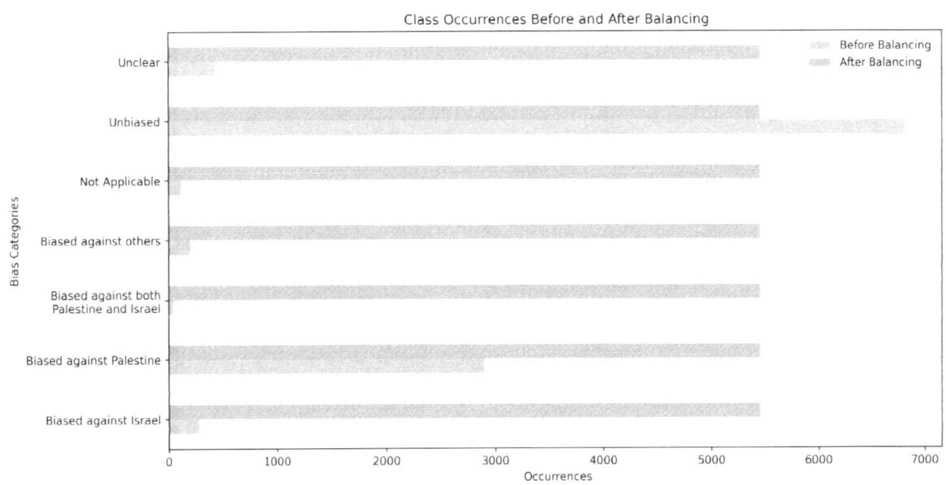

Figure 2: Bias Class Distribution

capture long-term dependencies in sequential data. In our research, LSTMs generated embeddings by preserving context over sequences, aiding in comprehensive text representation.

- **Bi-LSTM:** Bidirectional LSTM (Huang et al., 2015) extends LSTMs by capturing context from both past and future sequences. This bidirectional capability enhanced the quality of embeddings for deeper textual analysis.

- **Bi-GRU with Attention:** Combining Bidirectional GRUs (Wang et al., 2017) and attention mechanisms, this model highlighted important text features. Its computational efficiency and focus on relevant input parts improved the embeddings for bias detection and information retrieval tasks.

3.2.6 Machine Learning Algorithms

We utilized several machine learning algorithms to classify biased text effectively. Below is a concise summary of the models implemented:

- **SVM:** Support Vector Machine (SVM) identifies the optimal hyperplane that separates classes. Using kernel functions (e.g., RBF), it handles non-linear separations efficiently. In our implementation, SVM demonstrated robust performance for binary classification tasks by leveraging its mathematical rigor.

- **Random Forest:** An ensemble method that combines multiple decision trees, leveraging bagging to avoid overfitting. Each tree trains on a random subset of data, and predictions are made via majority voting. We used 100 trees with a random state of 42 to ensure consistent results.

- **XGBoost:** A boosting algorithm that sequentially builds trees to minimize residual errors. Configured with 100 estimators, a learning rate of 0.1, and a maximum depth of six, XGBoost provided high accuracy by optimizing for performance with hyperparameters like subsample and column sampling.

- **Decision Tree:** This interpretable model splits data into subsets based on feature values but risks overfitting without proper pruning. Using the Gini impurity criterion, we trained the model with a random state of 42 to ensure reproducibility.

- **CatBoost:** A gradient boosting model optimized for categorical features. By using ordered boosting and innovative handling of categorical data, CatBoost provided high accuracy. Parameters like 150 iterations, a learning rate of 0.1, and depth 6 were used for optimization.

- **Logistic Regression:** A statistical model for binary classification, Logistic Regression assumes linear separability of classes. Configured with a maximum of 1000 iterations and a random state of 42, the model offered simplicity and interpretability.

- **Gaussian Naive Bayes:** A probabilistic model leveraging Bayes' theorem with Gaussian distributions to handle continuous features. It proved effective for text classification, with its simplicity making it ideal for high-dimensional data.

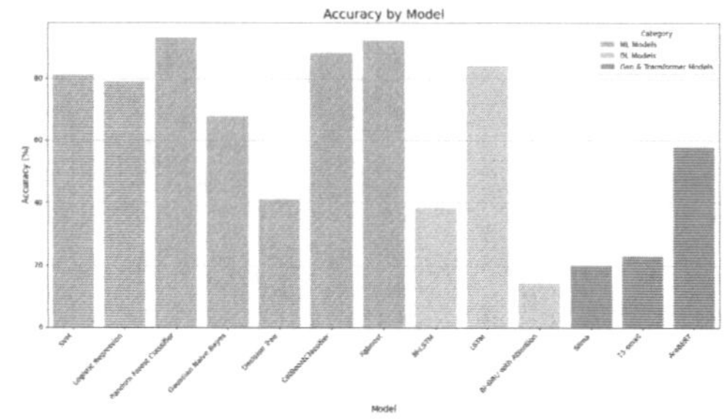

Figure 3: Accuracy

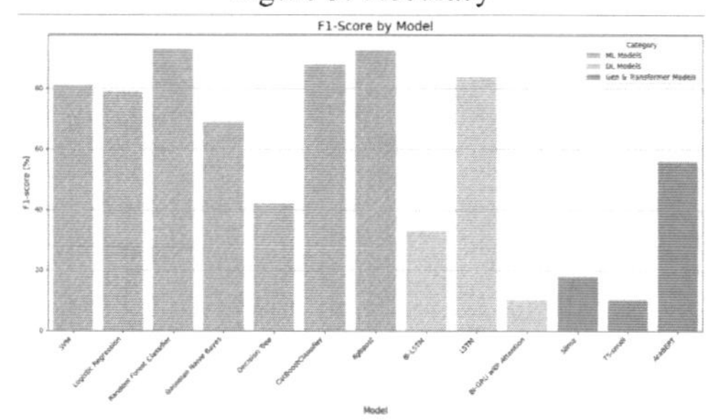

Figure 4: F1-Score

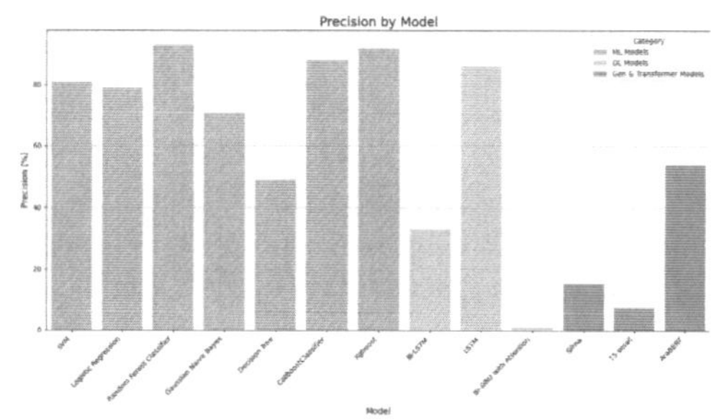

Figure 5: Precision

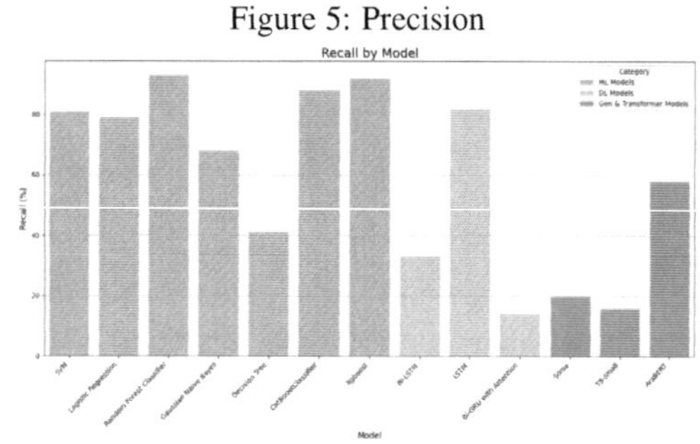

Figure 6: Recall

Figure 7: Performance Metrics Visualization

4 Results & Discussion

The models exhibit varying performance, with the accuracy and F1-scores for each summarized in table 1.

The table shows that in machine learning algorithms, the Random Forest Classifier has the highest performance with an accuracy of 93%, an F1-score of 93.23%, a precision of 93%, and a recall of 93%. XGBoost followed closely with an accuracy of 92%, an F1-score of 93%, a precision of 92%, and a recall of 92%, indicating strong performances along all metrics. Similarly, CatBoostClassifier achieved good performance with an accuracy of 88%, an F1-score of 88%, a precision of 88%, and a recall of 88Where for the Deep Learning

ML Algorithms				
Model	**Accuracy (%)**	**F1-score (%)**	**Precision (%)**	**Recall (%)**
SVM	81	81	81	81
Logistic Regression	79	79	79	79
Random Forest Classifier	**93**	**93.23**	**93**	**93**
Gaussian Naive Bayes	68	69	71	68
Decision Tree	41	42	49	41
CatBoostClassifier	88	88	88	88
XGBoost	92	93	92	92
Deep Learning Models				
Model	**Accuracy (%)**	**F1-score (%)**	**Precision (%)**	**Recall (%)**
Bi-LSTM	38.4	33	33	33
LSTM	**84**	**84**	**86**	**82**
Bi-GRU with Attention	14.18	10.2	8.9	14.18
Generative Models & Transformer Based Models				
Model	**Accuracy (%)**	**F1-score (%)**	**Precision (%)**	**Recall (%)**
Silma	20	18	15.32	20
T5-small	15.65	10.10	7.62	15.65
AraBERT	**58**	**56**	**54**	**58**

Table 1: Model Performance Summary by Type with Precision and Recall

models, the LSTM model achieved an accuracy of 84%, an F1-score of 84%, a precision of 86%, and a recall of 82%. Bi-LSTM and Bi-GRU with Attention achieved lower results: Bi-LSTM with an accuracy of 38.4%, an F1-score of 33%, a precision of 33%, and a recall of 33%, and Bi-GRU with Attention with an accuracy of 14.18%, an F1-score of 10.2%, a precision of 8.9%, and a recall of 14.18%. On the other hand, the generative models T5-small also had a low accuracy of 15.65%, an F1-score of 10.10%, a precision of 7.62%, and a recall of 15.65%. The generative model Silma, based on prompt engineering, performed with an accuracy of 20%, an F1-score of 18%, a precision of 15.32%, and a recall of 20%.

Among the traditional models, SVM achieved an accuracy of 81%, an F1-score of 81%, a precision of 81%, and a recall of 81%, which were reasonable but not high as compared to the ensemble methods. Logistic Regression also achieved a similar performance with an accuracy of 79%, an F1-score of 79%, a precision of 79%, and a recall of 79%. Gaussian Naive Bayes showed an accuracy of 68%, an F1-score of 69%, a precision of 71%, and a recall of 68%, while Decision Tree had a moderate performance with an accuracy of 41%, an F1-score of 42%, a precision of 49%, and a recall of 41%. AraBERT, a pre-trained language model specific to the Arabic language, achieved an accuracy of 58%, an F1-score of 56%, a precision of 54%, and a recall of 58%. While its performance outperformed the Decision Tree model and some of the Deep Learning models. It is shown that Generative and Transformer-based models such as SILMA and T5 performed worse than traditional machine learning (ML) models. This is due to many reasons, including that traditional ML models often benefit from feature engineering, where manually selecting and transforming relevant features can lead to better performance. Additionally, traditional ML models are designed for specialized tasks like classification, making them more effective for these specific problems compared to generative models optimized for generating new data. Moreover, traditional ML models have built-in inductive biases that make them well-suited for certain tasks, such as Random Forest being particularly adept at constructing multiple decision trees during training and outputting the mode of the classes, whereas transformers may require more data and computational resources to achieve similar results. Figures 3,4,5,6 illustrate the results of the Machine learning, Deep Learning, Generative and Transformer-based models for this work.

5 Conclusion

In this paper, we deal with the critical task of detecting bias in news reporting on the conflict between

Israel and Gaza. Applying an Arabic corpus of texts, advanced preprocessing methods, and several machine learning models, we have arrived at a robust framework for the detection of bias applicable to the nuanced and politically charged context of news reports on conflict situations. Among the tried methods, ensemble methods such as Random Forest and XGBoost showed better performance; thus, they are more suitable for this challenging classification. Our results indicate that although there are inherent difficulties arising from data imbalance, language-specific challenges, and subtle bias indicators, a good combination of data augmentation strategies such as Borderline-SMOTE along with state-of-the-art machine learning techniques can improve the detection of bias considerably. It is part of the larger aim of ensuring ethical journalism and offers a scalable methodology for media coverage analysis in sensitive geopolitical situations.

6 Limitations

This study has several limitations that are important to highlight. While the dataset is multilingual and extensive, it is limited to Facebook posts from a specific period, which makes it harder to generalize the findings to other platforms, time frames, or contexts. Annotating bias and propaganda is inherently subjective, especially in politically sensitive topics like the Israel-Gaza conflict, which could affect the quality of model training and evaluation. The transformer-based models we used, though effective, rely heavily on the training data and often struggle to identify subtle or context-specific biases shaped by historical and cultural factors. Similarly, addressing class imbalance with Borderline-SMOTE might oversimplify the complexity of real-world data, risking overfitting for minority classes and missing nuances in bias detection. Working with Arabic texts brought its own set of challenges, such as the language's rich morphology, diverse dialects, informal variations, and frequent code-switching, all of which made preprocessing more difficult and may have caused some loss of linguistic subtleties. Moreover, the lack of standardized resources for Arabic and domain-specific tools limited our ability to fully capture the complexity of biased reporting. Moving forward, we plan to address these limitations by expanding the dataset to include posts from other platforms and time frames, fine-tuning transformer models with domain-specific adaptations, and exploring hybrid approaches that combine linguistic insights with advanced deep learning techniques to better detect bias, particularly in Arabic texts.

References

Wissam Antoun, Fady Baly, and Hazem Hajj. 2020. AraBERT: Transformer-based model for Arabic language understanding. In *Proceedings of the 4th Workshop on Open-Source Arabic Corpora and Processing Tools, with a Shared Task on Offensive Language Detection*, pages 9–15, Marseille, France. European Language Resource Association.

Andy Donald, Apostolos Galanopoulos, Edward Curry, Emir Muñoz, Ihsan Ullah, M. A. Waskow, Maciej Dabrowski, and Manan Kalra. 2023. Bias detection for customer interaction data: A survey on datasets, methods, and tools. *IEEE Access*, 11:53703–53715.

Lina Duaibes, Areej Jaber, Mustafa Jarrar, Ahmad Qadi, and Mais Qandeel. 2024. Sina at fignews 2024: Multilingual datasets annotated with bias and propaganda. *Preprint*, arXiv:2407.09327.

Ana Sofia Evans, Helena Moniz, and Luísa Coheur. 2024. A study on bias detection and classification in natural language processing. *Preprint*, arXiv:2408.07479.

Hui Han, Wenyuan Wang, and Binghuan Mao. 2005. Borderline-smote: A new over-sampling method in imbalanced data sets learning. In *International Conference on Intelligent Computing*.

Sepp Hochreiter and Jürgen Schmidhuber. 1997. Long short-term memory. *Neural Computation*, 9(8):1735–1780.

Zhiheng Huang, Wei Xu, and Kai Yu. 2015. Bidirectional lstm-crf models for sequence tagging. *arXiv preprint arXiv:1508.01991*.

MU Nadeem and S Raza. 2021. Detecting bias in news articles using nlp models.

Colin Raffel, Noam Shazeer, Adam Roberts, Katherine Lee, Sharan Narang, Michael Matena, Yanqi Zhou, Wei Li, and Peter J. Liu. 2019. Exploring the limits of transfer learning with a unified text-to-text transformer. *CoRR*, abs/1910.10683.

Francisco-Javier Rodrigo-Ginés, Jorge Carrillo de Albornoz, and Laura Plaza. 2024. A systematic review on media bias detection: What is media bias, how it is expressed, and how to detect it. *Expert Systems with Applications*, 237:121641.

SinaLab. 2024. Biasfignews: A multilingual corpus of facebook posts annotated for bias and propaganda. GitHub.

Liang Wang, Nan Yang, Xiaolong Huang, Linjun Yang, Rangan Majumder, and Furu Wei. 2024. Multilingual e5 text embeddings: A technical report. *arXiv preprint arXiv:2402.05672*.

Nan Wang, Jin Wang, and Xuejie Zhang. 2017. Ynu-hpcc at ijcnlp-2017 task 4: Attention-based bi-directional GRU model for customer feedback analysis task of English. In *Proceedings of the IJCNLP 2017, Shared Tasks*, pages 174–179, Taipei, Taiwan. Asian Federation of Natural Language Processing.

NakbaTR: A Turkish NER Dataset for Nakba Narratives

Esma F. Bilgin Taşdemir
Medeniyet University
İstanbul, Turkey
esmabilgin.tasdemir@medeniyet.edu.tr

Şaziye Betül Özateş
Boğaziçi University
İstanbul, Turkey
saziye.ozates@bogazici.edu.tr

Abstract

The narratives of the ongoing Nakba are of significant importance for both the Palestinian people and the global community. The creation of language resources is crucial to automating the processing of written content related to this historical event. This paper introduces an annotated Named Entity Recognition (NER) dataset derived from a collection of 182 news articles about the Nakba and its witnesses. Given their prominence as a primary source of information on the Nakba in Turkish, news articles were selected as the primary data source. An initial analysis on the constructed dataset is also presented.

1 Introduction

The Nakba, which is translated as "catastrophe" in Arabic, is a term used for the mass displacement and dispossession of Palestinians starting from the 1948 Arab-Israeli war. During many Nakba events suffered by the Palestinian people, hundreds of thousands were forced to flee their homes, property, and belongings. The expulsion of native people to the degree of ethnic cleansing has several catastrophic results, including a refugee crisis and generational trauma that continues to this day. Today, there are again genocide and Nakba events against the Palestinian people, which have been escalating since the end of 2023.

The narratives about the Nakba events are important in many aspects, including cultural, legal, and historical significance. There are different types of sources where the narratives can be found. The news content from different outlets is one of the main sources of narratives in the Turkish language. In this work, we generated a manually annotated Named Entity Recognition (NER) dataset from websites of two news agencies. Both annotations and collected text can be used for several NLP tasks such as relation extraction, sentiment analysis, and topic modeling related to the Nakba event. Furthermore, it will serve as a new language resource for Turkish, a language often considered underrepresented in NLP research.

2 Related Work

Early studies on Named Entity Recognition (NER) began in the 1990s. Since then, numerous researchers have explored various aspects of NER tasks (Li et al., 2022; Yadav and Bethard, 2018). A NER dataset can be generated as a general purpose dataset or it can be a domain-specific dataset. Among different sources of text corpora, news texts are one of the popular sources as they are easy to collect especially in digital format. PERSON, LOCATION, and ORGANIZATION are the most common entity types in news NER datasets (Zhang and Xiao, 2024).

Most studies on NER in Turkish texts have focused on modern texts, which can be categorized as either formal or informal (noisy). Formal texts adhere to standard grammatical and orthographic rules, while informal texts may exhibit variations and deviations from these norms. In Akkaya and Can (2021), a transfer learning approach is used for NER in informal data with rarely-seen entity types. They add a CRF layer that is trained on both formal text and a noisy text to a BiLSTM-CRF model. They report 61.53% F1 score on noisy text. Safaya et al. (2022) experiment with several datasets and architectures with a goal of providing a benchmarking platform for various NLP tasks. They achieve 93.8% F1 score on the WikiANN dataset (Pan et al., 2017) using BiLSTM-CRF model and 93.07% F1 score with BERTurk-CRF model. Kılıç et al. (2020) report 82.31% F1 score on formal Turkish texts which is obtained through a multilingual cased BERT model. Finally, Ozcelik and Toraman (2022) present results for several models evaluated on some public datasets. They report, an

Proceedings of the Proceedings of the 1st International Workshop on Nakba Narratives as Language Resources, pages 122–126
January 20, 2025. ©2025 Association for Computational Linguistics

F1 score of 96.10% achieved by ELECTRA-tr on a dataset of news articles and 92.26% F1 score obtained by ConvBERTurk on the WikiANN dataset.

3 Methodology

3.1 Dataset

We created NakbaTR, a new and domain-specific dataset, using news texts published online. The content is limited to news containing testimonies from witnesses of the Nakba currently taking place. This section gives details on data collection and annotation processes we employed for creating the NakbaTR dataset.

3.1.1 Data Collection

Testimonies in Turkish related to the ongoing Nakba can be found mostly in news sources. The NakbaTR dataset was curated from websites of two state-owned news outlets; Anadolu Ajansı (AA)[1] and TRTHaber.[2]

Texts are scraped semi-automatically using a pipeline of searching, downloading and cleaning. We decided on two Turkish phrases; "anlattı" (told) and "konuştu" (spoke) which are used as searching keywords. We made searches for each keyword in each outlet, four searches in total. Web pages containing keywords along with "Gazze" (Gaza) are downloaded automatically. We downloaded 120 pages per website in this manner and 480 pages are downloaded in total. Pages that include video or photographic content are removed from the collection resulting a set of 369 pages (215 from TRTHaber and 181 from AA). The collected text are cleaned from irrelevant elements first automatically by exploiting the web page structure followed by manual cleaning of any remaining noise. The items of the dataset are comprised of text of the news, its URL and date it was published, and the source. Both sources are news agencies, so they use a similar, formal language.

We aimed to generate a collection of news in which expressions of Nakba witnesses are contained. We employed a rigorous manual filtering process based on existence of testimonies within the content. As a result, news texts that do not contain a witness testimony are removed from the collection. The final collection contains 182 news articles (74 news articles from TRTHaber and 107 news articles from AA). The testimonial expressions can be given with both direct and indirect speech. It should be noted that content other than the testimony part which gives contextual information regarding the testimony are kept in the dataset as well.

[1] `http://aa.com.tr`

[2] `http://trthaber.com`

3.1.2 NER Dataset Generation

NakbaTR dataset is annotated with PERSON, LOCATION, and ORGANIZATION types while words of other type of tags are all marked with O. We use the following definitions of tags:

- PERSON : People, including fictional.
- LOCATION: GPE and Non-GPE locations including countries, cities, states, mountain ranges and bodies of water.
- ORGANIZATION: Collectives such as companies, political groups, government bodies, and public organizations.

Annotation of NakbaTR is done in two steps. A BERT-based language model, which is detailed in Section 3.2 is employed for automatic annotation in the first step. In the second step, its output is corrected and verified by two human annotators. The data is prepared in CoNLL-2003 format with multiple word entities marked with B- and I- prefixes. Figure 1 depicts two example annotated sentences from the dataset. To assess the reliability of the annotations, we calculated the inter-annotator agreement between human annotators on 100 randomly selected sentences which contain 295 named entities in total, achieving a Cohen's Kappa score of 0.968, indicating a high level of consistency in annotations.

The resulting NakbaTR NER dataset contains 3,957 sentences, 2,289 PERSON, 5,875 LOCATION, and 1,299 ORGANIZATION tags in total. Details regarding the sources are given in Table 1. The NakbaTR dataset can be accessed at `https://github.com/sb-b/NakbaTR`.

3.2 BERT-based Language Model

Various pre-trained Language Models (PLMs) were previously utilized for the NER task on Modern Turkish (see Section 2). We observed that among different architectures and models, BERTurk (Schweter, 2020), a Turkish language model utilizing the BERT architecture and pre-trained on Turkish text, reached the highest F1

Source	News	Number of Sentences	Tokens	Person	Number of Location	Organization
AA	107	2,482	70,188	1,457	3,878	893
TRTHaber	74	1,550	41,639	832	1,997	406
TOTAL	181	4,032	111,827	2,289	5,875	1,299

Table 1: Dataset statistics.

```
#doc_id = https://www.trthaber.com/haber/dunya/gazzede-israilin-saldirilarinda
          -yaralanan-filistinli-cocuklar-cektikleri-aciyi-anlatti-826779.html
#metadata = 06.01.2024 12:29
#sent_id = 375
#text = Gazze'de, İsrail'in saldırılarında yaralanan Filistinli çocuklar
        çektikleri acıyı anlattı
Gazze'de B-LOC
, O
İsrail'in B-LOC
saldırılarında O
yaralanan O
Filistinli O
çocuklar O
çektikleri O
acıyı O
anlattı O

#sent_id = 376
#text = Gazze Şeridi'nin güneyine yönelik İsrail saldırılarında yaralanan
        Filistinli 2 kız çocuğunun yaşadıkları, gözlerinin önünden gitmiyor.
Gazze B-LOC
Şeridi'nin I-LOC
güneyine O
yönelik O
İsrail B-LOC
saldırılarında O
yaralanan O
Filistinli O
2 O
kız O
çocuğunun O
yaşadıkları O
, O
gözlerinin O
önünden O
gitmiyor O
. O
```

Figure 1: Annotations of the first two sentences of a news document in the NakbaTR dataset. Sentence translations: *(First sent.)* "In Gaza, Palestinian children injured in Israeli attacks described their suffering." *(Second sent.)* "The experiences of two Palestinian girls injured in Israeli attacks on the southern Gaza Strip remain vivid in their minds."

score for the NER task on the Turkish split of the WikiANN NER dataset. Hence, we opted to utilize BERTurk that is fine-tuned on a large Turkish NER dataset (Tür et al., 2003) as the Turkish NER model in the automatic annotation process.

The utilized BERTurk model has 12 transformer layers each consisting of 12 attention heads. The number of hidden units is 768. A total of 110 million parameters are fine-tuned during the pre-training phase on a large corpus of Turkish text data, allowing the model to learn contextual representations that capture intricate syntactic and semantic relationships within the language.

In the automatic annotation phase, the BERT-based model achieves an impressive F1 score of 87% in predicting named entities. Its performance on individual entity types is as follows: 89% for LOCATION entities, 76% for ORGANIZATION entities, and 90% for PERSON entities. The precision score of the model on all entity types is 100%, indicating that whenever the model predicts a named entity, it is always correct. However, the recall scores are 81% for LOCATION entities, 61% for ORGANIZATION entities, and 81% for PERSON entities. The low recall indicates that there are named entities that the model cannot detect.

It is important to note that these model performance metrics were derived from aligned sentences between the output of the BERTurk NER model and the manual annotation step. Segmentation and tokenization errors that occurred while preparing the news data in CoNLL-2003 format propagated throughout the dataset, necessitating significant effort during the manual correction phase.

4 Dataset Analysis

We conducted some basic analyses regarding the annotated named entities on the NakbaTR dataset. We plotted the mention frequencies of frequently occurring location names over time. Figure 2 illustrates these plots for the TRTHaber and AA sections of the dataset, respectively. Note that, we excluded the locations *Gazze (Gaza), Filistin (Palestine)*, and *İsrail (Israel)* from this plot since the mention frequency of these location names are much more higher than any other location in the dataset. The figure is helpful in understanding the changing focus of the news. For instance, the coverage of the intensive assault of Israeli army on Northern Gaza civilian areas like Jabaliya and Beit Lahia is clearly traceable from both plots. Although there are some common patterns between the two news sources, they have different coverage rates. This can be attributed to the difference in their focus, target audience, and perspective since AA provides a broader, more international one, while TRTHaber has more local perspective.

We also conducted an analysis of the co-occurrence patterns of named entities within the dataset to explore relationships between entities. Specifically, we counted the frequency of each named entity pair appearing in the same sentence throughout the dataset. To enhance the clarity of

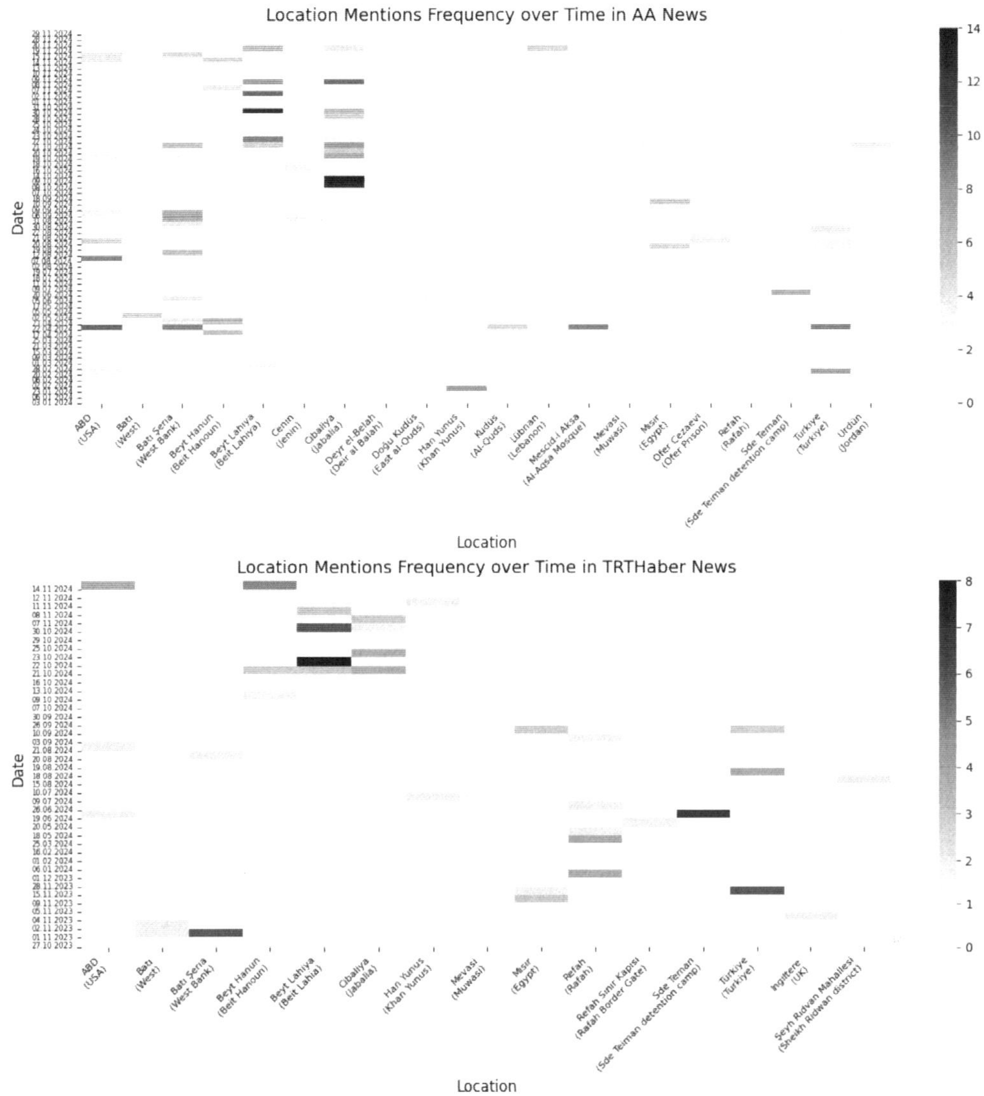

Figure 2: Mention frequency plots of frequently occuring location names in the AA and TRTHaber sections of the dataset over time.

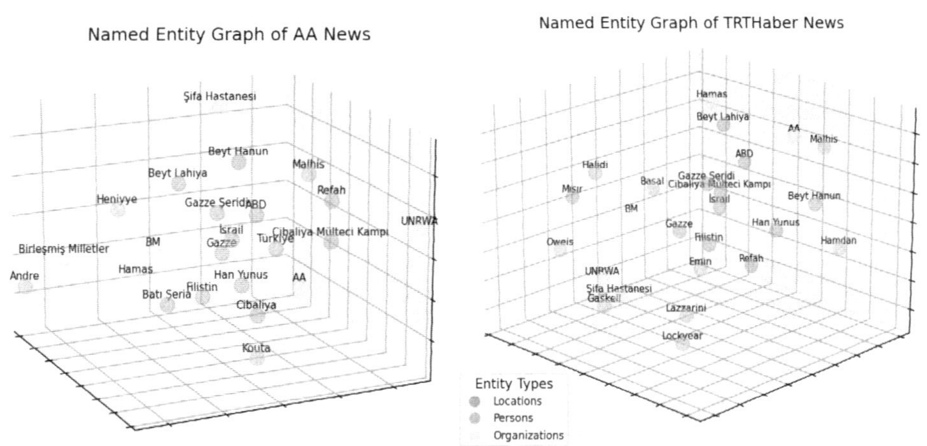

Figure 3: Co-occurence graph of named entities in AA and TRTHaber sections of the dataset.

the visualization, we applied a filtering step to exclude entity pairs with a co-occurrence frequency lower than 10 for the TRTHaber section and a co-occurrence frequency lower than 18 for the AA section. The resulting co-occurrence graph provides a visual representation of frequently co-occurring entities, highlighting key connections within the data. Figure 3 illustrates co-occurrence graphs, showing the relations between named entities in the AA and TRTHaber news in the NakbaTR dataset. In the figure, different entity types are represented in different colors. Although only the entity pairs that are most frequently observed in the dataset are included for clarity, this co-occurrence graph provides insights into the relationships among the entities in the narratives. For instance, the organization entity `UNRWA` and the person entity `Lazzarini` are located near in the TRTHaber graph which makes sense as Philippe Lazzarini is the commissioner-general of the UNRWA organization. Other visible relationships are between the person entity `Oweis` (Saleem Oweis, communications specialist at UNICEF Middle East and North Africa) and the organization entity `BM` (United Nations) in the TRTHaber graph and districts in the north Gaza located together in the AA graph. Some real life entities can have multiple names as in the case with `BM` (UN) and `Birleşmiş Milletler` (United Nations). This situation is clearly visible in the AA graph in the figure. Unifying multiple names for a single entity will therefore be beneficial before extracting relationships between entities.

5 Conclusion

In this work, we introduced a novel, manually annotated, Turkish NER dataset. The dataset comprises 3,957 news sentences collected from the websites of two prominent news agencies. We applied a filtering process to make sure that only the news which contain witness testimonies regarding the ongoing Nakba are included in the dataset. After a semi-automatic annotation for entities of types Person, Location, and Organization, we obtained a NER dataset of 2,289 PERSON, 5,875 LOCATION, and 1,299 ORGANIZATION tags. The dataset can be extended to be useful in several NLP tasks such as relation extraction or sentiment analysis for the Nakba event while providing a new language resource for Turkish. As future work, we aim to improve the dataset by increasing the number of news and entity types.

References

Emre Kagan Akkaya and Burcu Can. 2021. Transfer learning for Turkish named entity recognition on noisy text. *Nat. Lang. Eng.*, 27(1):35–64.

Yüksel Pelin Kılıç, Duygu Dinç, and Pınar Karagöz. 2020. Named entity recognition on morphologically rich language: exploring the performance of bert with varying training levels. IEEE International Conference on Big Data (2020).

Jing Li, Aixin Sun, Jianglei Han, and Chenliang Li. 2022. A survey on deep learning for named entity recognition. *IEEE Trans. Knowl. Data Eng.*, 34(1):50–70.

Oguzhan Ozcelik and Cagri Toraman. 2022. Named entity recognition in Turkish: A comparative study with detailed error analysis. *Inf. Process. Manag.*, 59(6):103065.

Xiaoman Pan, Boliang Zhang, Jonathan May, Joel Nothman, Kevin Knight, and Heng Ji. 2017. Cross-lingual name tagging and linking for 282 languages. In *Proceedings of the 55th Annual Meeting of the Association for Computational Linguistics (Volume 1: Long Papers)*, pages 1946–1958, Vancouver, Canada. Association for Computational Linguistics.

Ali Safaya, Emirhan Kurtuluş, Arda Goktogan, and Deniz Yuret. 2022. Mukayese: Turkish NLP strikes back. In *Findings of the Association for Computational Linguistics: ACL 2022*, pages 846–863, Dublin, Ireland. Association for Computational Linguistics.

Stefan Schweter. 2020. BERTurk - BERT models for Turkish. `https://zenodo.org/records/3770924`. [Online; accessed 21-10-2023].

Gökhan Tür, Dilek Hakkani-Tür, and Kemal Oflazer. 2003. A statistical information extraction system for Turkish. *Natural Language Engineering*, 9(2):181–210.

Vikas Yadav and Steven Bethard. 2018. A survey on recent advances in named entity recognition from deep learning models. In *Proceedings of the 27th International Conference on Computational Linguistics, COLING 2018, Santa Fe, New Mexico, USA, August 20-26, 2018*, pages 2145–2158. Association for Computational Linguistics.

Ying Zhang and Gang Xiao. 2024. Named entity recognition datasets: A classification framework. *Int. J. Comput. Intell. Syst.*, 17(1):71.

Integrating Argumentation Features for Enhanced Propaganda Detection in Arabic Narratives on the Israeli War on Gaza

Sara Nabhani[1,2], Claudia Borg[1], Kurt Micallef[1], Khalid Al-Khatib[2]

[1]Department of Artificial Intelligence, University of Malta
{sara.nabhani.23, claudia.borg, kurt.micallef}@um.edu.mt
[2]Department of Computational Linguistics and Society, University of Groningen
{s.nabhani, khalid.alkhatib}@rug.nl

Abstract

Propaganda significantly shapes public opinion, especially in conflict-driven contexts like the Israeli-Palestinian conflict. This study explores the integration of argumentation features, such as claims, premises, and major claims, into machine learning models to enhance the detection of propaganda techniques in Arabic media. By leveraging datasets annotated with fine-grained propaganda techniques and employing cross-lingual and multilingual NLP methods, along with GPT-4-based annotations, we demonstrate consistent performance improvements. A qualitative analysis of Arabic media narratives on the Israeli war on Gaza further reveals the model's capability to identify diverse rhetorical strategies, offering insights into the dynamics of propaganda. These findings emphasize the potential of combining NLP with argumentation features to foster transparency and informed discourse in politically charged settings.

1 Introduction

Propaganda is a form of communication aimed at influencing attitudes and behaviors by presenting one-sided or misleading information. It often relies on emotional appeals rather than rational argumentation to manipulate public perception and advance specific agendas or ideologies.

In the digital era, the rise of social media has amplified the spread of propaganda, enabling its rapid dissemination to global audiences with little oversight. This has heightened its potential impact, as seen in events like the 2016 U.S. Presidential Election (Ali and ul abdin, 2021) and during the COVID-19 pandemic (Broniatowski et al., 2020), where social media platforms were used to polarize opinions and undermine trust in democratic institutions.

The detection of propaganda is especially critical in conflict-driven contexts, such as the narratives surrounding the Israeli war on Gaza. These narratives often employ polarizing rhetoric, emotionally charged language, and manipulative techniques to shape public opinion and justify political or military actions. Arabic media, both traditional and digital, plays a central role in constructing these narratives, given the geopolitical significance of the Arabic-speaking world. In such contexts, propaganda can be a powerful tool for inciting violence, manipulating perceptions, and influencing international discourse. However, detecting propaganda in Arabic poses unique challenges due to the language's rich morphology, diverse dialects, and limited annotated datasets.

Natural Language Processing (NLP) offers a promising avenue for automating propaganda detection by analyzing linguistic patterns and rhetorical cues . While significant progress has been made in high-resource languages like English, relatively little research has focused on Arabic. This disparity highlights the need for approaches tailored to Arabic's linguistic and cultural characteristics.

A promising direction for enhancing propaganda detection is the integration of argumentation features, such as claims and premises. Propaganda and argumentation often share a structural foundation: both involve presenting claims supported by reasoning. However, propaganda diverges by infusing these structures with emotionally charged content designed to manipulate public sentiment (Nettel and Roque, 2012). By identifying argumentation components within texts, it becomes possible to analyze how propaganda leverages these structures to influence audiences, distinguishing between logical persuasion and manipulative communication.

In this work, we aim to improve Arabic propaganda detection by integrating argumentation features into NLP models. We then apply the enhanced models to analyze narratives from Arabic media covering the Israeli war on Gaza. The code used in this study is available at our GitHub repository.[1]

[1]https://github.com/saranabhani/prop-arg

Proceedings of the Proceedings of the 1st International Workshop on Nakba Narratives as Language Resources, pages 127–149
January 20, 2025.

2 Related Work

2.1 Propaganda Detection in Arabic Texts

A shared task on Propaganda Detection in Arabic was organized at the WANLP 2022 workshop (Alam et al., 2022) to address the notable absence of research on Arabic language propaganda detection. In this shared task, one submission (Hussein et al., 2022) applied basic preprocessing steps like normalization and transformed the data into the BIO format to represent data spans within tweets accurately. They adopted a transfer learning approach by employing the Marefa-NER model, a pre-trained template designed for Named Entity Recognition (NER), demonstrating the model's adaptability to this propaganda detection task.

Building on the momentum of the WANLP 2022 shared task on Propaganda Detection in Arabic (Alam et al., 2022), the organizers introduced the ArAIEval shared task[2] (Hasanain et al., 2023) focusing on two critical areas: persuasion technique and disinformation detection in tweets and news articles. The top submission (Lamsiyah et al., 2023) achieved first place with a streamlined approach centered around a BERT-based Arabic pre-trained language model encoder coupled with a singular, efficiently structured classifier. In their exploration of input text encoding, the team assessed the performance of three BERT-based Arabic pre-trained language models: ARBERTv2 (Abdul-Mageed et al., 2021), MARBERTv2 (Abdul-Mageed et al., 2021), and AraBERT-large (Antoun et al., 2020). The AraBERT encoder was selected, and the model was trained using an asymmetric multi-label loss.

Capitalizing on the progress achieved by the ArAIEval shared task, the 2024 edition (Hasanain et al., 2024) continued to advance the field of propaganda detection in Arabic text. Task 1 of the shared task focused on Unimodal Propaganda Detection, specifically targeting the identification of persuasive techniques within tweets and news articles written in Arabic. The dataset used for this task comprised tweets derived from Arabic news sources on Twitter, along with news paragraphs sourced from the AraFacts dataset (Sheikh Ali et al., 2021). The annotation process for this dataset involved labeling text snippets with a set of 23 persuasion techniques, building on the work of Piskorski et al. (2023). The top submission for this task came from Labib et al. (2024), which achieved the highest F1 score by integrating data augmentation techniques with model fine-tuning. Their approach involved leveraging a pre-trained Arabic-BERT model (Safaya et al., 2020), which was specifically fine-tuned on the task's annotated data. To address the challenge of class imbalance, the team employed data augmentation strategies such as synonym replacement, which enhanced the model's ability to generalize across different types of persuasive techniques. Another strong submission was from Riyadh and Nabhani (2024), who took advantage of a multilingual BERT model (mBERT) (Devlin et al., 2019) to capture the complexities of Arabic text. Their approach was distinctive in its focus on experimenting with different hidden layers of the model to determine the most effective layer for the task.

Overall, the recent advancements in propaganda detection in Arabic text have predominantly relied on fine-tuning transformer-based architectures and leveraging data augmentation techniques.

2.2 Contextual Features in Propaganda Detection

Relatively few studies have explored the integration of contextual features to enhance the performance of propaganda detection systems. A notable exceptions involve the addition of discourse features to token embeddings, which has shown potential for improving the accuracy of propaganda detection. This study by Chernyavskiy et al. (2024) explored the integration of discourse features into token embeddings to enhance the detection of propaganda in English and Russian. For this they used the dataset from SemEval-2023 (Piskorski et al., 2023). Their approach involved conducting a discourse analysis of the text to identify higher-level organizational structures utilizing the Two-Stage discourse parser (Wang et al., 2017). By embedding these discourse features directly into the token representations, the model gained a richer understanding of the text's structure, which proved beneficial in identifying propagandistic content.

This study highlights the significant impact of incorporating contextual features into token embeddings. This approach provides models with a deeper understanding of the context surrounding propaganda, beyond just the surface-level content of the text. While research in this area is still relatively sparse, the positive outcomes from these studies support the potential of our methodology in this work, suggesting that further exploration could lead to significant advancements in propaganda de-

[2] https://araieval.gitlab.io/

tection.

3 Data

3.1 Propaganda Detection Dataset

For the propaganda detection task, we utilized the dataset provided by the ArAIEval 2024 shared task on propaganda detection in Arabic text (Hasanain et al., 2024), specifically focusing on Task 1: Unimodal (Text) Propagandistic Technique Detection. This dataset encompasses two primary text genres: tweets and paragraphs extracted from Arabic news articles. Details regarding the data collection and annotation processes are thoroughly documented in the shared task paper (Hasanain et al., 2024). The dataset is publicly accessible via the ArAIEval GitLab repository.[3]

The dataset is pre-split into training, validation, and test sets, which were directly utilized in this work without modification. Each entry in the dataset contains a unique identifier, the raw text (either a tweet or a news paragraph), and annotations describing the propaganda techniques identified within specific spans of text. Each annotation includes the technique name, the exact text span where the technique occurs, and the character positions marking the start and end of the span. Text spans can be associated with multiple propaganda techniques, and overlapping spans are common.

The dataset includes 23 fine-grained propaganda techniques, derived from the taxonomy proposed by Piskorski et al. (2023). Detailed explanations of each technique, as defined in Piskorski et al. (2023), can be found in Appendix A.

The dataset's structure allows for a comprehensive analysis of propaganda in Arabic texts, accommodating both sequence labeling (to identify specific spans of propaganda) and multilabel classification (to categorize the techniques used).

Table 1 presents detailed statistics, including the sizes of the training, validation, and test sets and the total number of tokens. Figures 1a and 1b in Appendix B visualize the distribution of propaganda techniques across the datasets. Techniques such as Loaded Language and Name Calling are the most frequent, while others, like Straw Man and Guilt by Association, appear less commonly. The label distribution across the training, validation, and test sets is relatively consistent, despite the uneven number of different labels.

[3] https://gitlab.com/araieval/araieval_arabicnlp24

	Train	Dev	Test
# Documents	6,997	921	1,046
# Tokens	228,373	27,867	35,204
Avg. Tokens/Doc	32.63	30.25	33.65
Unique Tokens	59,193	13,443	16,108

Table 1: Propaganda dataset statistics

3.2 Argumentation Mining Dataset

To incorporate argumentation features into our study, we utilized the Persuasive Essays (PE) corpus by Stab and Gurevych (2017), as no suitable Arabic datasets aligned with our requirements. This English-language resource, widely used in cross-lingual argumentation tasks, comprises 402 essays randomly selected from essayforum.com, each accompanied by writing prompts and annotated with key argumentation components. These components include: Major Claim, representing the central argument typically introduced in the introduction and reinforced in the conclusion; Claim, which supports or challenges the major claim by addressing specific aspects or perspectives; and Premise, consisting of evidence or reasons that justify a claim and explain its validity. The corpus is pre-divided into training and test sets, which we used without modification. Table 2 provides detailed statistics about the corpus. By adapting this robust English dataset through a cross-lingual framework, we aim to extend its applicability to Arabic, leveraging its detailed annotations to enhance our study.

	Train	Test	Total
# Essays	322	80	402
# Paragraphs	1,786	449	2,235
# Tokens	118,645	29,537	148,182
MajorClaim	598	153	751
Claim	1,202	304	1,506
Premise	3,023	809	3,832

Table 2: Argumentation dataset statistics

3.3 Analysis Dataset: News Media Narratives on the Israeli War on Gaza

The dataset used for analyzing news media narratives about the Israeli war on Gaza originates from the FIGNEWS shared task (Zaghouani et al., 2024). This initiative focused on the early stages of the Israel-Gaza conflict, curating a multilingual corpus covering five languages: Arabic, English, French, Hebrew, and Hindi.

The dataset was annotated with multiple layers, including bias labels ("biased against Palestine", "biased against Israel", "unbiased") and propaganda labels ("propaganda", "not propaganda").

The qualitative analysis for this work (Section 8) utilized a sample of 17 examples with Arabic source language from the top-performing system in the shared task, developed by team NLPColab (Abdul Rauf et al., 2024).

4 Baseline for Propaganda Detection

In this study, we use the best-performing system from the ArAIEval 2024 shared task on propaganda detection in Arabic texts by Labib et al. (2024) as our baseline. This system, built on Arabic-BERT (Safaya et al., 2020), achieved an F1 score of 0.2995 by fine-tuning for detecting propagandistic spans and classifying them into 23 techniques. Key features include the BIO tagging scheme for accurate span identification and data augmentation to address class imbalance for less frequent techniques.

While this system was not originally developed as a baseline, we adopt it in this role for our study. Its performance in the shared task makes it an ideal reference point for evaluating the improvements introduced by our approach.

5 Proposed Methodology

This study investigates the enhancement of propaganda detection models by integrating argumentation features. Argumentation features, such as *Major Claim*, *Claim*, and *Premise*, provide a structured representation of the persuasive elements within a text. By leveraging the overlap between argumentation and propaganda, we aim to enrich the model's understanding of the underlying rhetorical strategies.

5.1 Model Architecture

The proposed model builds on a transformer-based architecture with AraBERTv2 (Antoun et al., 2020) as the backbone. This pre-trained model generates rich contextual embeddings for each token, capturing linguistic characteristics in Arabic text. To incorporate argumentation features, we augment these embeddings with additional input, as described below.

Input Representation Each token in the input text is represented by a combination of contextual embeddings and argumentation features. The token embeddings, derived from AraBERTv2, capture the linguistic and contextual information of each token. Additionally, a one-hot encoded vector of length four represents argumentation features, assigning each token one of four values: *Major Claim*, *Claim*, *Premise*, or *None*. These argumentation features, generated by an argumentation analyzer, are concatenated with the token embeddings to create a richer and more comprehensive representation.

Output Representation The model is designed for multi-label classification at the token level, where each token is assigned a binary vector representing the propaganda labels. The vector length corresponds to the number of propaganda techniques considered in the study (23 techniques). A value of 1 in the vector indicates the presence of a specific propaganda technique, while a value of 0 denotes its absence.

5.2 Model Workflow

The proposed model's workflow begins with embedding generation, where the input text is tokenized and processed through AraBERTv2 to produce contextual embeddings. These embeddings are then augmented with argumentation features, which are concatenated to enrich the representation of each token. The enhanced embeddings are passed through a classification layer to compute probabilities for various propaganda techniques. Finally, propagandistic spans are identified by grouping consecutive tokens with identical labels.

6 Argumentation Annotation Methodology

To generate argumentation annotations, we employed two primary approaches:

1. **GPT-4 Prompting**: This method involved using GPT-4 to automatically annotate the data.

2. **Trained Argumentation Model**: A dedicated argumentation model was developed and trained on the Persuasive Essays (PE) argumentation data. Once trained, this model was applied to annotate the propaganda dataset.

By implementing these two approaches, we aimed to compare their effectiveness in augmenting the propaganda detection task with argumentation features. This comparison allowed us to evaluate and determine the optimal method for integrating argumentation annotations into the overall framework.

6.1 Argumentation Annotation with GPT-4

We utilized GPT-4o,[4] an advanced variant of GPT-4, to annotate the propaganda dataset with argumentation features. This approach leverages GPT-4o's ability to adapt without extensive task-specific training, serving as both an evaluation of its effectiveness and a baseline for comparison with trained argumentation models.

Prompt Design and Testing We experimented with different prompting strategies to guide GPT-4o in classifying spans as *Major Claim*, *Claim*, *Premise*, or *None*, using a sample of 10 sentences from the training data. Both sentence-level and word-level approaches were tested, with sentence-level prompts generally producing cleaner and more accurate annotations. In contrast, word-level prompts faced challenges such as fragmented spans and inconsistent labeling, requiring significant post-processing. Additionally, an Arabic, human-translated, version of the most effective sentence-level prompt was tested, maintaining clarity but necessitating further validation through extensive post-processing.

6.2 Argumentation Model Development

To train an argumentation analysis model for Arabic texts, we explored two strategies: monolingual modeling and multilingual modeling. These strategies effectively leveraged annotated English resources while addressing the scarcity of Arabic argumentation datasets.

Monolingual Modeling Monolingual modeling involved using English argumentation data and applying translation techniques to bridge the gap between English and Arabic. Two approaches were employed:

Translate-Train The Translate-Train approach involved translating the English Persuasive Essays (PE) argumentation dataset into Arabic. Annotation projection techniques were then applied to transfer English annotations onto the translated Arabic text, ensuring the preservation of argumentative structures. The resulting Arabic dataset was used to fine-tune a model based on AraBERTv2 (Antoun et al., 2020).

Translate-Test In this approach, RoBERTa-large (Liu et al., 2019), trained on the English PE dataset, was utilized for argumentation detection. Arabic propaganda texts were translated into English, allowing the English-trained model to annotate the translated texts. The resulting annotations were projected back onto the original Arabic texts using alignment techniques. This approach avoided direct training on Arabic data while still enabling argumentation detection.

Multilingual Modeling Multilingual modeling leveraged pre-trained multilingual transformer models, XLM-RoBERTa-large (Conneau et al., 2019), to perform argumentation detection across languages without requiring extensive annotated resources in Arabic.

Zero-Shot Multilingual Modeling The zero-shot approach involved training a multilingual model on the English PE dataset and directly applying it to Arabic propaganda texts.

Translate-Train Multilingual Modeling The Translate-Train Multilingual approach extended the Translate-Train method by combining English PE data and its translated Arabic counterpart into a single training dataset. This approach exposed the multilingual model to both languages, allowing it to learn language-specific features alongside shared linguistic patterns.

Translation and Annotation Projection For both Translate-Train and Translate-Test approaches, translation and annotation projection were critical components. ***Translation Methods:*** Two machine translation tools were employed: (1) NLLB 1.3B (Team et al., 2022), a multilingual translation model designed to handle diverse languages, including low-resource ones, and (2) Google Translate, which allowed for comparison of translation quality's impact on model performance. ***Annotation Projection:*** FastAlign (Dyer et al., 2013), a statistical word alignment tool, was used to align annotations between English and Arabic, preserving argumentative structures across translations.

By combining translation methods, annotation projection, and diverse models, our framework effectively addressed the challenges of generating argumentation annotations for Arabic texts, enabling argumentation detection in resource-constrained settings.

Mitigating the Impact of Annotation and Translation Errors The Translate-Train and Translate-Test models rely heavily on automatic translation

[4] Accessed in July 2024

and annotation projection, both of which can introduce errors that affect model performance. To address these challenges, we conducted targeted investigations to evaluate and mitigate the impact of these errors.

Annotation Projection Errors To understand the effect of annotation projection errors, we manually corrected samples of 100 and 200 instances from the training data. These corrected annotations were used to assess their impact on the performance of both the argumentation detection and the propaganda detection models. Due to the labor-intensive nature of manual corrections, this effort was focused on the Translate-Train Monolingual approach.

Translation Quality Errors Translation quality was identified as a critical factor influencing model effectiveness, particularly in the Translate-Test approach. Inspired by the findings of Artetxe et al. (2023), two key strategies were implemented to mitigate the impact of translation errors. First, **Domain Adaptation** was applied by fine-tuning the machine translation model on domain-specific data, ensuring translations better aligned with the characteristics of the argumentation detection task. Second, **Training Data Adaptation** involved augmenting the training data by translating it into Arabic and then back-translating it into English, incorporating the back-translated content to expose the model to the variability introduced by translation. These strategies highlighted the sensitivity of the Translate-Test approach to translation quality.

7 Propaganda Detection Evaluation and Discussion

The effectiveness of incorporating argumentation features into the propaganda detection task was evaluated using various approaches, including cross-lingual, multilingual, and GPT-4-based annotation methods. Table 3 summarizes the Micro F1 scores for the development and test sets, highlighting the impact of these methods on performance compared to the baseline.

7.1 Cross-Lingual Approaches

Translate-Test Using Google Translate, this method achieved a Micro F1 score of 0.3948 on the development set and 0.3978 on the test set. The NLLB translation model performed comparably, with scores of 0.3981 and 0.4024 on the development and test sets, respectively. Training data adaptation improved performance for Google Translate, reaching 0.4089 on the development set and 0.4018 on the test set. However, domain adaptation reduced performance, highlighting that this approach was not beneficial in mitigating poor translation quality.

Translate-Train Monolingual Using the NLLB-translated dataset improved performance to 0.3695 on the development set and 0.3701 on the test set. Manual corrections of annotation projection for 100 and 200 samples boosted scores on the test set to 0.3952 and 0.3947, respectively, underscoring the importance of high-quality annotation alignment.

7.2 Multilingual Approaches

Zero-Shot Multilingual achieved a Micro F1 score of 0.3981 and 0.3930 on the development and test sets, respectively. This result indicates that the model could generalize across languages, although linguistic differences between English and Arabic pose challenges.

Translate-Train Multilingual using Google Translate, achieved Micro F1 scores of 0.4033 and 0.3931 on the development and test sets, respectively. NLLB yielded similar results, with scores of 0.3988 and 0.3929. These results demonstrate a very marginal improvement over the Zero-Shot Multilingual model, indicating the benefit of multilingual exposure during training is very limited.

7.3 GPT-4 Annotation Approach

The GPT-4-based approach, using an English prompt to annotate the propaganda dataset with argumentation features, achieved the highest Micro F1 scores of 0.4077 on the development set and 0.4025 on the test set. This method demonstrated consistent performance across both datasets, outperforming other approaches.

7.4 Discussion

The results reveal several key findings. All methods incorporating argumentation features outperformed the baseline Micro F1 score of 0.2995, demonstrating the effectiveness of integrating argumentation information into propaganda detection models. Translation quality played a crucial role, as the Translate-Test approaches showed better performance with higher-quality translations, although gains were limited without adaptation techniques. The accuracy of annotation projection was also

Approach	MT Model	Adaptation	#Corrected Annotation	Micro F1 Dev	Micro F1 Test
Baseline	-	-	-	-	**0.2995**
Zero-Shot Multilingual	-	-	-	**0.3981**	**0.3930**
Translate-Test	Google Translate	-	0	0.3948	0.3978
	Google Translate	Training Data	0	**0.4089**	0.4018
	NLLB	-	0	0.3981	**0.4024**
	NLLB	Training Data	0	0.3918	0.4006
	NLLB	Domain	0	0.3773	0.3799
Translate-Train Monolingual	NLLB	-	0	0.3695	0.3701
	NLLB	-	100	0.3889	**0.3952**
	NLLB	-	200	**0.4033**	0.3947
Translate-Train Multilingual	Google Translate	-	0	**0.4033**	**0.3931**
	NLLB	-	0	0.3988	0.3929
GPT-4 - Prompt6(AR)	-	-	-	0.4004	0.3914
GPT-4 - Prompt1(EN)	-	-	-	**0.4077**	**0.4025**

Table 3: F1 Scores of Propaganda Detection Models with Argumentation Feature Augmentation Across Different Approaches and Adaptation Strategies - Test Set

pivotal, with manual corrections significantly enhancing the performance of Translate-Train Monolingual models, underscoring the importance of precise alignment in cross-lingual tasks. GPT-4 achieved the highest scores, though with modest margins over specialized models, indicating the strong competitiveness of those models. Lastly, the results highlighted the critical impact of training data quality, as the Translate-Test approach outperformed Translate-Train due to the latter embedding errors from machine translation and annotation projection directly into the training data.

8 Qualitative Analysis on the Media Narratives on the Israeli War on Gaza

To assess the performance of the proposed model in detecting propaganda techniques, we conducted a qualitative analysis on the FIGNEWS subset (Section 3.3). These examples were selected to be annotated as propagandistic and to represent both narratives biased against Palestine and those biased against Israel. All annotated examples are in Appendix C.

The analysis of the examples reveals diverse strengths and shortcomings in the model's identification of propaganda techniques. Several examples showcase the model's ability to detect and label effectively, while others highlight areas for improvement in span detection and labeling accuracy.

The model performed strongly in identifying a variety of propaganda techniques, particularly in cases involving *Appeal to Fear*, *Appeal to Hypocrisy*, and *Loaded Language*. For instance, in Example 13: "حذَّرنا إسرائيل من عواقب ملاحقة مسؤولين من حماس خارج فلسطين" (We warned Israel about the consequences of pursuing Hamas officials outside Palestine) was accurately labeled as *Appeal to Fear*, as the phrase evokes concern about potential repercussions. Similarly, for *Appeal to Hypocrisy*, Example 7 includes: "في الوقت الذي تحارب فيه إسرائيل إبادة شعب تُتهم هي بإبادة شعب" (While Israel is fighting genocide, it is accused of genocide), which effectively exposes perceived inconsistencies in criticism. Another strong example of *Appeal to Hypocrisy* appears in Example 8: "أين كرامة الإنسان، أين حقوق الإنسان، أين احترامه فالجواب هي إسرائيل" (where human dignity is, where human rights are, and where respect is, the answer is Israel). These instances highlight the model's ability to identify rhetorical strategies that challenge or question the credibility of opponents.

The model also demonstrated proficiency in recognizing *Appeal to Time*, as seen in Example 6 with "المذبحة القادمة" (The next massacre) and "لن تنتهي الحرب قبل" (The war will not end before). Both spans emphasize urgency and the inevitability of action, aligning well with the intended technique. Additionally, the model's performance in labeling *Questioning the Reputation* was consistent across multiple exam-

ples. In Example 7, the span:
"أين كانت جنوب إفريقيا عندما قُتل وشُرد الملايين في سوريا واليمن على يد شركاء حماس"
(Where was South Africa when millions were killed and displaced in Syria and Yemen by Hamas's partners?) effectively critiques perceived hypocrisy, making the label appropriate. Similarly, in Example 8, "أين كرامة الإنسان" (Where is human dignity) and in Example 9,
"نتنياهو لا يفوت فرصة لالتقاط الصور لرفع أسهمه المتهاوية سياسياً" (Netanyahu never misses a chance to take pictures to boost his declining political ratings), were correctly identified as instances of questioning credibility.

The model's labeling of *Flag Waving* was another area of strength. For instance, in Example 7, the span:
"سنواصل الحفاظ على حقنا في الدفاع عن أنفسنا وتأمين مستقبلنا حتى النصر الكامل"
(We will continue to preserve our right to defend ourselves and secure our future until complete victory) was aptly labeled, as it appeals to patriotism and unity.

For *Exaggeration-Minimization*, Example 7 includes "الملايين" (Millions), while Example 5 includes "عملية عالية الجودة" (High-quality operation). Both spans are persuasive through their amplification of scale or quality, making the assigned labels fitting. Similarly, the *False Dilemma* technique is well-demonstrated in Example 12 with:
"لا تفاوض مع جيش الاحتلال بشأن تبادل الأسرى حتى انتهاء العدوان"
(No negotiations with the occupation army over prisoner exchange until the end of the aggression), which frames the situation as lacking alternatives. In Example 5, the span "وكل قادة حماس مصيرهم الموت" (All Hamas leaders are destined for death) similarly constructs a binary scenario, reinforcing the label's validity.

8.1 Limitations

Overprediction of Labels The model exhibited instances of overprediction, particularly for the *Loaded Language* label. For example, in Example 10, "تلقي" (Receiving) was labeled as *Loaded Language*, despite being neutral. Similarly, in Example 13, "حذّرنا" (We warned) was labeled as *Loaded Language*, though it does not carry an emotive or charged tone. Mislabeling was also seen in Example 12, where "قطاع" (Strip) was inaccurately labeled as *False Dilemma*, which does not align with the text's intent. In Example 6, "المخطوفين" (The captives) was labeled as *Name Calling*, but it is more descriptive than propagandistic.

Overly Broad or Irrelevant Spans The model demonstrated a tendency to select overly broad spans or include irrelevant elements within spans. For instance, in Example 13, the span "عواقب ملاحقة" (Consequences of pursuing) was labeled as *Loaded Language*, but only "consequences" carries the intended emotional charge, while "pursuing" is neutral. Similarly, in Example 8, "على دواعش حماس" (Over Hamas's Daesh) was labeled as *Questioning the Reputation*, but the inclusion of "على" (Over) extends the span unnecessarily.

Unidentified Propagandistic Content The model failed to identify certain propagandistic content. For Example 4, no spans were identified as propagandistic, yet the span
"إن القضاء على 'حماس' هو الطريقة الوحيدة لاستعادة الرهائن"
(Eliminating Hamas is the only way to retrieve the hostages) could be labeled as *False Dilemma* or *Appeal to Fear* due to its framing of a singular solution and invocation of threat.

In summary, the model demonstrates strong performance in recognizing clear techniques such as *Loaded Language*, *Name Calling*, and *Appeal to Fear*, but occasionally mislabels neutral phrases or includes extraneous content in spans. These findings underscore the importance of refining span selection and improving the accuracy of labels to handle nuanced cases effectively.

9 Conclusion

This work highlights the effectiveness of integrating argumentation features into propaganda detection models for Arabic texts. By combining claims, premises, and other argumentative elements with advanced NLP methodologies, we demonstrate consistent improvements over baseline models. Our analysis of Arabic media narratives reveals the model's ability to detect diverse propaganda techniques, offering valuable insights into rhetorical strategies in politically sensitive contexts.

While translation and annotation quality present challenges, the findings underscore the potential of this approach for fostering transparency in conflict-driven discourse. Future research should focus on refining annotation and translation methods. These advancements will contribute to building robust NLP tools capable of analyzing and mitigating the impact of propaganda in sensitive geopolitical contexts.

Acknowledgments

We acknowledge the assistance of the LT-Bridge Project (GA 952194) and DFKI for the use of their Virtual Laboratory.

References

Muhammad Abdul-Mageed, AbdelRahim Elmadany, and El Moatez Billah Nagoudi. 2021. ARBERT & MARBERT: Deep bidirectional transformers for Arabic. In *Proceedings of the 59th Annual Meeting of the Association for Computational Linguistics and the 11th International Joint Conference on Natural Language Processing (Volume 1: Long Papers)*, pages 7088–7105, Online. Association for Computational Linguistics.

Sadaf Abdul Rauf, Huda Sarfraz, Saadia Nauman, Arooj Fatima, SadafZiafat SadafZiafat, Momina Ishfaq, Alishba Suboor, Hammad Afzal, and Seemab Latif. 2024. NLPColab at FigNews 2024 shared task: Challenges in bias and propaganda annotation for news media. In *Proceedings of The Second Arabic Natural Language Processing Conference*, pages 573–579, Bangkok, Thailand. Association for Computational Linguistics.

Firoj Alam, Hamdy Mubarak, Wajdi Zaghouani, Giovanni Da San Martino, and Preslav Nakov. 2022. Overview of the wanlp 2022 shared task on propaganda detection in arabic. *Preprint*, arXiv:2211.10057.

Khudejah Ali and Khawaja Zain ul abdin. 2021. Post-truth propaganda: heuristic processing of political fake news on facebook during the 2016 u.s. presidential election. *Journal of Applied Communication Research*, 49(1):109–128.

Wissam Antoun, Fady Baly, and Hazem Hajj. 2020. AraBERT: Transformer-based model for Arabic language understanding. In *Proceedings of the 4th Workshop on Open-Source Arabic Corpora and Processing Tools, with a Shared Task on Offensive Language Detection*, pages 9–15, Marseille, France. European Language Resource Association.

Mikel Artetxe, Vedanuj Goswami, Shruti Bhosale, Angela Fan, and Luke Zettlemoyer. 2023. Revisiting machine translation for cross-lingual classification. In *Proceedings of the 2023 Conference on Empirical Methods in Natural Language Processing*, pages 6489–6499, Singapore. Association for Computational Linguistics.

David Broniatowski, Daniel Kerchner, Fouzia Farooq, Xiaolei Huang, Amelia Jamison, Mark Dredze, and Sandra Crouse Quinn. 2020. The covid-19 social media infodemic reflects uncertainty and state-sponsored propaganda. *arXiv preprint*.

Alexander Chernyavskiy, Dmitry Ilvovsky, and Preslav Nakov. 2024. Unleashing the power of discourse-enhanced transformers for propaganda detection. In *Proceedings of the 18th Conference of the European Chapter of the Association for Computational Linguistics (Volume 1: Long Papers)*, pages 1452–1462, St. Julian's, Malta. Association for Computational Linguistics.

Alexis Conneau, Kartikay Khandelwal, Naman Goyal, Vishrav Chaudhary, Guillaume Wenzek, Francisco Guzmán, Edouard Grave, Myle Ott, Luke Zettlemoyer, and Veselin Stoyanov. 2019. Unsupervised cross-lingual representation learning at scale. *CoRR*, abs/1911.02116.

Jacob Devlin, Ming-Wei Chang, Kenton Lee, and Kristina Toutanova. 2019. Bert: Pre-training of deep bidirectional transformers for language understanding. In *Proceedings of the 2019 Conference of the North American Chapter of the Association for Computational Linguistics: Human Language Technologies, Volume 1 (Long and Short Papers)*, pages 4171–4186.

Chris Dyer, Victor Chahuneau, and Noah A. Smith. 2013. A simple, fast, and effective reparameterization of IBM model 2. In *Proceedings of the 2013 Conference of the North American Chapter of the Association for Computational Linguistics: Human Language Technologies*, pages 644–648, Atlanta, Georgia. Association for Computational Linguistics.

Maram Hasanain, Firoj Alam, Hamdy Mubarak, Samir Abdaljalil, Wajdi Zaghouani, Preslav Nakov, Giovanni Da San Martino, and Abed Freihat. 2023. ArAIEval shared task: Persuasion techniques and disinformation detection in Arabic text. In *Proceedings of ArabicNLP 2023*, pages 483–493, Singapore (Hybrid). Association for Computational Linguistics.

Maram Hasanain, Md. Arid Hasan, Fatema Ahmed, Reem Suwaileh, Md. Rafiul Biswas, Wajdi Zaghouani, and Firoj Alam. 2024. Araieval shared task: Propagandistic techniques detection in unimodal and multimodal arabic content. *Preprint*, arXiv:2407.04247.

Ahmed Samir Hussein, Abu Bakr Soliman Mohammad, Mohamed Ibrahim, Laila Hesham Afify, and Samhaa R. El-Beltagy. 2022. NGU CNLP atWANLP 2022 shared task: Propaganda detection in Arabic. In *Proceedings of the The Seventh Arabic Natural Language Processing Workshop (WANLP)*, pages 545–550, Abu Dhabi, United Arab Emirates (Hybrid). Association for Computational Linguistics.

Momtazul Labib, Samia Rahman, Hasan Murad, and Udoy Das. 2024. CUET_sstm at ArAIEval shared task: Unimodal (text) propagandistic technique detection using transformer-based model. In *Proceedings of The Second Arabic Natural Language Processing Conference*, pages 507–511, Bangkok, Thailand. Association for Computational Linguistics.

Salima Lamsiyah, Abdelkader El Mahdaouy, Hamza Alami, Ismail Berrada, and Christoph Schommer. 2023. UL & UM6P at ArAIEval shared task:

Transformer-based model for persuasion techniques and disinformation detection in Arabic. In *Proceedings of ArabicNLP 2023*, pages 558–564, Singapore (Hybrid). Association for Computational Linguistics.

Yinhan Liu, Myle Ott, Naman Goyal, Jingfei Du, Mandar Joshi, Danqi Chen, Omer Levy, Mike Lewis, Luke Zettlemoyer, and Veselin Stoyanov. 2019. Roberta: A robustly optimized bert pretraining approach. *Preprint*, arXiv:1907.11692.

Ana Laura Nettel and Georges Roque. 2012. Persuasive argumentation versus manipulation. *Argumentation*, 26(1):55–69.

Jakub Piskorski, Nicolas Stefanovitch, Giovanni Da San Martino, and Preslav Nakov. 2023. SemEval-2023 task 3: Detecting the category, the framing, and the persuasion techniques in online news in a multilingual setup. In *Proceedings of the 17th International Workshop on Semantic Evaluation (SemEval-2023)*, pages 2343–2361, Toronto, Canada. Association for Computational Linguistics.

Md Riyadh and Sara Nabhani. 2024. Mela at ArAIEval shared task: Propagandistic techniques detection in Arabic with a multilingual approach. In *Proceedings of The Second Arabic Natural Language Processing Conference*, pages 478–482, Bangkok, Thailand. Association for Computational Linguistics.

Ali Safaya, Moutasem Abdullatif, and Deniz Yuret. 2020. KUISAIL at SemEval-2020 task 12: BERT-CNN for offensive speech identification in social media. In *Proceedings of the Fourteenth Workshop on Semantic Evaluation*, pages 2054–2059, Barcelona (online). International Committee for Computational Linguistics.

Zien Sheikh Ali, Watheq Mansour, Tamer Elsayed, and Abdulaziz Al□Ali. 2021. AraFacts: The first large Arabic dataset of naturally occurring claims. In *Proceedings of the Sixth Arabic Natural Language Processing Workshop*, pages 231–236, Kyiv, Ukraine (Virtual). Association for Computational Linguistics.

Christian Stab and Iryna Gurevych. 2017. Parsing argumentation structures in persuasive essays. *Computational Linguistics*, 43(3):619–659.

NLLB Team, Marta R. Costa-jussà, James Cross, Onur Çelebi, Maha Elbayad, Kenneth Heafield, Kevin Heffernan, Elahe Kalbassi, Janice Lam, Daniel Licht, Jean Maillard, Anna Sun, Skyler Wang, Guillaume Wenzek, Al Youngblood, Bapi Akula, Loic Barrault, Gabriel Mejia Gonzalez, Prangthip Hansanti, John Hoffman, Semarley Jarrett, Kaushik Ram Sadagopan, Dirk Rowe, Shannon Spruit, Chau Tran, Pierre Andrews, Necip Fazil Ayan, Shruti Bhosale, Sergey Edunov, Angela Fan, Cynthia Gao, Vedanuj Goswami, Francisco Guzmán, Philipp Koehn, Alexandre Mourachko, Christophe Ropers, Safiyyah Saleem, Holger Schwenk, and Jeff Wang. 2022. No language left behind: Scaling human-centered machine translation. *Preprint*, arXiv:2207.04672.

Yizhong Wang, Sujian Li, and Houfeng Wang. 2017. A two-stage parsing method for text-level discourse analysis. In *Proceedings of the 55th Annual Meeting of the Association for Computational Linguistics (Volume 2: Short Papers)*, pages 184–188, Vancouver, Canada. Association for Computational Linguistics.

Wajdi Zaghouani, Mustafa Jarrar, Nizar Habash, Houda Bouamor, Imed Zitouni, Mona Diab, Samhaa R. El-Beltagy, and Muhammed AbuOdeh. 2024. The fignews shared task on news media narratives. *Preprint*, arXiv:2407.18147.

A Propaganda Techniques Definition

In this section, we provide the definitions of the propaganda techniques included in the dataset, as outlined in (Piskorski et al., 2023).

A.1 ATTACK ON REPUTATION

- **Name Calling-Labelling:** a form of argument in which loaded labels are directed at an individual, group, object or activity, typically in an insulting or demeaning way, but also using labels the target audience finds desirable.

- **Guilt by Association:** attacking the opponent or an activity by associating it with another group, activity, or concept that has sharp negative connotations for the target audience.

- **Doubt:** questioning the character or the personal attributes of someone or something in order to question their general credibility or quality.

- **Appeal to Hypocrisy:** the target of the technique is attacked based on their reputation by charging them with hypocrisy/inconsistency.

- **Questioning the Reputation:** the target is attacked by making strong negative claims about it, focusing specially on undermining its character and moral stature rather than relying on an argument about the topic.

A.2 JUSTIFICATION

- **Flag Waiving:** justifying an idea by exhaling the pride of a group or highlighting the benefits for that specific group.

- **Appeal to Authority:** a weight is given to an argument, an idea or information by simply stating that a particular entity considered as an authority is the source of the information.

- **Appeal to Popularity:** a weight is given to an argument or idea by justifying it on the basis that allegedly "everybody" (or the large majority) agrees with it or "nobody" disagrees with it.

- **Appeal to Values:** a weight is given to an idea by linking it to values seen by the target audience as positive.

- **Appeal to Fear-Prejudice:** promotes or rejects an idea through the repulsion or fear of the audience towards this idea.

A.3 DISTRACTION

- **Straw Man:** consists in making an impression of refuting an argument of the opponent's proposition, whereas the real subject of the argument was not addressed or refuted, but instead was replaced with a false one.

- **Red Herring:** consists in diverting the attention of the audience from the main topic being discussed, by introducing another topic, which is irrelevant.

- **Whataboutism:** a technique that attempts to discredit an opponent's position by charging them with hypocrisy without directly disproving their argument.

A.4 SIMPLIFICATION

- **Causal Oversimplification:** assuming a single cause or reason when there are actually multiple causes for an issue.

- **False Dilemma-No Choice:** a logical fallacy that presents only two options or sides when there are many options or sides. In extreme, the author tells the audience exactly what actions to take, eliminating any other possible choices.

- **Consequential Oversimplification:** is an assertion one is making of some "first" event/action leading to a domino-like chain of events that have some significant negative (positive) effects and consequences that appear to be ludicrous or unwarranted or with each step in the chain more and more improbable.

A.5 CALL

- **Slogans:** a brief and striking phrase, often acting like an emotional appeal, that may include labeling and stereotyping.

- **Conversation Killer:** words or phrases that discourage critical thought and meaningful discussion about a given topic.

- **Appeal to Time:** the argument is centered around the idea that time has come for a particular action.

A.6 MANIPULATIVE WORDING

- **Loaded Language:** use of specific words and phrases with strong emotional implications (either positive or negative) to influence and convince the audience that an argument is valid.

- **Obfuscation-Vagueness-Confusion:** use of words that are deliberately not clear, vague, or ambiguous so that the audience may have its own interpretations.

- **Exaggeration-Minimisation:** consists of either representing something in an excessive manner or making something seem less important or smaller than it really is.

- **Repetition:** the speaker uses the same phrase repeatedly with the hope that the repetition will lead to persuading the audience.

B Distribution of propaganda techniques across the datasets

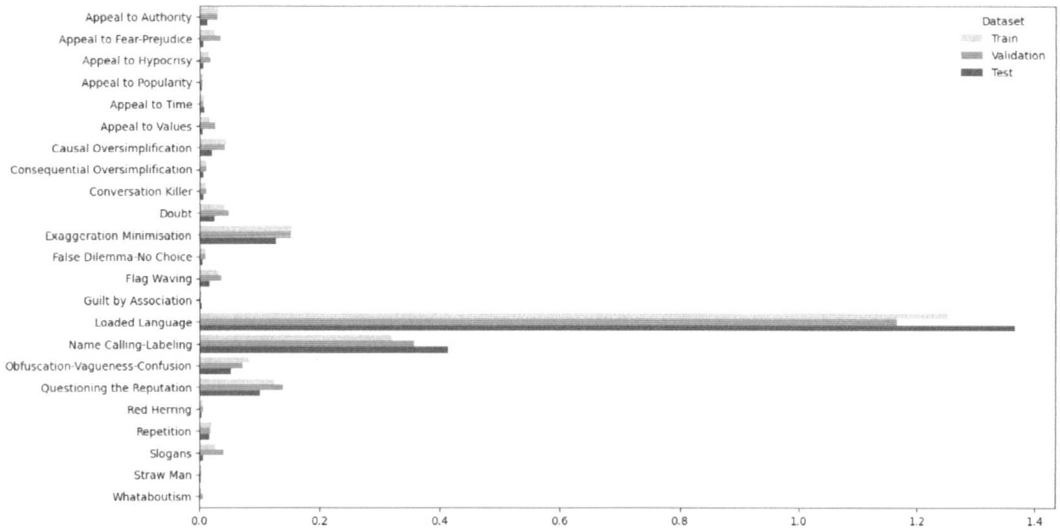

(a) Ratio of Labeled Documents to Total Documents

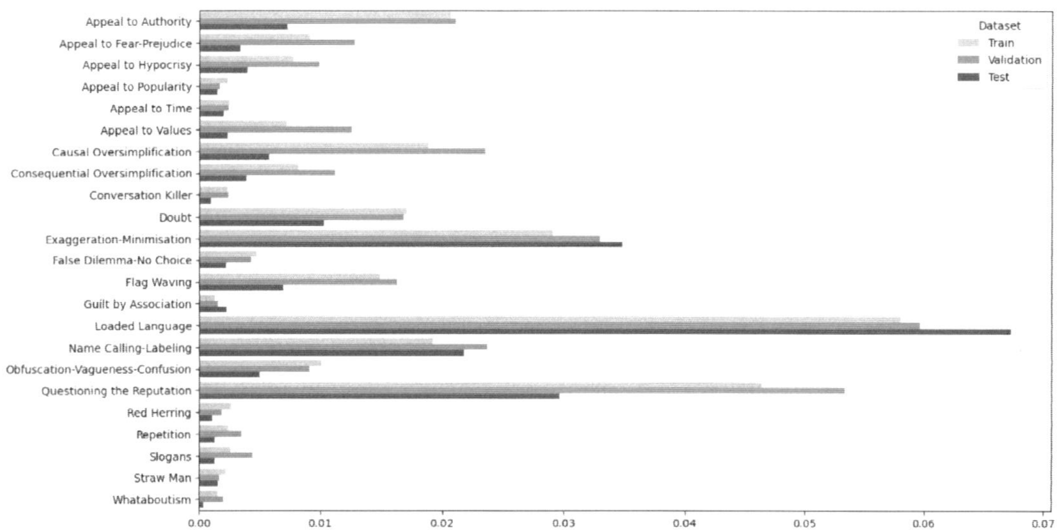

(b) Ratio of Labeled Tokens to Total Tokens

Figure 1: Propaganda Techniques Distribution: Ratios of Labeled Tokens and Documents

C Propaganda annotated examples of the narratives of the Israeli war on Gaza

Arabic	رسالة الى سكان حي الزيتون انتم تعرفون ان الحي مكتظ ومليئ بأوكار لحماس ولذلك وحفاظا على سلامتكم وعلى سلامة عائلاتكم واحبائكم توجهوا الى جنوب وادي غزة. كونوا متاكدين ان قادة حماس يتحصنون ويحاولون حماية أنفسهم
Translation	A message to the residents of the Zeitoun neighborhood: You know that the neighborhood is crowded and full of Hamas hideouts. Therefore, for your safety and the safety of your families and loved ones, move to the south of Wadi Gaza. Be assured that Hamas leaders are sheltering themselves and trying to protect themselves.
Labeled Spans	• مكتظ ("crowded") - Loaded Language • ومليئ ("full") - Loaded Language • متاكدين ("be assured") - Loaded Language • يتحصنون ("sheltering themselves") - Loaded Language

Table 4: Example 1 - Biased against Palestine

Arabic	الاتحاد الأوروبي يدرج رئيس المكتب السياسي لحركة حماس في قطاع غزة يحيى #السنوار على قائمة 'الإرهاب' المجلس الأوروبي: 'يندرج هذا القرار في إطار رد الاتحاد على التهديد الذي تشكله حماس وهجماتها الوحشية على #إسرائيل في السابع من أكتوبر' لتفاصيل أكثر
Translation	The European Union lists the head of Hamas' political bureau in the Gaza Strip, Yahya Sinwar, on the "terrorism" list. European Council: "This decision is part of the Union's response to the threat posed by Hamas and its brutal attacks on Israel on October 7." For more details.
Labeled Spans	• الإرهاب ("terrorism") - Loaded Language, Name Calling/Labeling • التهديد ("threat") - Loaded Language • وهجماتها الوحشية ("its brutal attacks") - Loaded Language

Table 5: Example 2 - Biased against Palestine

Arabic	الرئيس الأميركي جو_بايدن يعتبر أن استمرار المعارك في غزة قد يؤدي إلى تنفيذ أهداف حركة حماس بايدن: 'حماس شنت هجوماً إرهابياً لأنها لا تخشى شيئاً أكثر من أن يعيش الإسرائيليون والفلسطينيون جنباً إلى جنب في سلام' لتفاصيل أكثر
Translation	U.S. President Joe Biden considers that the continuation of battles in Gaza may lead to the achievement of Hamas' goals. Biden: "Hamas launched a terrorist attack because it fears nothing more than Israelis and Palestinians living side by side in peace." For more details.
Labeled Spans	• المعارك ("battles") - Loaded Language • شنت هجوماً إرهابياً ("launched a terrorist attack") - Loaded Language, Exaggeration/Minimization • تخشى شيئاً ("fears nothing") - Loaded Language • أن استمرار المعارك في غزة قد يؤدي إلى تنفيذ أهداف حركة حماس ("the continuation of battles in Gaza may lead to the achievement of Hamas' goals") - Causal Oversimplification • حماس شنت هجوماً إرهابياً لأنها ("Hamas launched a terrorist attack because") - Causal Oversimplification • حماس شنت هجوماً إرهابياً لأنها لا تخشى شيئاً أكثر من أن يعيش الإسرائيليون والفلسطينيون جنباً إلى جنب في سلام ("Hamas launched a terrorist attack because it fears nothing more than Israelis and Palestinians living side by side in peace") - Flag Waving

Table 6: Example 3 - Biased against Palestine

Arabic	وزير المالية الإسرائيلي بتسلئيل سموتريتش يقول إن القضاء على 'حماس' هو الطريقة الوحيدة لاستعادة الرهائن الأخبار حرب
Translation	The Israeli Minister of Finance, Bezalel Smotrich, says that eliminating 'Hamas' is the only way to retrieve the hostages.
Labeled Spans	None

Table 7: Example 4 - Biased against Palestine

Arabic	عاجل | 'يديعوت أحرونوت عن مسؤولين إسرائيليين': 'اغتيال العاروري عملية عالية الجودة وكل قادة حـ.ماس مصيرهم الموت'
Translation	Breaking: 'Yedioth Ahronoth citing Israeli officials': 'The assassination of al-Arouri is a high-quality operation, and all Hamas leaders are destined for death.'
Labeled Spans	• اغتيال (Assassination) - Loaded Language • عالية الجودة (High-quality) - Loaded Language • وكل قادة حـ.ماس مصيرهم الموت (All Hamas leaders are destined for death) - False Dilemma-No Choice • مسؤولين إسرائيليين (Israeli officials) - Obfuscation-Vagueness-Confusion • اغتيال (Assassination) - Name Calling-Labeling • عالية الجودة (High-quality) - Name Calling-Labeling • اغتيال العاروري عملية عالية الجودة وكل قادة حـ.ماس مصيرهم الموت (The assassination of al-Arouri is a high-quality operation, and all Hamas leaders are destined for death) - Appeal to Fear-Prejudice • اغتيال (Assassination) - Exaggeration-Minimisation • عملية عالية الجودة (High-quality operation) - Exaggeration-Minimisation

Table 8: Example 5 - Biased against Palestine

Arabic	عاجل | نتنياهو: - لن ننسى الفظائع التي وقعت في السابع من أكتوبر - نحن مصممون على تحقيق كل أهداف الحرب - لا بديل لنا عن النصر الساحق وإعادة مختطفينا في قطاع #غزة - لدينا الحق في الدفاع عن أنفسنا ولا أحد بإمكانه منعنا من ذلك - المذبحة القادمة بحق أبنائنا مسألة وقت لذلك يجب القضاء على حماس - وجهت الحكومة للقيام بمزيد من التفعيل لبرنامج صناعات دفاعية محلي لكي نعتمد على أنفسنا أكثر - أي تحقيقات يجب أن تتم بعد انتهاء الحرب - العلاقات مع #مصر تدار بشكل جيد ولكل بلد مصالحه التي يقلق بشأنها - لا أتراجع عن أي كلمة قلتها بخصوص #قطر - لن أتراجع عن أي مسار من مسارات الضغط على #حماس وقطر يمكنها القيام بهذا الضغط - قطر تستضيف قادة في حماس وبالتالي يمكنها ممارسة ضغط بخصوص المخطوفين - الموقف لا يزال على حاله بخصوص عدم إقامة مستوطنات في غزة - هدفنا القضاء على سلطة حماس ولا يمكن أن نسمح ببقاء قوات مسلحة في غزة ولن تنتهي الحرب قبل إكمال المهمة - محكمة العدل الدولية لم تجبرنا على إنهاء الحرب #حرب
Translation	Breaking: Netanyahu: - We will not forget the atrocities that occurred on October 7 - We are determined to achieve all the goals of the war - There is no alternative to decisive victory and the return of our captives in the Gaza Strip - We have the right to defend ourselves, and no one can prevent us from doing so - The next massacre against our children is a matter of time; therefore, Hamas must be eliminated - The government has been directed to further activate a local defense industries program to rely more on ourselves - Any investigations should take place after the war - Relations with Egypt are well-managed, and every country has its own interests to worry about - I do not back down from anything I said about Qatar - I will not back down from any pressure path on Hamas, and Qatar can exert such pressure - Qatar hosts Hamas leaders and can therefore exert pressure regarding the captives - The stance remains unchanged regarding the non-establishment of settlements in Gaza - Our goal is to eliminate Hamas authority, and we cannot allow armed forces to remain in Gaza; the war will not end before completing the mission - The International Court of Justice has not forced us to end the war.
Labeled Spans	• الفظائع (Atrocities) - Loaded Language • النصر الساحق (Decisive victory) - Loaded Language • المذبحة (Massacre) - Loaded Language • يقلق (Worried) - Loaded Language • الضغط (Pressure) - Loaded Language • المخطوفين (The captives) - Name Calling-Labeling • العلاقات (Relations) - Doubt • المذبحة القادمة (The next massacre) - Appeal to Time • مسألة وقت لذلك يجب القضاء على حماس (A matter of time; therefore, Hamas must be eliminated) - Appeal to Time • تنتهي الحرب قبل (Before the war ends) - Appeal to Time

Table 9: Example 6 - Biased against Palestine

Arabic	#عاجل | #نتنياهو: - في الوقت الذي تحارب فيه إسرائيل إبادة شعب تتهم هي بإبادة شعب - رأينا اليوم عالما مقلوبا رأسا على عقب ونحن نحارب الإرهابيين والأكاذيب - صراخ نفاق جنوب إفريقيا يصل إلى السماء - أين كانت جنوب إفريقيا عندما قتل وشرد الملايين في #سوريا واليمن على يد شركاء حماس - سنواصل الحفاظ على حقنا في الدفاع عن أنفسنا وتأمين مستقبلنا حتى النصر الكامل #حرب_غزة
Translation	#Breaking | #Netanyahu: - While Israel is fighting genocide, it is accused of genocide - Today we saw an upside-down world as we fight terrorists and lies - The hypocritical cries from South Africa reach the heavens - Where was South Africa when millions were killed and displaced in #Syria and Yemen by Hamas's partners? - We will continue to preserve our right to defend ourselves and secure our future until complete victory.
Labeled Spans	• إبادة شعب (Genocide) - Loaded Language • بإبادة شعب (Accused of genocide) - Loaded Language • الإرهابيين والأكاذيب (Terrorists and lies) - Loaded Language • صراخ نفاق (Hypocritical cries) - Loaded Language • وشرد الملايين (Displaced millions) - Loaded Language • في الوقت الذي تحارب فيه إسرائيل إبادة شعب تتهم هي بإبادة شعب - رأينا اليوم عالما مقلوبا رأسا على عقب ونحن نحارب الإرهابيين والأكاذيب - صراخ نفاق جنوب إفريقيا يصل إلى السماء - أين كانت جنوب إفريقيا عندما قتل وشرد الملايين في #سوريا واليمن على يد شركاء حماس (Where was South Africa when millions were killed and displaced in Syria and Yemen by Hamas's partners?) - Questioning the Reputation • في الوقت الذي تحارب فيه إسرائيل إبادة شعب تتهم هي بإبادة شعب - رأينا (While Israel fights genocide) - Appeal to Hypocrisy • مقلوبا (Upside-down) - Appeal to Hypocrisy • الإرهابيين (Terrorists) - Name Calling-Labeling • شركاء حماس (Hamas's partners) - Name Calling-Labeling • سنواصل الحفاظ على حقنا في الدفاع عن أنفسنا وتأمين مستقبلنا حتى النصر الكامل (We will continue to preserve our right to defend ourselves and secure our future until complete victory) - Flag Waving • أين كانت جنوب إفريقيا عندما قتل وشرد (Where was South Africa when killed and displaced) - Doubt • في #سوريا واليمن على يد شركاء حماس (In Syria and Yemen by Hamas's partners) - Doubt • الملايين (Millions) - Exaggeration-Minimisation

Table 10: Example 7 - Biased against Palestine

Arabic	سألني صديقي الجزائري من جديد: يا أفيخاي ما سر تفوق شعب إسرائيل على دواعش حماس ليس فقط عسكريًا. فأجابته: فإن سألت أين كرامة الإنسان، أين حقوق الإنسان أين احترامه فالجواب هي إسرائيل. وأشكر الله على كوني يهوديا وصهيونيا لإني منهما تعلمت ماذا يعني الحياة وماذا تعني الإنسانية.
Translation	My Algerian friend asked me again: Oh Avichai, what is the secret of Israel's superiority over Hamas's Daesh, not only militarily? I replied: If you ask where human dignity is, where human rights are, and where respect is, the answer is Israel. I thank God for being Jewish and Zionist because from them I learned what life and humanity mean.
Labeled Spans	• تفوق شعب (Superiority of a people) - Questioning the Reputation • على دواعش حماس (Over Hamas's Daesh) - Questioning the Reputation • أين كرامة الإنسان (Where is human dignity) - Questioning the Reputation • أين حقوق الإنسان أين احترامه فالجواب هي إسرائيل (Where are human rights and respect? The answer is Israel) - Questioning the Reputation • سألت (Asked) - Appeal to Hypocrisy • أين كرامة الإنسان، أين حقوق الإنسان أين احترامه فالجواب هي إسرائيل (Where is human dignity, where are human rights and respect? The answer is Israel) - Appeal to Hypocrisy • دواعش حماس (Hamas's Daesh) - Name Calling-Labeling • يهوديا وصهيونيا (Jewish and Zionist) - Name Calling-Labeling • سر تفوق شعب إسرائيل على دواعش حماس (The secret of Israel's superiority over Hamas's Daesh) - Doubt

Table 11: Example 8 - Biased against Palestine

Arabic	رئيس الوزراء الإسرائيلي يزور #غزة في 'وقت الهدنة' مع #حماس.. ورئيس منتدى الشرق الأوسط للدراسات السياسية والاستراتيجية: '#نتنياهو لا يفوت فرصة لالتقاط الصور.. لرفع أسهمه المتهاوية سياسياً' #فلسطين #إسرائيل #الحدث
Translation	The Israeli Prime Minister visits Gaza during the "time of the truce" with Hamas. The President of the Middle East Forum for Political and Strategic Studies says: "Netanyahu never misses a chance to take pictures to boost his declining political ratings."
Labeled Spans	• الهدنة (Truce) - Loaded Language • المتهاوية (Declining) - Loaded Language • #نتنياهو لا يفوت فرصة لالتقاط الصور.. لرفع أسهمه المتهاوية سياسياً (Netanyahu never misses a chance to take pictures to boost his declining political ratings) - Questioning the Reputation • الهدنة (Truce) - Name Calling-Labeling • الهدنة (Truce) - Appeal to Time

Table 12: Example 9 - Biased against Israel

Arabic	لحظة تلقّي والد الأسير المحرر بصفقة وفاء الأحرار والناطق باسم حركة حماس عن مدينة #القدس محمد حمادة نبأ استشهاد نجله المُبعد إلى #غزة من بلدة صور باهر' #حرب_غزة #فيديو
Translation	The moment the father of the released prisoner under the "Wafa al-Ahrar" deal and spokesman for the Hamas movement in Jerusalem, Muhammad Hamada, received the news of the martyrdom of his son, who was displaced to Gaza from the town of Sur Baher.
Labeled Spans	• تلقّي (Receiving) - Loaded Language • المحرر (Released) - Loaded Language • استشهاد (Martyrdom) - Loaded Language • الأسير المحرر (Released Prisoner) - Name Calling-Labeling • وفاء الأحرار (Wafa al-Ahrar) - Name Calling-Labeling

Table 13: Example 10 - Biased against Israel

Arabic	مقال في صحيفة 'لوموند' الفرنسية جاء فيه أن مشاعر التعاطف مع ضحايا هجوم حماس عبر العالم تحوّلت بعد الهجوم على غزة نحو المدنيين الفلسطينيين بسبب معاناتهم.. أبرز ما ورد في الصحافة الدولية بشأن الحرب الإسرائيلية على قطاع غزة #حرب_غزة #الأخبار
Translation	An article in the French newspaper "Le Monde" stated that feelings of sympathy for the victims of Hamas's attack worldwide shifted after the attack on Gaza toward Palestinian civilians due to their suffering. Highlights from international press coverage of the Israeli war on Gaza.
Labeled Spans	• التعاطف (Sympathy) - Loaded Language • ضحايا هجوم (Victims of Attack) - Loaded Language • تحوّلت (Shifted) - Loaded Language • الهجوم (Attack) - Loaded Language • معاناتهم (Their Suffering) - Loaded Language • هجوم (Attack) - Name Calling-Labeling • عبر العالم (Worldwide) - Exaggeration-Minimisation

Table 14: Example 11 - Biased against Israel

Arabic	القيادي في حماس صالح العاروري في آخر لقاء تلفزيوني على شاشة #الجزيرة قبل استشهاده: لا تفاوض مع جيش الاحتلال بشأن تبادل الأسرى حتى انتهاء العدوان على قطاع #غزة #حرب_غزة #الأخبار
Translation	Hamas leader Saleh Al-Arouri in his last televised interview on Al Jazeera before his martyrdom: No negotiations with the occupation army over prisoner exchange until the end of the aggression on the Gaza Strip.
Labeled Spans	• استشهاده (Martyrdom) - Loaded Language • العدوان (Aggression) - Loaded Language • لا تفاوض مع جيش الاحتلال بشأن تبادل الأسرى حتى انتهاء العدوان (No negotiations with the occupation army over prisoner exchange until the end of the aggression) - False Dilemma-No Choice • قطاع (Sector/Strip) - False Dilemma-No Choice • جيش الاحتلال (Occupation Army) - Name Calling-Labeling • العدوان (Aggression) - Name Calling-Labeling

Table 15: Example 12 - Biased against Israel

Arabic	عاجل | رويترز عن مسؤول بالمخابرات التركية: 'حذرنا إسرائيل من عواقب ملاحقة مسؤولين من حماس خارج فلسطين بما فيها تركيا'
Translation	Breaking | Reuters quoting a Turkish intelligence official: 'We warned Israel about the consequences of pursuing Hamas officials outside Palestine, including in Turkey.'
Labeled Spans	• حذرنا (We warned) - Loaded Language • عواقب ملاحقة (Consequences of pursuit) - Loaded Language • حذرنا إسرائيل من عواقب ملاحقة مسؤولين من حماس خارج فلسطين (We warned Israel about the consequences of pursuing Hamas officials outside Palestine) - Appeal to Fear-Prejudice

Table 16: Example 13 - Biased against Israel

Arabic	ذكرت وسائل إعلام تابعة لحركة #حماس أن أكثر من 30 شخصا قتلوا وأصيب العشرات في قصف إسرائيلي لمخيم #جباليا في شمال.
Translation	Media affiliated with the Hamas movement reported that more than 30 people were killed and dozens injured in an Israeli bombing of Jabalia camp in the north.
Labeled Spans	• قصف (Bombing) - Loaded Language

Table 17: Example 14 - Biased against Israel

Arabic	هنية: اغتيال العاروري ورفاقه عملٌ إرهابيّ مكتمل الأركان وحماس لن تُهزَم
Translation	Haniyeh: The assassination of Al-Arouri and his companions is a fully-fledged terrorist act, and Hamas will not be defeated.
Labeled Spans	• اغتيال (Assassination) - Loaded Language • عملٌ إرهابيّ (Terrorist Act) - Loaded Language • العاروري ورفاقه (Al-Arouri and his companions) - Questioning the Reputation • الأركان (Fully-fledged) - Questioning the Reputation • لن تُهزَم (Will not be defeated) - Questioning the Reputation • مكتمل الأركان (Fully-fledged) - Obfuscation-Vagueness-Confusion • اغتيال العاروري (Assassination of Al-Arouri) - Name Calling-Labeling • عملٌ إرهابيّ (Terrorist Act) - Name Calling-Labeling • عملٌ إرهابيّ مكتمل الأركان وحماس لن تُهزَم (Fully-fledged terrorist act, and Hamas will not be defeated) - Exaggeration-Minimisation • هنية (Haniyeh) - Appeal to Authority • عملٌ إرهابيّ مكتمل الأركان (Fully-fledged terrorist act) - Appeal to Authority

Table 18: Example 15 - Biased against Israel

Arabic	ترحيب عربي بتدابير محكمة العدل الدولية بشأن منع الإبادة الجماعية في غزة، و'الصحة العالمية' ترفض اتهامات إسرائيلية بـ'التواطؤ مع حماس' تعرَّف أبرز أخبار اليوم
Translation	Arab approval of the measures by the International Court of Justice regarding preventing genocide in Gaza, and 'WHO' rejects Israeli accusations of 'collaboration with Hamas.' Discover the top #news of the day.
Labeled Spans	• الإبادة الجماعية (Genocide) - Loaded Language • اتهامات (Accusations) - Loaded Language • التواطؤ (Collaboration) - Loaded Language • 'الصحة العالمية' ترفض اتهامات إسرائيلية بـ'التواطؤ مع حماس' ('WHO rejects Israeli accusations of collaboration with Hamas') - Questioning the Reputation • 'التواطؤ مع حماس' ('Collaboration with Hamas') - Name Calling-Labeling

Table 19: Example 16 - Biased against Israel

Arabic	حركة حماس : تم الاتفاق مع الأشقاء في قطر ومصر على تمديد الهدنة الإنسانية المؤقتة لمدة يومين إضافيين بنفس شروط الهدنة السابقة.
Translation	Hamas Movement: Agreement was reached with the brothers in Qatar and Egypt to extend the temporary humanitarian truce for an additional two days under the same terms as the previous truce.
Labeled Spans	• الهدنة الإنسانية المؤقتة (Temporary Humanitarian Truce) - Loaded Language • الأشقاء (Brothers) - Name Calling-Labeling • الإنسانية (Humanitarian) - Name Calling-Labeling

Table 20: Example 17 - Biased against Israel

Author Index

Association for Computational Linguistics
209 N. Eighth Street
Stroudsburg, Pennsylvania 18360

ISBN 979-8-3313-1372-2

CURRAN ASSOCIATES INC.
proceedings.com